THE MORALITY OF MONEY

Remove Fear and Discover Financial Freedom
Through Simple Economic Principles
and Universal Truths

RENÉE E. BRYAN

Library of Congress Control Number: 2026908036
ISBN: 979-8-9954497-0-6 (paperback)
ISBN: 979-8-9954497-1-3 (hardcover)
ISBN: 979-8-9954497-2-0 (ebook)
ISBN: 979-8-9954497-3-7 (audiobook)

Printed in the United States of America

Published by Bryan Ventures, Inc
St. Paul, MN ~ https://bryanventures.com
Author site: https://reneelizbryan.info

About the Author

As a successful business owner for over twenty-five years, Renée E. Bryan has advised major players in the financial services industry on how legislation, tax changes, and economic impacts have helped or hindered Americans. With a growing gap between the wealthy and the struggling middle- and lower-classes, now is the time to secure your future using this straightforward strategy. By sharing her personal journey of self-discovery, Renée presents a way to eliminate fear from your finances and embark on the path to personal freedom.

Blogs & Insightful Considerations ~ https://wrongwaylizzie.me
Economic Education & Financial Classes ~ https://bryanventures.com
YouTube Video Creations & Unleashed Commentary ~
https://www.youtube.com/@Fearless_Finances

Reviews gratefully accepted at Amazon, Goodreads,
and wherever you purchased this book.

Dedication

To my kids, who helped me grow up while I was raising them.
You are the best of what I wish to embody.
With you, I gratefully leave a legacy that makes the world better.

Acknowledgements

Veronica Belmont and Gary Forget,
who freely shared their passion for the written word to help me improve this book.

The agents and financial advisors who have attended my classes.
You helped refine my craft and consider money in broader, deeper ways.

My mother, who always believed in me,
telling me I was so smart that I could be whatever I wanted.
Those words fortified me and provided a vision I didn't always see.
I love you and miss you.

CONTENTS

INTRODUCTION

You might wonder, "Who is this lady, and why should I listen to anything she says about morality and money?" Let me start with the easiest of the two—I'm an expert in financial matters.

If you have a financial advisor, they have likely attended the type of classes I created and still instruct. I train them and have spent my entire 35-year career in the financial services industry—first as a sales representative and then as a marketing director for an investment firm. I helped brokerage houses and their representatives understand how certain investment products fit into their clients' portfolios and the various tax benefits or consequences of specific trades, transactions, and liquidations.

I also had these fabulous financial professionals, true gurus in the field, share their knowledge with me. Over the last two decades, this synergy of information and experience with licensed agents has helped them remain relevant to their clients and enlightened me about the global need for financial literacy.

I know money and investments, and how to protect them. Equally impactful, I worked through bear and bull markets, recessions and prosperity, and high- and low-interest-rate conditions. I have researched and seen how legislation, tax changes, and economic impact have helped or hindered they typical American. I have also seen the effect of the national debt, chronic deficit spending, and a growing disparity between the rich and the striving middle class.

Over the years, I have also changed my mind about the best course of action and the most moral choice, which brings me to the faith component of my approach to managing money morally.

In 2012, I began to explore a faith-filled life. Even though I was at the height of financial success, many of my relationships were not going well. I was a single mom with teenage kids. While they faced typical challenges, I wanted to ensure a balanced success for them. My family and friends were less than helpful in achieving this goal. As you explore the pages of this book, you'll discover that many of these relationships were harmful.

If I look beyond these external causes and consider my true motivator for faith, I realize I wasn't living my authentic life. At the time, I was not living the way GOD had intended for me, and something was missing. My life lacked wholeness and contentment. I was miserable and struggling.

I started attending a local megachurch, where I tried to connect by volunteering and other forms of involvement in the ministry. I noticed an interesting and painful correlation. The deeper I dove into my faith, the lower my bank balance tanked. The more I committed to spiritual principles, the less my financial returns. Fewer customers started a new relationship with me as I began my new life. It seems overly dramatic, but it is nonetheless true. When I made this change, my business sales dried up, and my financial security collapsed. It was like living in a barren desert.

I knew this was coming. I ran a successful insurance continuing education business for over a decade, and I knew legislative changes in 2010 would dramatically impact my business model. The prior two years' sales dropped, so I adjusted and hoped for a leveling off. Instead, my modest six-figure income fell to one-sixth of what it had been before. Yes, ONE-SIXTH!

I was freaking out and in a fearful free fall. I had lived my entire adult life with a comfortable income. I had a sizable mortgage and clear, achievable savings goals. My two kids were college-bound with graduate studies in mind. I was, I am, the quintessential poster child of the person who hopes to achieve success in the face of many obstacles. A divorced single mom who left an abusive relationship and started a successful woman-owned business. Except it was falling apart.

When I had every worldly reason to turn my back on all this Christian nonsense, I knew GOD was taking me on a tour of faith-filled finances. The correlation between my commitment to faith and the instantaneous drying up of my financial world was too grand a parallel to miss. I was about to learn lessons that probably few in a boardroom would share, grasp, or conceive. I sensed GOD saying, "You've learned many financial lessons, but it's time to see this through Our lens. Let Us show you a few things."

Show me, They* did.**

Many who have suffered profound tragedy frequently say, "It was one of the best things to happen to me." I am one of those people. I would not have this new perspective and enlightened faith without this loss. This book explores the lessons I've learned because they work. I've transitioned from the depths of financial loss to financial recovery. I once again have clear, attainable goals and a plan to achieve them. My kids and I are living lives we couldn't have imagined back in 2012.

No, I didn't win the lottery or marry a sugar daddy. My parents didn't leave me a million dollars. I don't think they ever owned a million. I applied the simple strategies we'll explore in this book. These concepts, if used consistently, will bring you financial security. You, too, will have a plan that can bring you to a life you have not yet conceived, and all it takes is commitment to a few simple choices.

*If you have concerns or questions about "THEY" as a pronoun for GOD or Higher Power, please see Appendix I at the back of the book.

**If you are not a person of faith, please don't run away from the content of this book. Even though my journey includes a reliance on the teachings of Jesus, whom I met in the Gospels, you are not required to share that faith or any faith to explore the financial concepts in this book. The "Preface" on the following pages will explain further.

PREFACE

"Faith does not need to push the river because faith is able to trust that there is a river. The river is flowing. We are in it." —Richard Rohr

This is not a traditional financial planning book. You probably figured as much, given that the title contains "morality" and "money."

I never intended to write six chapters that appeared in the first draft. I started with an outline and a computer. As I began to peck out the key strategies I planned to share, Creative Energy seemed to take over. Ideas that I hadn't planned began to Flow. Helpful strategies and suggestions that were not part of the original plan were incorporated into the text. I would question this new material: "Will people want to read about that?" Then, the Universe would answer through a friend. They'd ask how they should decide their next steps. My response? "I just wrote a chapter about that. Would you like to read it?"

The first few editors told me, "I think this should be multiple books." I toyed with that idea, knowing that authors who publish more than one book typically achieve financial success and broader readership more quickly. Upon reflection, I realized the unexpected chapters were just as important, if not more so, than the planned content.

When I reviewed everything for a final edit, I realized two chapters deserved further exploration. They are a helpful part of my strategy and will likely be expanded in a second book designed to nurture our ability to seek and find answers. Both offer guidance on better solutions for your life. Sure, that includes money, but many of the things we do or choose to do can affect our financial health. If we don't consider and maybe even confront these thoughts and behaviors, any plan we adopt will have little success.

My journey to these principles was unique. My faith became intertwined with my view of financial concepts; hence, this book attempts to merge them.

This merger, however, is challenging. The text jumps back and forth between faith and finance, or focuses on money, and then moves on to morality. In my experience, the two are neither mutually exclusive nor do they naturally intersect.

Like two magnets that repel on opposite sides, one must actively seek the areas where a connection can form. Once attached, it takes a significant force to separate them again. They become one while touching, but reconnecting them may require turning and twisting when separated. I've experienced this when faith is combined with finances or morality is sought in money.

Of course, these two magnets never need to be connected. This is how most of the world operates, or so it seems. This would even be the case in faith-based circles, where principles appear to be left in the pews. One can seemingly attach a magnet to their finances, and the other to their faith, without ever trying to pair them. The magic begins when the magnets' strength is intensified by correctly aligning both. It is the same for us when we orient ourselves (and our magnets) toward the Flow, operating in formidable synergy.

Some editors tried to correct my view of tapping the Flow. They were Christian with a more traditional view and thought this book should adopt that tone. They further believed my market for this book would be fellow Christians. I see it differently.

Devout Christians can benefit from the Spiritual principles offered in this book when they open their minds beyond a black-and-white, binary, rule-based religious system and seek greater reliance on what is sensed but unseen. The Flow relies on Spirit, or if you prefer, the Flow is Energy. This requires flexibility, responsiveness, and buoyancy—not rigidity, pronouncements, or dominance. We go with the Flow. We can never control or contain it.

If you are squeamish about religious concepts or feel that the widely accepted notion of GOD has been twisted into something to run from, I understand. I've been there. Having experienced horrid behavior from those who claim to be faith-filled people, I was also skeptical of those professing a Higher Order in the Universe. The first time I stepped back into a church after my hiatus, I felt like an interloper. Having questioned GOD, experienced anger at a Creator, and voiced frustration with the Church, I felt like a hypocrite sitting in a pew. I did not feel comfortable being there. I get it, and I won't force any belief on you.

Whatever Spiritual place you are in or not in, you are welcome here. You can be an atheist, agnostic, or current believer of any doctrine and fully tap the Flow. The Flow will be your guide to many decisions, and anyone at any time can step into the deep purpose of the River. All that is required is an open and willing mind for your heart and spirit to connect.

This is why the Spiritual principles in this book are essential. Every day, at nearly every moment, we must make choices about what to do with our time, money, and talents—which people we should connect with and rely on, which job to take, who to vote for, where to live—the list goes on and on. Our financial stability depends on these choices. When we have the Flow as our guide, our measure of success changes and becomes easier to find.

While I have faith and my own beliefs, I respect your autonomy to choose yours. On occasion, I might offer a Bible verse or two. Most of those verses are attributed to Jesus—those in red from the four gospels. I offer these simply because I think, and so do a lot of other people, that Jesus was an awesome dude. I quote various sources, too. The Flow taps everyone regardless of religious affiliation or doctrine. When we cultivate our ability to sense the Flow, it becomes evident that the Creative Energy of the Universe is a magnet that pulls us ever closer whenever we choose to orient ourselves toward it.

I know some people who have struggled with religion and concepts around faith. If this is your journey, here are some suggestions that I know have helped friends navigate faith-filled writings to gain the essence of the story without getting bogged down in the GOD question.

- View the word GOD as an acronym for Good Orderly Direction, Great Out-Doors, Glimpse One's Destiny, Great Omnipotent Designer, Gift Of Defense, Guard On Duty, Grace Over Doubt, Giver Of Delight—GOD. Whatever you prefer. I have ALL CAP GOD in these paragraphs to help you.
- Replace "GOD" with something universal we can all feel good about, like LOVE, PEACE, HARMONY, GRACE, GOODNESS, CREATIVE

ENERGY—you get the idea. GOD and GOOD are close. Maybe that is something you could try.

- Develop your concept. Common ones I'll use are Universe, Source, or Creator. If you prefer, you can use FATHER TIME or MOTHER EARTH. In the book *The Shack*, GOD is Papa, or you could use Momma. Anything that feels good to you is perfect.
- A special friend of mine used an option I love. Each time he encountered the word GOD, he would replace it with NOT {your name}. So, if I were doing this, I would replace GOD with NOT RENÉE to reinforce my reliance on something other than me.
- A pet-loving friend who had difficulty conceiving a GOD but saw deep, unconditional love and acceptance in her DOG would envision her cute little pup's face when she hit that word, and all was well.

The important thing is to avoid getting bogged down in words, the need to label, or even the need to understand the Flow. We only need to acknowledge that there might be a Loving Power out there that can assist and guide us and that everyone, regardless of their history or experiences, can tap into it. That's it.

CHAPTER ONE

START SAVING NOW

ASSETS = SECURITY

"'A part of all I earn is mine to keep.' Say it in the morning when you first arise. Say it at noon. Say it at night. Say it each hour of every day. Say it to yourself until the words stand out like letters of fire across the sky."
—George Clason, The Richest Man in Babylon

PAY YOURSELF FIRST

Whatever you do, start saving now. This concept is so vital to your financial plan that I rearranged the entire book to address it first. Before the Flow became integral to this book, I initially planned to start with extensive evidence showing that carrying debt is less costly to your financial future than waiting to save would be. My indignation was aimed at one author and one book, Dave Ramsey—"*Financial Peace University*." For those unaware, he's made multimillions, marketing to churches with his one-size-fits-all philosophy of financial planning. I even acknowledged that contempt with my working title, "What Dave Ramsey Got Wrong." My list of grievances about his plan and his approach was so long I might have filled a three-volume set. I'll tell you more about my concerns with his approach in later sections.

I spent some time on pages of that, which promptly got thrown into a folder I created called the "Chopping Floor" after the first few friends who read it said things like, "Who is Dave Ramsey?" or "Why so negative, Renée? Is that the tone you want?" There was even an, "You seem angry. That's not like you." I'm surprised she didn't add, "Are you okay?"

As much as I oppose almost all of the advice offered by Dave Ramsey and pundits like him, I want this book to be hopeful, helpful, and inviting. Your financial future is promising. This book will help you; I want you to feel comfortable in this space. Feedback and insight are ways the Flow can guide us. There are plenty of reasons to be ticked off about how others' greed can negatively affect our financial future; putting our energy into a positive construct is more helpful. This book will offer advice on detecting bad actors and avoiding their schemes, as these skills are crucial for a secure financial future. It's also my belief that when tapping the Flow, such ploys become apparent. When our magnetized connection to a Greater Good is fully synced, this type of undertaking becomes less appealing—even repellent.

While I typed those first few "Chopping Floor" chapters, I kept thinking of you, the reader: Spending time on that information first would rob you of greater financial security later. You might wonder, "Renée, how can reading pages offering sound financial advice rob someone of security? It seems the opposite would be true."

You would be right: investing our time, money, and effort in endeavors that build something we value is beneficial, not a waste. Of greater importance, however, is the loss of compounded value. Every day, we fail to set aside money in an interest-bearing account, thereby robbing ourselves of free money. This missed opportunity delays or diminishes our future wealth and security. The time spent on those pages would be costly to your future if it delays establishing the habit of saving.

I will show you the value in real-life examples later, but it is critical that you start packing away every penny you can. Financial security is achieved through assets that pay us, and the only way we can get those assets is by starting to save now.

BUILD ASSETS

"Rich people acquire assets. The poor and middle class acquire liabilities that they think are assets." —Robert Kiyosaki, Rich Dad, Poor Dad

It starts with "Pay Yourself First". This phrase comes from one of my favorite financial planning books, *The Richest Man in Babylon* by George Clason, quoted in the prior section. Still, it probably gained most notoriety through another excellent wealth-creation book by Robert Kiyosaki, *Rich Dad, Poor Dad.* Today, the phrase "PAY YOURSELF FIRST" is frequently used in financial planning circles.

The concept is simple: PUT MONEY IN SAVINGS BEFORE YOU DO ANYTHING ELSE—pay yourself first. This is how a 401(k) contribution works. It comes from one's paycheck before the net deposit is made to their account. (A 401(k) is an employer-sponsored retirement plan. In later chapters, we'll discuss the basics of retirement accounts and more.)

"Pay Yourself First" is so critical that I rearranged the entire book so that you could start saving now. Settle on an amount you can save immediately and start putting it away. We'll discuss how to find more money to save and where to put it in this chapter and then explore these topics further throughout the book. If you are wondering how to find the money to do this, given your tight budget right now, I understand—I do. Remember, I'm the lady whose income dropped to one-sixth of her previous earnings. I tucked money in savings every month, no matter what—and didn't touch it. These pages explain precisely how I did it; you can do it, too.

Before getting into the "how," I want to drive the "Pay Yourself First" concept home with something that blew my mind. In *Rich Dad, Poor Dad,* Kiyosaki tells us that RICH DAD was so tied to the "Pay Yourself First" concept that he would put money into savings before anything else got paid: the mortgage, the electricity, the car payment, the food, and even the taxes. Building assets is so profoundly fundamental to a secure financial future that RICH DAD paid himself before absolutely anyone else.

Please do not interpret this as a suggestion to neglect your other financial responsibilities. There is no morality in failing to pay our debts. Taking care of our responsibilities is the right thing to do—we can't consider our approach "moral" if we don't honor our commitments by paying what we owe. RICH DAD explains it this way (paraphrased), "After I pay myself first, if I don't have enough money for my other obligations, then I have to figure out a way to pay for them."

Granted, RICH DAD is an entrepreneur, which means he might have more latitude to "figure out a way," but to some degree, I want you to adopt that same attitude. If you don't have enough income to "Pay Yourself First" with enough money to create the financial security you wish, what should you do (or even what might you consider changing) to make that happen? We will dive deeper into this idea later in the text as well.

For now, start putting money away. If you are unsure how to begin, keep reading, and we'll devise a plan.

YOU CAN'T AFFORD NOT TO

"Do not save what is left after spending; instead, spend what is left after saving."
—Warren Buffett

Sometimes, people will say (and it could be true), "I can't afford to save." The truth is actually, "You can't afford not to." To have real financial security, you must build up long-term savings. It is the number one thing to do.

There are many mathematical and logical reasons for saving in this book, but consider this: "If you had enough money saved and invested so that you could pay off all your debts and generate enough income to pay all your expenses, wouldn't you feel financially secure?" The response, of course, is, "Yes!" This is the definition of financial security.

The lack of financial security is a source of fear, and decisions we make out of fear are rarely good choices. Let's consider Dave Ramsey, the author of "*Financial Peace,*" again. He filed for bankruptcy because of too much debt. This experience, his fear, is the primary reason he advocates for everyone to get out of debt first. Instead, I think he should consider other contributing factors for his bankruptcy, such as why he took on the debt, his education, discernment regarding this choice, and whether he had other assets or income to cover it. It's not the debt that's bad. It's the circumstances in which debt is created.

The idea of paying off all my debts and then focusing on saving means I MUST work longer to generate income to keep money moving first to debts and then to savings. The person who saves the money first creates an asset that works for them. People retire with debt all the time. It is not the end of the world. If we do this properly, it might create a bigger and better world for our future.

When I instruct our financial classes and discuss the pros and cons of paying off a mortgage early, people in the class will say, "There is a warm fuzzy feeling when you own your home debt-free." Absolutely, without one ounce of doubt, that is very true.

You know what else? I also get a warm, fuzzy feeling when I see tens of thousands of dollars in a savings account. It is particularly cozy if the balance in that account exceeds my mortgage payoff amount and increases by more than the monthly installment. That is impactful. That is security.

Think about everyone practicing the Dave Ramsey plan over the last few recent years (2019 to 2023), with mortgage interest rates in the 2 percent range and the stock market increasing by sizable double digits each year. It is absurd to advise someone to take their extra money to pay off debt at 2 percent instead of capitalizing on a 20 percent gain. The fact that he has not come out and corrected his advice as the market has changed is where morality comes in.

You might think, "Yeah, but those market gains disappeared with the 2022 volatility." Yes, but since editing this section in 2026, we've seen double-digit gains for the last 3 plus years.

We'll develop investment strategies in the coming pages. That is why I want you to start this savings strategy now. If you wish to return to a philosophy like Dave Ramsey's after seeing the value this book offers, you can apply the money you have saved to your debt. This brings me to another important point:

SAVING IS NOT AN EXPENSE

"Someone's sitting in the shade today because someone planted a tree a long time ago."
—Warren Buffett

When you take the money from your checking account, where you usually spend it, and put it in a savings account where you don't use it, it is still your money, right? It is there for you whenever you choose. It's more powerful if you leave it there and let it grow, but saving money is not an expense. It's just putting it in an account where you don't spend it now.

If you are unconvinced, let me tell you a little story about my mother. She worked for a school district in the Minneapolis area. She had to pay union dues and contribute to the pension as part of her employment contract. She would say, "I hate that they make me put this money away. I could use it now." My response: "But mom, you will NEED it later."

The same applies to all of us. We will need it later. Please don't fall victim to the urge to spend it now. Benjamin Franklin had it right when he said, "A penny saved is a penny earned." That one penny becomes many more pennies through the power of compounding. We gain the greatest benefit from the power of compounding when we have more time to let our pennies multiply. It is essential to start sooner rather than later.

Perhaps you are sitting there thinking, "Sure, Renée, all that sounds great, but my 'earlier' is past me. I'm (pick whatever age you are), and I didn't do this savings stuff when I was younger. It's too late for me." Oh, no—no, no—no, it is NEVER too late. If the earliest you can begin saving is today, you will be far better off having done it than continuing to put it off. Believe me, your future self will thank you.

A PENNY SAVED

"A penny saved is two pence clear."
—Benjamin Franklin, 1737 Poor Richard's Almanac
(Often paraphrased as "A penny saved is a penny earned.")

I'm hoping you are on board with saving now. If you are, you might be thinking, "Where the heck am I going to get this extra money to tuck away, Renée? I'm barely scraping by." While I have no idea about your current financial situation, there are a couple of things you can do right now to find the cash.

First, if you have been following Dave Ramsey's philosophy and allocating all your extra money to pay off debt, stop. Take that money and save it instead.

Pay your bills, and if you have any credit card debt that is not at some low special financing rate, pay it off or consolidate it to a loan with a lower interest rate. This is one of the things that Dave Ramsey got right. If we have a balance on high-interest-rate credit cards or any loan, that is a bad financial situation. But because of his fear of debt, he doesn't suggest moving to a lower-interest-rate loan. Doing so saves you money immediately, and Ben Franklin would be proud. This accelerates your path to financial freedom simply by reducing interest costs.

This is true of any debt charging above the current lending rate or the interest rate for which you can qualify. If you've had a rocky road to a good credit score, move that debt again to reduce the cost of interest as it improves. This is debt management: We need to periodically evaluate whether we can save a few pennies by moving our debt to a more favorable option. Ben would be proud!

To decide the best option for you, I want you to consider the cost of the loan, not so much the rate. Although the interest rate is essential, the term (the time it will take to pay off the loan) and other fees are also crucial. We'll discuss all this in more detail later, but in the meantime, move that debt to lower interest rates and shift any 'extra' dollars you were allocating to debt reduction under Dave's system into your savings pocket.

WHAT DID JESUS DO

"...give, and it will be given to you. Good measure, pressed down, shaken together, running over, will be put into your lap. For with the measure you use it will be measured back to you." —Jesus of Nazareth, Luke 6:38

If you follow the Dave principle of tithing 10 percent to the church each month, you might be able to stop that as well. Notice my tone is less emphatic than his. I am not in any position to dictate to you what GOD wants you to do with your financial capital. That is not my place, or Dave Ramsey's. That is between you and our Creator—that decision comes from the Flow.

I can tell you that Jesus did not mention tithing in the Gospels. He also said nothing about abortion, homosexuality, or a whole host of things that many Christians point to that somehow followers must adhere to. If these things were most essential to Jesus, I believe He would have discussed them...yet not a word.

Case in point for Jesus' thoughts on giving, in Mark 12:43-44, He says, *"this poor widow put in more than all the other contributors to the treasury; for they gave out of their surplus, but she, out of her poverty, gave all she owned, all she had to live on."* This demonstrates tremendous faith. Especially as a widow in ancient Israel, she had limited ability to earn a reasonable income. She felt compelled to give and gave it. When I say, 'compelled,' I mean something we sense when we ask GOD what we should do, and we feel a nudge in a specific direction.

Please notice, however, that Jesus didn't say, "She gave more than her tithe." He didn't say, "The other contributors stuck with their tithe." There is no mention of a tithe, and this woman's act of faith reflects the lack of fear we should all strive for in our financial decisions. She gave this without concern for her other needs.

Does Jesus call us to be generous? Yes. Would the Universe work much better if we all only kept what we needed and gave the rest away? I think it would be. After all, if this were the principle we all practiced, we'd all have the security of housing, and no one would be hungry. Yet, Jesus offers no mandate for either of these, so I won't tell you what you should do with your charitable giving.

If we genuinely believe in Spiritual guidance, then what GOD calls us to give will differ. We should search our hearts, pray, and seek advice from those we admire. The answers will come if we seek them and are responsive regarding what we should do for gifts, giving, and charity.

In Mark 10, Jesus tells the rich man to give it all and follow Him. When this young man could not do so, Jesus remarked, "It is easier for a camel to go through the eye of a needle than for a rich person to enter the Kingdom of GOD." [Here in the United States, our poor are wealthier than half the world's population. We'll spend some time discussing that in this book because you already are more affluent than you may believe.] What does this story say about what we do with our financial resources? On the one hand, Jesus says to give it all away, and on the other, to give freely.

Both can be true. If you are a person of faith, and even if you are not, we all see that each of us has different talents, gifts, passions, and callings. Maybe you will be asked to give monetarily, or your gift could be of time, talent, or experience. The important thing is to be receptive to what the Flow would have you do.

IT'S NOT A SLOT MACHINE

"One person gives freely, yet gains even more; another withholds unduly

but comes to poverty." —Proverbs 11:24

Generosity does not mean money will 'flow' back to us. Some consider this the Prosperity Gospel; Jesus gave it all away. He refused every opportunity to cash in on his position. In Matthew 8:20, Jesus says, "Foxes have dens and birds have nests, but the Son of Man has no place to lay his head."

When I first recommitted myself to faith, I was giving 10 percent to the church at a time when I could least afford it. I believed it to be obligatory. I cheerfully gave, and even now, I do not regret it, but underneath it all, I felt as if I kept giving the 10 percent, GOD would reward me in some way. During my financial struggle, I even remember praying in the pew one Sunday, "GOD, if you reward me financially, I promise to give all the extra to charity. I commit to being generous with what you've given me."

That didn't work. It seemed GOD had other plans for me. It turns out that I always seemed to have just enough, no matter what I gave or didn't give financially. This is GOD's economy, and we'll spend some time on it in the next chapter.

This is why I say that if you are tithing 10 percent and need to find a place to tap into to begin saving, I encourage you to look at these contributions and search your heart for what GOD would like you to do. As you consider this, I want to emphasize that there is no mandate to allocate all your charitable resources to the church or other religious organizations. GOD may have laid other charities and social needs on your heart. This is how all the necessary work gets done.

As I searched my soul in this area, I discovered other ways to give—through volunteering. I don't donate as much in cash as I used to, but I volunteer in all sorts of areas, and I believe this is what GOD wants me to do with my resources. Your time, talent, gifts, passions, education, and experiences are all a part of the resources GOD has blessed you with and calls us to share. If you tap into all this wealth, chances are your giving will exceed 10 percent. I know mine did.

Whatever you do, pray, soul-search, contemplate, ask for advice, and try some different things. See what feels right for you.

REDUCE EXPENSES

"He who buys what he does not need, steals from himself."
—Swedish Proverb

As with the other points before this, I cannot tell you the perfect way to reduce your expenses because we all spend our money differently. However, reducing your expenses is a surefire way to find money to save.

I can tell you a few things I do regularly:

- **Pack a lunch—**I met a friend at an outdoor coffee shop and brought a sandwich. When traveling for work, I pack a cooler with a few meals. I packed a salad mix, a sandwich, grapes, beverages, and some leftovers on my last trip. I still ate out a little during the two-day trip, but I significantly reduced the expense by grabbing a few things from my fridge before I left.
- **Walk or ride**—It's part of why I moved to the city. I walk or ride as much as possible. I bike fourteen miles to church on Sunday. (Thank GOD for e-bikes!) As I write this, I'm at a park, four miles from home, with my bike behind me. Yesterday, I had to get in the car for the first time all weekend to drive to a party 30 miles from my home, which is not the norm. Many days go by with the car in the garage and precious gas saved.
- **Eliminate cable and the landline**—If you live in an area like mine where you can tap antenna TV and the cell coverage is good, get rid of those other expenses if you still have them.
- **Check your food budget**—Are there things you can eliminate or reduce? I know this will sound unbelievable, but I usually spend only about $40 on groceries each week. Granted, I live alone and eat out a few times a week, but I no longer buy junk food. I invested in a freezer to stock up on sale

items. In the summer, I garden, then can and freeze in the fall. I also don't eat three meals a day. I am grateful for the science of intermittent fasting because my natural pattern is one to two meals per day.

- **Thrift stores and secondary markets**—It goes without saying that buying something used in good condition can provide natural savings. Recently, I've been doing this more and more for my clothing. Americans buy so much in excess that the second-hand clothing market has practically new items.
- **Reduce beauty, electronics, coffee, happy hour drinks, nicotine, you name it**—We all have things we might spend our money on that we can tap into to kick this off. For me, in the early days, it was the beauty stuff. I spent about $100 per month to get my nails done. I could not justify continuing to do that when my income went down. Do I miss it? Yes. As I typed this section, I looked at my stubby, imperfect nails and missed those manicures, but—and this is an important BUT—I like vacations, time off, events with family, and my new e-bike a lot more than those pretty nails. I can't afford it all, so I must prioritize.

This is by no means a complete list. Consider your budget, invite GOD in, listen, and see what you can and should rearrange to afford a little cushion in your finances.

One last thing: Be patient with yourself and do your best to stay on track. Early in my journey, I knew GOD wanted me to quit smoking and drinking. Both were a significant drain on my budget. One was killing me, and the other was utterly unnecessary, BUT it took me a while to let them go. Old habits die hard. If you feel the pull to let an item go but are afraid or have some difficulty, that's okay. Stay the course, ask GOD for help, and follow the path toward healing and freedom. You'll get there.

WHERE TO PUT YOUR PENNIES

"If you're saving, you're succeeding."—Steve Burkholder

In this book, we'll discuss strategies to find a financial advisor and get better educated about savings options to help you determine where to put your pennies and create an investment mix that helps build wealth through all sorts of market trends. For now, here are some simple strategies to get started.

1. Start with your 401(k) first if you are not taking advantage of the maximum employer match in your work-related retirement plan. Each matching dollar your company puts in that account is FREE money—in every sense of the word, FREE. If you go this route, you will not be able to return to the Dave Ramsey plan and use these dollars to pay off debt without penalty. In the end, please believe me, you will not regret your contribution to this account. Your future retired self will thank you.
2. If you are already taking advantage of the full employer match in your retirement plan, I would put the money in a Roth IRA. Consider making the maximum contribution here as well. For 2026, the annual limit is $7,500, or about $625 monthly. Those ages 50 or older can add an extra $1,000 per year, or $8,500 ($708 monthly). If you've been told your AGI (Adjusted Gross Income) is too high for a Roth, Google "Backdoor Roth IRA" and follow the directions. The IRA limits are indexed for inflation, so be sure to check the current amounts.

I recommend establishing a monthly, weekly, or per-pay-period contribution. This has an advantage for two reasons:

1. You don't know your finances at the end of the year. Coming up with $7,500 or $8,500 in a lump sum is more complicated than $310.00 twice a month.
2. Routine contributions mean you can DOLLAR COST AVERAGE. We'll discuss this in more detail in the fifth chapter, "Tools & The Trade Off." To summarize, instead of trying to time the market and invest at the lowest price to maximize gain, you 'average' this risk by buying routinely. Sometimes, you will buy high, and sometimes, you will buy low, but by buying regularly, you will reduce the risk of buying high with a large sum.

If you cannot afford the full Roth contribution, that's okay--contribute what you can. However, I encourage you to stretch your budget to find every available penny. Remember, you are PAYING YOURSELF FIRST, and YOU are your most important outlay. Each extra penny you can get into your savings helps your future security.

As you decide on your contribution amount, I also encourage you to consider possible fluctuations and your financial needs. For example, my business is seasonal. Like most of us, insurance agents like to have their schedule freed up during the holidays, so my sales go down in November and December. As a result, I contribute $850 (one-tenth of the current $8,500 catch-up contribution limit) per month to my Roth IRA from January to October (ten months) and then nothing for the last two months of the year. This also means my budget isn't as tight when I have all the holiday spending.

NOTE: The bonus with this seasonal method is that historically, the year's final quarter often sees a rise in the stock market. It's not guaranteed, of course, but it also means I have a greater likelihood of buying low through the year with a bump in value by year's end.

Consider something similar, depending on your financial needs. The important thing is to start saving and do it consistently. If these two bundles are full, that is, you're taking complete advantage of the employer match at work, and you have the total allowed contribution to a Roth IRA, then take the extra amount you've established and put it away. Save it, and don't touch it. The other thing I'd like you to do is pat yourself on the back. You are doing more for your financial future than most Americans.

A PENNY FOR YOUR THOUGHTS

"One penny may seem to you a very insignificant thing, but it is the small seed from which fortunes spring." —Orison Swett Marden

The final consideration is where to put your pennies. For now, I suggest you put them in an S&P 500 INDEX FUND. The S&P 500 is considered a good gauge of large-cap U.S. equities and represents about 80 percent of the U.S. equity market by capitalization. As of October 2025, the index had an aggregate market cap of over $57 trillion.

We'll discuss different investment options and basic diversification strategies later in the book. You could put the pennies in a money market or savings account, but traditionally, a large-cap index fund will outperform a savings account over the long term. While the Dow Jones Industrial Average is a viable option, the S&P 500 offers greater diversification. Conversely, the NASDAQ may present higher volatility.

IMPORTANT POINT—even though the S&P 500 might be less volatile than the NASDAQ, that does not mean you will not experience any volatility. Your account will fluctuate in value. That is the nature of the beast, BUT the S&P 500 averaged a gain of about 10 percent per year over the 30 years from 1992 to 2021. You can also go back to the 1950s and the turn of the last century to see the same trend. If we adjust that for inflation, that is about 7 percent per year—again, not bad.

These are "averages." For example, I wrote this section during the summer of 2022—the market had been down about 20 percent since January. Many people were whining, and some were even acting as if the world might end. I was editing this about two years later, in September 2024, and the previous 2022 value of about 3,700 had risen to a record high of almost 5,800, representing a gain of over 55 percent. I'm working on another edit in October 2025, and the value is at 6,552 with a 12-month yield of 11.65 percent. Not quite as good as the prior two years, but a nice gain nonetheless.

It is essential to put this into perspective. The last ten years of the S&P 500 have produced tremendous gains, with double-digit returns in the 20 percent range over a couple of years. Sure, there were some minor losses during those years, and it matters when you invest, but most people who have had some money invested in the market in the last few years are way ahead.

Importantly, none of us knows what the future will bring, and another major correction could be on the horizon at any time. This can cause anxiety, but fear is your enemy in creating a peaceful and prosperous future. Don't worry or fret—take the most significant amount you can afford, put it away, and don't think about it. Don't look at the value every day. Don't concern yourself with the value except a few times per year when it's time to determine if your plan is still the best for you. More on that in the chapter regarding investment strategies entitled "More FREE Pennies". It's time to discuss planning the direction of your life by considering "GOD's Economy".

CHAPTER TWO

GOD'S ECONOMY

A SPIRITUAL GUIDE TO TRUE PROSPERITY

"Follow your instincts. That's where true wisdom manifests itself."
—Oprah Winfrey

THE PLAN IS IN YOU

Fear is the enemy in all sorts of endeavors. It can stop us from pursuing a dream, chatting with the person we are attracted to, trying for that new job, starting a business, making a significant purchase, and all sorts of opportunities GOD might be calling us to do or be. Fear can also rob us of peace, joy, serenity, and financial security.

One of the best ways to eliminate fear is to have a plan and be confident in it. The mechanics of making wise financial choices will be discussed in the later chapters of this book. These include paying off debt or savings, selecting investments, and deciding whether to buy this insurance policy or that one. I promise to offer you tools to navigate all that, but before we get there, it's vital to discuss methods for tapping into your own inner wisdom.

Financial planning is not one-size-fits-all. Just as we are not all equally productive or capable in the same career, the financial strategy that works for me may not work for you. Some principles govern how money, interest rates, and economic trends generally apply, but there are always exceptions. What is far more valuable is for you to know and understand how these things work and hone the sense to determine the best choice—an intuition, if you will. As important, the best financial choice can vary over time. It is essential to be able to determine when a change is needed and apply a strategy to carry out that change.

Most of these points are common sense and things that many of us do automatically. Making good choices is not rocket science. It means listening to that still, soft voice that we too often get used to ignoring.

OPPOSITE WORLD

"Moral outrage is the opposite of GOD; it only divides and separates what GOD wants for us, which is to be united in kinship. Moral outrage doesn't lead us to solutions — it keeps us from them."

—Gregory Boyle, Barking to the Choir

You will be making money and choosing financial directions in the real world, but we will gain the most wealth if we tap into GOD's economy, which is an opposite world. It is often counterintuitive to the transactional, what's in-it-for-me, quid pro quo, selfish reality of this world. In GOD's economy, glasses are not half full or half empty; they are overflowing.

- GOD's economy gives us greater freedom and autonomy when we give up control. (Mark 8:35)
- When we feel unlovable, we are offered grace and unsurpassable worth. (Romans 5:6-8)
- We gain power through our weakness and can boast with gratitude in hardship. (2 Corinthians 12)
- The tiniest faith moves mountains. (Matthew 17:20)
- The smallest offering feeds many. (Matthew 14:13-21)
- Water is turned to wine. (John 2:1-11)
- We give something away, and we get more in return. (Luke 6:38)

You might be reading this and thinking, "Sure, Renée, I've read all that stuff before. It makes great stories, but the real world doesn't operate like that." You are correct. Sometimes, the process doesn't work as described above, and I do not claim to have all the answers. I cannot guarantee you worldly riches. I can, however, assure you that a change in perspective changes everything.

CREATOR ACCOUNTING

"It's simply a matter of creative accounting." —Mel Brooks

Have you heard of "creative accounting"? This method of accounting capitalizes on loopholes to falsely portray a better financial image. In GOD's economy, there's a unique method called "Creator Accounting". Let me use a personal story to illustrate.

Early on, as I explored my faith, I thought one way I could benefit GOD's plans and improve my finances was to work in ministry. You probably think, "Renée, unless you've got a fascinating notion of GOD's economy, most people in ministry don't make much money."

You are right, but even a low-paying job can equal more money to me. Part of my insurance continuing education business is online classes. I could work in ministry and still have the income from our online courses. I would have a dual income that equates to more money and helps (hopefully) a good cause. In this grand plan, instead of seeking GOD's will for me, I prayed for what I wanted—a new job.

The problem was that no new job came. I would apply at my church for jobs I was overqualified for—nothing. I would submit my resume to other non-profits for which I was a perfect fit—nothing. All the while, I was praying for what I wanted and getting increasingly pessimistic about the blessing I had been given—a fantastic business with clients who loved me, which generated an income that had sustained my family and me for years. I couldn't see and feel the beautiful gift GOD had given me because I was so wrapped up in my plans.

That's when GOD took me on another journey to learn another life lesson. I met a woman on a mission trip who was the Executive Director at a Christian women's shelter. I told her of my desire to enter the ministry, and shortly after our return, she had an opening for a Case Manager. Since we had gotten to know each other in the field, I went through a quick interview process, and my grand plan worked. I was working in a ministry! Even better, I thought, I could offer a lot of help from my personal experiences. I was hired at an hourly rate higher than that of any other Case Manager. My plan was working!

But not entirely—and this is where Creator Accounting comes into the mix. The whole time I worked there, my books never balanced. After I started working there, balancing two jobs, I did not have enough money to pay all my bills. I kept going into the red and wasn't spending more than before. It just did not make any sense. I should have been making a lot more money—I should have had money to save, but whenever I sat down to balance the books, I could not stretch each dollar far enough. It was like the story of the loaves and fishes in Matthew 14 in reverse. Instead of lunch for one feeding thousands, my presumed excess turned into five loaves and two fish.

Equally important, I was heartbroken at the job. My friends would say, "I've never seen you so negative about something." And I was—and I couldn't shake it. Instead of working with the women, they had me collecting donations, which is not a job I would have accepted or wanted. I kept telling myself, "This is GOD's will for you. You should do the best job you can." Colossians 3:23 became my mantra, "Work willingly at whatever you do, as though you were working for the Lord rather than for people."

I was not working willingly—I was angry and frustrated. Through all of this, I never really considered GOD's will for me. I assumed that being in Christian ministry was a noble and helpful job, so naturally, it was GOD's will. Looking back, it was my will run amok.

My negative attitude got me fired after three months, but here is another GOD moment for you. After discussing with the Executive Director about how I was not a good fit for the job, I went to my car. I was upset, and all the while,

I was in a mind trap: "How will I get another ministry job?" I was still seeing what I thought was best. I was a frazzled mess, and I didn't know what to do next when my phone rang. On the other end was a long-time customer and an excellent businessman.

He asked, "Renée, I know you took another job, but your live classes for next year are still on the website. Are you planning to instruct them?" At that moment, I gushed out all that was happening—how frustrating the job was. I told him they gave me one job working with the women and then put me in the office. I told him I had just been fired and didn't know what to do.

He then said, "Well, Renée, just come back. Your classes are still posted here. Just come back." Even thinking about it now, I don't understand why I couldn't see that before he said it. I left those classes there so I could return, but I was so wrapped up in the idea that I should be in ministry—that working for a non-profit was GOD's will for me —that I could not see what was right before my eyes the entire time.

PRAYERS ARE ANSWERED

"GOD sometimes answers our prayers by giving us what we would have asked for had we known what He knows." —J. D. Greear

I truly believe that GOD answered my prayers for a job in ministry to show me what it's like out there and how I am right where I should be, creating and instructing educational material. Running my education business and writing this book allows me to share many concepts that help people. I returned to my business with new excitement and vigor. That was almost 10 years ago, and not a day goes by now that I don't thank GOD for the opportunity to share, research, and educate on a wide range of topics. I love my job, and I have no idea why I thought I should leave it.

After this experience went full circle, when I thought back, I envisioned GOD hearing all these prayers from me, "Give me a job. Give me a job. Give me a job. Give me a job. Hey GOD—give me a job." All the while, GOD was watching and thinking—and probably whispering, "Hey, Renée, I've given you this great blessing. You have a job that is perfect for you. I gave you the talent and passion for it. You help people through your work. If you listen more, there are more great ideas and suggestions for you." But I couldn't hear any of this, I couldn't sense it—I couldn't recognize it because I am running around thinking, "I've got the plan."

In all this, I imagine GOD saying, "Okay, Renée, you can't recognize the BIG plan right now. Here's a job to show you what you desire so much." I was sent on another journey of revelation—not to punish me but to show me how to be of maximum service right where I am. I also learned that the world is more harmonious when I am GOD-reliant and seek GOD's will first.

On an interesting note, when I came back to my business, my books were finally balanced. Even though I had one less job, I now had enough money. That is Creator Accounting in GOD's economy. When we are in GOD's will, or the Flow, things will flow through and to us, and the books will balance on the plus side.

I know it doesn't make rational sense. It's like the shortfall I experienced during the faith journey that I shared in the introduction. There was no rational reason for my finances to change so dramatically then or for this interesting correlation to occur. But it did happen, it did—and it further strengthened my reliance on seeking GOD's plan for my life. It convinced me that life works better in the Flow, and it's worth twisting those magnets around so the energy connection is strong.

Here is another thing I began to recognize during this experience: If I have a negative feeling that I can't shake with prayer, acceptance, or the power of positivity (as happened with my ministry job), I generally need to consider doing something different. A change is likely necessary to get back into the "Flow." I didn't fully recognize the power of this until after a few more lessons.

FINDING THE FLOW —GET ORGANIZED

"A river doesn't just carry water, it carries life."
—A.D. Posey, Write It Down (2017)

Late in 2021, my income began to fall again. I mentioned earlier how these seasonal changes are typical, so I didn't think much of it. When it hit March, and my income wasn't on a solid uptick, I began to worry. I had been concerned that many of my customers were retiring, and I wasn't picking up enough new clients to replace them. That is not a sustainable business plan. To make matters worse, in 2020 and 2021, I received COVID-19 relief funds through the "Paycheck Protection Program." There would be none of that for 2022.

Having been through this before, I started considering all my options and looking at what I should do. In truth, I was figuring out what GOD would have me do. I started with a list of options to help me bring in more money or reduce my expenses. It resembled this:

- Get a job
- Spruce up my resume
- Work part-time as a Flight Attendant
- Write my book
- Prep for house rental
- Advertise on the internet
- Improve website search rankings
- Create pre-licensing classes
- Rebrand my business

The list wasn't static. Whenever I had a new idea or a friend suggested something, I'd add it to the list. Many of these items need more than just one step to research or begin. When starting the process for any item, I would add to or cross off items on my list depending on what I had learned. It was very fluid, and I would look at the list each day and determine which item I felt like pursuing.

Depending on your objective, your list may be vastly different. Maybe you've been trying, unsuccessfully, to conceive a child. Your list might include appointments with healthcare providers, reviewing adoption services, exploring foster care options, savings or financing options for fertility treatments, and more. Maybe going back to school is a possibility, so your list is checking out colleges, degree options, financial aid, and determining whether to use personal savings or income, etc. Your focus could be on achieving a secure retirement. Your list would likely include reviewing expenses to reduce monthly costs, exploring savings alternatives, and using educational tools to learn more about investing, among other financial strategies.

Whatever your goal, there is a list to help you stay on task and get organized. Nearly every list will include a financial consideration, which is why the information discussed in this book is so important.

1

Get organized—write a list of opportunities to pursue. Remember that the list will change over time as new ideas are presented to you, and many items will have multiple tasks associated with them. Keep it organized and fluid.

THE FLOW HAS ENERGY

"Those who flow as life flows know they need no other force." —*Lao Tzu*

Over the years of seeking GOD's will for my life, I have begun to understand that the item I have energy for is likely what I should do. In my experience, energy is part of the life source of the Flow. For years, I would push myself in ways that exhausted me or stay in relationships that drained me, but now I try to stay in the Flow and go where my energy takes me. Granted, there are things I must push myself to do, but the truth is, rarely is anything so important that it can't be rescheduled, postponed, or canceled.

The first one, "Get a Job", was simple and easy to do, and I have the energy for simple and easy. A friend told me that a woman in our social circle would help me spruce up my resume. It is part of her full-time employment, and she wants to help the women she knows succeed, so she offers this service free of charge. If you go to her website, the revised resume and social media profile will cost about $2,500, so having her help me at no cost was a fantastic gift.

I reached out to her, and she was excited to help. I emailed her my resume with the other information she requested. We also set an appointment to discuss my objectives. When we met a few days later, she said, "I noticed on your resume that you are a business owner. Do you want a job? Or would you prefer to develop your business further?"

This is a no-brainer—I reply, "Further develop my business." I explain some of the challenges in my business, like prior attempts to gain more market share, and why I am thinking it's best to see what the employment market offers to maximize my income before I retire.

She says, "Helping people with resumes is a side gig for extra money. My day job is helping women business owners become multi-millionaires. Would you like to make a million a year or more?"

Don't feel alone if you are feeling a bit of shock and awe, and even doubting this story. When this happened, I felt like I had entered the Twilight Zone. I wanted to start looking around for a Candid Camera, but the surprises were not over yet. Then she said, "Our services normally cost in the $24,000 range, but I would be happy to help you for free."

Oh yes, you read that right. FREE! Nothing—zero dollars. I get to keep all my pennies. At this point, I stopped looking for any camera, and my shock and awe turned to suspicion with thoughts like, "Is this a joke? Is she running a scam? This cannot be for real." As my head swam with all these thoughts, she kept talking about strategies in legitimate language. I started to recognize that this could be a real opportunity. After we spoke further and set a plan for our next meeting, I crossed "Get a Job" off my list and added "Re-Brand My Business".

YAY, GOD! We'll discuss many perspectives on this little gem of a GOD shot later in other sections of the book.

2

Go where the Energy is—work on the motivating items. We have harnessed an energy force that craves accomplishment when in the Flow. If you are not feeling particularly 'motivated,' that's okay. It happens—try to find something you would like to accomplish that day.

GO WHERE THE DOORS OPEN

"Follow your bliss and the universe will open doors where there were only walls."
—Joseph Campbell

The next one I tackled was "Work as a Part-time Flight Attendant." Years earlier, on a flight to Mexico, I was in the back of the plane and befriended the attendants stationed there. I had often thought it would be a fun gig to fly around and attend to the traveling passengers. The real motivation was the benefits of free travel. They told me a little about their pay—not fantastic—and the hours—not fabulous either, but it might help bring in a few bucks.

When I did the research, however, each lead fizzled. This is the other thing I know about seeking GOD's will: When it is something I should be doing, doors open, and things happen. If I hit roadblocks or the options don't work out, it's time for me to put my energy elsewhere. This would be challenging if I were determined to achieve at all costs, but I have come to understand the importance of maintaining the Flow over time.

Also, it is imperative to note that sometimes obstacles are things we should work to overcome. For example, my daughter wanted to go to medical school, but she had a low MCAT score because her test date overlapped with the death of her grandmother, my mom. It was a crushing blow, and she thought she had ruined her chances to get into a career she'd dreamed about and planned for several years. Even though some might consider this a sign that a door was closing, she did not let this one hindrance stop her.

She began applying to various schools, worrying that this might not work out and that she'd have to give up on her life's dream. I kept telling her, "When GOD puts a passion in your heart for something, GOD will make a way." I believe this, too. Our passions and dreams come from the Flow. She received some declines, but with her first acceptance (yes, she had more than one), she called me up, super excited, to share the news, and I uttered words I don't typically say, "I told you so."

If you have a passion or a dream, in my experience, GOD will make a way, so persevere and take risks. I am confident you will be rewarded. Being a flight attendant was a passing fancy, not a life's dream. When I encountered roadblocks, this employment idea got crossed off the list.

3

Go where the doors open—GOD will make way for you in the Flow. Doors will open, good things will happen, and new ideas will be presented. If some doors close, it's no big deal. Look at the other ideas on your list.

FEELING THE FLOW

"Going with the flow is responding to cues from the universe. When you go with the flow, you're surfing life force." —Danielle LaPorte

The next item I considered was "Prep the House for Rental." This requires more explanation. I enjoy traveling and do it as much as I can. I am also blessed with friends and family who live in various places in North America and like me enough to let me stay with them. This dramatically reduces my travel expenses, allows me to stay longer, and lets me spend time with people I love. It is also a fantastic perk of the job I tried to leave for ministry work. It never ceases to amaze me how much better things are when I leave the choices to GOD.

With all this travel, I am sometimes away from my home for weeks at a time. From the 12 months beginning in August 2021, I was away from home for about three months or a quarter of the year. My house is left vacant while I still pay the mortgage and utilities. Listing it on short-term rental sites would cover expenses and generate income.

I started by getting a bid to build walls in my basement to store my items. The cost was more than expected, but I was still not ready to cross this item off the list. Next, I started checking the rental rates for other houses in my area. These were lower than I had hoped. Even though things were not moving in my favor, I still hadn't given up on this one because a friend of mine knew someone who transitioned these properties—cleaning them, replenishing items, and assisting guests with requests. This is the type of service I would need to rent my home, as I would be out of town and unable to take care of it. I also thought a connection like this was too serendipitous to be a coincidence. This must be part of the Flow.

I reached out to the contact. He asked for my ad. I replied that I was gathering information at this stage and asked for his rates, but I received no response for days. That is not a great sign, but I was still willing to give him the benefit of the doubt. Occasionally, things fall through the cracks. We are all guilty of missing a text or forgetting to hit the send button.

I tried again, and his response came out of left field. He started talking about problems with his email when we'd been texting. I sent him a screenshot to clarify my request, but there was no response. As you'd imagine, "Prep House for Rental" got crossed off the list. As much as I thought this might be a great idea, there were risks involved with this income alternative, and my overall feeling about this was not comfortable.

In addition to going where the Energy is and staying in a lane where the doors are open, I rely heavily on my feelings to navigate where GOD might want me to be. This one can be a little sticky. After all, I can convince myself that certain feelings I might have are GOD's will for me, and then I will act on impulse for all sorts of things that are not helpful to me or those around me. Here, I try to rely on a two-point test:

1. **Feeling** is like intuition or a sixth sense and is sometimes counterintuitive to what I 'think' I should do. It is not the same as a feeling that could be whimsical, sad, or insecure today. This is a read on how comfortable (or anxious) an idea or a situation makes me feel.
2. **Wisdom** is more profound than pure knowledge, yet still very reliant on facts, and is more educational than feelings. Wisdom depends on the sense of what is right and might also be called discernment. This point is like saying, "You want to have your wits about you."

In American culture, 'feelings' are frequently shamed or minimized. Many people will tell us not to rely on our 'feelings.' I think this is wrong. Our emotions and other primal senses are GOD-given, reflect our Creator, and keep us connected to GOD. Regardless of your beliefs, many see Jesus as a great prophet, and He was a very emotional man. Flipping tables (Matthew 21:12-13, Mark 11:15-18), openly weeping at a friend's passing (John 11:35), and His fears the night before His death (Luke 22:43—46) are just three examples of how Jesus also used feelings to navigate through this world. This fabulous man gave us a road map worthy of following, and in my experience, interpreting our feelings is necessary to navigate the Flow.

4

Honor your feelings—how we feel about things can guide us to and through the Flow. Stay where things feel safe. Avoid things that feel uncomfortable. Although it appears straightforward, I have often persuaded myself not to adhere to this crucial instinct. Trust yourself.

REVISIT OLD IDEAS

"Yesterday's the past, tomorrow's the future, but today is a gift. That's why it's called the present." —Bil Keane

I didn't spend much time on "Create Pre-Licensing Classes". I had considered creating these courses before, and it was just too much work for the Return on Investment (ROI). There was a limited market. Ultimately, I had no energy for it —I crossed it right off the list.

The other two, "Advertise on the Internet" and "Improve Website Search Rankings," were winners. In 2021, we launched a new website to improve our SEO (Search Engine Optimization). Better SEO means your website ranks higher in relevant searches. I created new pages to drive more traffic from common searches and returned to Google to see whether some advertisements would increase sales.

This is why it can pay off to "Revisit Old Ideas". In years past, I was paying way too much for Google ads for the sales we were gaining in return. Google now has a method to synchronize things for us. The results improved. Today, all our results are up. Our year-to-date performance for 2023 increased by 15 percent compared to 2022.

A benefit of old ideas is that they generally don't take too much time to assess. Since we have experience analyzing them, we can typically quickly decide whether this route will work or not. Look how quickly we went through three ideas from the list.

5

Revisit old ideas—continuing to put ideas that didn't work before on the list doesn't always pay off, but sometimes things change, and an old idea that didn't work before might bring benefit today.

TALK ABOUT IT

"Find a group of people who challenge and inspire you; spend a lot of time with them, and it will change your life." —Amy Poehler

Even though I worked through several items on my list by June 2022, my income hadn't turned around. I was left with two time-consuming items on my list: "Write My Book" and "Rebrand My Business," and neither one of them made my heart sing.

Since I wasn't sure what I should do and had exhausted the options I had thought of, I began talking about it. Whenever anyone I trust, value, appreciate, or respect asked, "How are you doing?" I would tell them.

Granted, I didn't just blurt out all of my issues, but if appropriate, I would say, "Not so great. My income is down, and I'm trying to figure out what to do." If they asked for more, I would share. Often, a conversation would ensue. GOD will provide us with guidance from those around us at opportune moments. Two crucial guidepost conversations took place around this time, and each helped me make decisions about my remaining items.

I loved working with the woman who became my consultant to rebrand my business. She was high-energy—just my style. I loved our conversations. We were very much alike and became fast friends. She had me use a model she incorporated with other business owners. It was an opportunity for me to reflect on and consider the direction of my company; using her model provided some research so she could get to know my products, market, and business model.

The work on the model was an energy drag (and we know what that means—I likely was out of step with the Flow), but I also knew I couldn't give up on it because of how I felt at that moment. If I saw the process through, there still could be something to learn. Practical life skills are valuable as we seek the Flow.

Something interesting (and emotional) was happening at these meetings. Sometimes, when we talked about my company or the data, I would begin to cry as I tried to answer. Anyone who knows me realizes I am an emotional person on the full spectrum from elation to sorrow and sometimes anger. But to cry in a business meeting discussing facts? No—tears are generally not part of the process.

I knew these feelings were telling me something, and even as I reflect now, I am not sure why that was coming up and flowing out. It might have been a release from some of the fear and grief. I knew things would change in my business, and I was unsure what would happen. What is more accurate is that I do not understand why I was emotional. It wasn't the first time I was anointed with tears for no rational reason. I knew the tears were telling me something, and I should honor them—the reason why was of no importance compared to acknowledging their validity in this process.

Around this time, I was walking with a friend, and the opportunity was presented to discuss it. She was interested because she has a writer's heart like me. As we chatted, the conversation returned to my business when an idea struck her. This is GOD at work for me. Random thoughts from seemingly nowhere, I believe, are coming from Somewhere, and she said, "You know, I have a friend whose business model is a little like yours. Maybe he can be of help to you, too. I'll contact him to see if he has time to talk with you."

These moments are why the list is fluid. GOD will keep revealing new things to us, and I was excited about this opportunity to speak with her friend. The energy and positive feelings were good signs for finding the Flow.

As often happens, arranging a time to talk to her friend took a while. I liked his energy, too, and, as my friend suggested, many aspects of his story were like mine. As he described his process of reviving his business and lifestyle, my interest started to wane. As he continued, I didn't believe much of what he shared would benefit me, but I kept listening in case a GOD nugget was in the mix.

In the conversation, he said, "What are you thinking of doing?" I started to talk about some of the business plans I had been developing. When I was done, he said, "At first, when you talked about your customers and course content, you sounded energized, but as soon as you started discussing the strategies to rebrand your business, I thought you might have more fun watching paint dry."

That was the heart of the matter—I was following this lead because I thought it was what I should do to make the most money. The opportunity had presented itself, but I was not excited about rebranding Bryan Ventures. I liked it the way it was, and so did my customers. Here's a little secret about that, too—even though I told myself that I didn't want to make a million a year, I kept following this method that brought me no energy or joy because I thought I would secretly find a million in my business. Doing things solely for the money is counter to the Flow.

I started telling him that I would like to take all I'd learned from my financial career and put it in a book. I wanted to help people build wealth, find freedom from fear, and create real happiness. I said I didn't know where it would go or if it would do anything, but it would be worth it if I could help even a few people. There is too much bad advice, and I wanted to give people a plan.

When I finished, he said, "Well, there you go. That's what you should do. I could feel energy and joy through the phone. I have no idea where this will go for you, but if people are one-tenth as passionate as you are about this, it's sure to take off."

When it's over, and the idea is settled, it seems so obvious. Thinking back, I don't know why I couldn't see it. I also recognize that the process—the uncertainty, new connections, various ideas, searching, making determinations, learning new things, and being vulnerable—is an opportunity to grow and become more reliant on things I instinctively know through seeking and dependence on the Flow.

I had one immediate obstacle. I had to tell a remarkable, accomplished woman who had graciously offered to help me create a new business strategy that I now had a different plan. What I thought would be an obstacle turned out to be an open door. When I shared the book idea with her, she said, "Renée, why didn't you share this with me earlier? Part of the intention of this process is to discover other ideas about which you are passionate. Whatever brings us joy will always produce positive results."

With those words, I could nearly hear heaven sing. Everything had come together in perfect harmony, and the height of irony was that, soon after, the cash-flow logjam in my business began to bust apart, and more revenue started streaming in. I had my usual winter holiday dip, but since I started writing this book, money has not been as much of a concern as before.

It is even hard for me to believe, but when I consider all of this, GOD might have orchestrated some of the financial concerns, or at least utilized them, to motivate me to get this book written. I had this outline collecting dust for years, and who knows how much longer I would have continued this literary atrophy. This seeming hardship brought something good. That's the norm in GOD's economy—what we think is a drawback or a hindrance may instead be a stepping stone or a breakthrough.

6

Talk about it—GOD speaks through the people around us, so discussing possibilities and concerns with the people we trust and respect can bring guidance and new ideas.

LET YOUR HEART SING

"Every single day, do something that makes your heart sing."
—Marcia Wieder

Even though it was an enormous undertaking, I wanted to write this book. I did, but I had another hurdle to overcome. Part of my writing process is to get out of my home space. In 2017, I created a blog after I started biking to the cathedral each morning. Close to sunrise, I'd pedal hard until I hit the steps of that beacon of faith. It's grand and beautiful—two things that reflect how I feel when I feel Spiritually awakened. I have always been drawn to this place—even if my faith wanes, I sense GOD there.

I would sit at the top of the steps, near the fifteen-foot doors, overlooking the city, and pray. Then, I would head to a nearby coffee shop to read the gospels. During each ride or reading, the Flow would bring me an idea I would write as a daily devotional or prayer. The writings fill a blog, and maybe I'll publish them someday. Those moments of connection to Divine creativity generally do not happen sitting at my home office.

It was 2022, and I'd hardly written for a few years. In 2019, I had to move further from the city. I couldn't afford to buy a home in those areas around the cathedral, and the distance and the hills kept me from my bike. I missed it terribly. Cycling is not only helpful for my writing inspiration but also for my health and weight. It's also fabulous for my wallet and the planet, as I can get where I want without a drop of gasoline. It rings so many bells for me and makes my heart sing—and remember, "When GOD puts a passion in our heart, GOD will make a way."

I thought the solution was a new e-bike. For those unfamiliar with these bikes, they have an electric motor and offer pedal assistance, making hills and longer rides more enjoyable. I'd been shopping for various models, but buying one during a financial downturn did not seem prudent. GOD's economy, however, sometimes has other ideas about wise financial choices.

I knew I would have to make this investment if I hoped to write this book. I lived in this area of giant hills, an hour's bike ride from the city, for three years and had ridden my bike twice. I wrote some, I did, but most of that was inspired by other travels. If I hoped to get these pages written, I had to get out of the house. There were two financial reasons I decided to make this purchase:

1. I had the money in my savings. It was in the stock market, and my pennies were making more pennies, so I didn't want to pull it out, but I did have the money for it if necessary.
2. They offered me a good financing deal. I thought it would be zero percent, but they gave me over 4 percent after the application process. I was upset with this new offer—it felt like a bait-and-switch. (Bait-and-switch is when they lure you in with a promotion and then switch it once you are hooked.) With further consideration, the cost of interest on the bike over an 18-month term was only $60, or $5 per month, so I took it. We'll discuss decisions like these in the chapter "Debt is NOT Bad".

This bike was riddled with problems—horrible brakes, fenders falling off, a charging station not working, a tire blowout—you name it, this bike had issues. At times, the company has been great. Other times, horrible. When I wrote this, I finally received a new charging dock after waiting 4 months. But this bike has also brought me so much joy. In the four months I rode it that summer, the odometer clocked nearly 2,000 miles. Since I used this bike to run errands around the city, I also figured that was 2,000 fewer miles on my car and 100 fewer gallons of gas purchased. In the summer of 2022, gas prices were around $4.00 per gallon, so I saved about $400 in fuel. Maybe that wasn't joy, but it made me happy—and I started writing again.

7

Let your heart sing—we work hard not just to make money but to use that money for what brings joy to the people around us and ourselves. Our happiness is a motivator.

PRACTICE MAKES PROGRESS

"Continuous improvement is better than delayed perfection."
—Mark Twain (pseudonym of Samuel Langhorne Clemens (1835 - 1910))

At this point, you might be sitting there thinking, "Okay, Renée, I hear you, and to some extent, tapping into this Flow makes some sense. However, I don't seem to pick up on those signals." This is super common—and do not worry about that. The signals are there—GREAT BIG arrows are pointing to the Flow, and awareness is the most effective way to become more attuned.

There are countless easy methods to tap the Flow. It is not a one-size-fits-all route. Your route may vary from mine, yet just like so many things in GOD's economy, while I tell you this can be effortless, navigation can be hard work. It may require a change of heart or mind to find the Flow, or a daily commitment to try, like moving magnets, to attract rather than repel.

All of that might feel intimidating right now. I understand, but please don't worry about that. Stay present right now, at this moment, and each part of the plan we need will be revealed when we need it. Tapping the Flow is simple: Step into the Universe for solutions and follow the signs.

Following, or even sensing, those signs brings us to number eight: "Practice Makes Progress." Unlike the saying, "Practice Makes Perfect," our aim is "**PROGRESS**." Aiming for perfection and never quite making it can be a pitfall and a reason not even to try. Yet practicing anything, even if we fail, sometimes *especially* when we fail, can bring progress.

As I wrote these words, trying to explain the avoidance of perfection as a goal, I wanted to add something like, "Everything in GOD'S world is imperfect." That statement isn't correct because how many want to say, "Everything in GOD'S world is PERFECT!"

That is another truism in GOD's economy—both are correct. In all the little imperfections in you, me, butterfly wings, and the battered moon in our night sky lies the endless perfection of it all. We don't need to make everything an either-or situation. We can hold more than one truth at a time. We each may have a different image of GOD, yet it is all the same. GOD is Energy that exists both inside and outside of us. There is no need to pick one or the other; it can all be true simultaneously. Our objective is to remain open to new ideas. GOD is showing and revealing new things to us at any given time. Part of the solution is to keep our minds open.

Although there are many means to connect to the Flow through the measures of faith addressed in these pages, with an open mind, all it takes is a willingness to begin. It is as simple as turning each page.

8

Practice makes progress—Dropping perfection can sometimes be difficult, but the only thing that matters with the Flow is to try. That's it. Take the pressure off, and if you need to know your next step, ask. GOD will surely point you in the right direction.

Let's look at what we have so far. It's a handy checklist for anything we might want to accomplish.

1. **Get Organized**—Write a list of opportunities to pursue. The list will change over time, and many items will have multiple tasks. Keep it organized and fluid.
2. **Go Where the Energy Is**—We have harnessed an energy force that craves accomplishment. Channel it into what you're motivated to pursue.
3. **Go Where the Doors Open**—GOD will make way for you in the Flow. If some doors close, it's no big deal. Look at the other ideas on your list.
4. **Honor Your Feelings**—How we feel about things can guide us. Stay where things feel safe. Avoid things that feel uncomfortable. Trust yourself.
5. **Revisit Old Ideas**—Sometimes things change, and an old idea that didn't work before might bring benefit today.
6. **Talk About It**—GOD speaks through the people around us, so discussing possibilities and concerns can bring guidance and new ideas.
7. **Let Your Heart Sing**—We work hard to use money for what brings joy to the people around us and ourselves. Our happiness matters to GOD.
8. **Practice Makes Progress**—Take the pressure off, and if you need to know your next step, ask. GOD is sure to respond when we seek an answer.

CHAPTER THREE

THE HEART OF THE MATTER

REMOVING FEAR FROM YOUR FINANCES

"I win because I learned years ago that scared money always loses. I never care, so I win." —Hedy Lamarr

ARE YOU AFRAID?

We all have fears about our finances. Some days, mine are more crushing and heart-pounding than others, but making choices about money from a place of fear equates to loss. This is why faith was so important to me. After many sleepless nights spent worrying, it all worked out. Maybe not the way I planned—sometimes even better—yet in the midst, I could not drop the fear.

Fear isn't bad. It motivates us and, in that way, can help us get to a better place. Anger works in the same way. Both are designed to create an unsettled feeling and move us to make a change. Just as dealing with anger and resentment is fundamental to making good, healthy choices, working through fear is equally essential to creating a solid financial future. When we make long-term financial decisions out of fear, it can create lasting disadvantages. Here's an example.

A Planet Money podcast from NPR, "A New Way to Pay for College—Income Sharing," featured a young woman who attended a well-known Midwestern university. Tuition was about $30,000 annually. She was "concerned" (another name for fear) about her student loans. The financial aid officer told her about "Income Sharing". In a nutshell, they would give her $50,000 for her college costs. It was not a loan. She committed to sharing her income with the school when she graduated. It was like the university was investing in her with a bit of capital.

The terms: 15 percent of her income for 8 years. Immediately, I thought, "NO WAY! I'd never do that." NEVER—EVER—EVER! Granted, there is a cap. The maximum she must pay is $125,000, but even that is ridiculous.

Consider this: $50,000 at 10 percent (and you know her rate would be lower in today's market) means the following year, it's $55,000 in total, then $60,500 in year two. In this example, it takes almost ten years before the balance is the same, $125,000, and that is if she's making no payments. Chances are she would **never, ever, ever** pay $125,000 total on the $50,000 of debt.

Part of the problem is that we have no idea what she will pay under this income-sharing arrangement. I thought, "If she makes $50,000 annually, her 15 percent is $7,500. That is less than the loan would have cost, but it's dropping her income to $42,500."

My next thought is, "That is criminal. It is horrible to do that to a brand-new graduate." All else being equal, with her income remaining constant for the entire 8-year term, she will have paid $60,000 on her $50,000 loan. Not too bad, but do you think that will be her story? A $50,000 income for 8 years with no increases? For her sake, let's hope not.

Here is her real story: She landed a job right out of the gate at $70,000. Her payment was $10,500 per year or $875 per month. She got a decent raise two years in, and the new payment mentioned in the podcast was over $950 per month. In a standard loan, her payment remains unchanged, and the interest cost decreases as she pays the balance. That is not the case here; as she does better, she pays more.

Further, consider this: Had she borrowed $50,000 at 10 percent, her monthly payment would be $660. If she made only these minimum payments, the interest over the term would be $29,000. If she had paid more, like $950 per month, she'd have paid it off in just under 6 years, and the total cost would have been $66,000, or $16,000 in interest.

Of course, my head is swimming in other financial planning concerns we cannot even deal with at this moment, like:

1. Is the payment based on gross or after-tax income?
2. Are the payments tax-deductible?
3. Is this negotiable in financial hardship? Waivers for disability?

These and other factors can further negatively impact this college student.

If our lovely young woman earns less income, she pays less, but would she want to make $30,000 per year so her payment to the darn school is lower? Consider living on 85 percent of $30,000, $25,500, per year. That would be just over $2,000 per month for our college graduate.

That is just one example of what can happen when we make financial decisions based on fear. Instead, facts, math, calculations, common sense, faith, and even gut instinct—but NEVER fear. We should be prudent with debt, considering any financial choice carefully. When we rashly make financial decisions tainted by fear, it is a losing proposition. Our lovely college graduate student found this out when she chose income-sharing through her university.

WHAT'S THE DEAL?

"We simply attempt to be fearful when others are greedy and to be greedy only when others are fearful." —Warren Buffett

Please don't get me wrong—I do not think our graduate is dumb. I think she was victimized. I feel bad for her and anyone who has been ripped off. Heck, we all have fallen victim to some shrewd or conniving strategy. I do not blame her for this choice. I blame the BIG GUYS—the university in this case, but this could be any college, bank, lending institution, automobile salesperson, landlord, housing authority, mortgage broker, investment firm, insurance company, and ad infinitum. Anytime, anywhere, the imbalance is such that it gives one entity an advantage, which it then uses to help itself, thereby harming someone else. (See Appendix II for more information on THE BIG GUYS reference.)

Whoever put together this program at this university knows the financial consequences to a graduate under this program, which is why they are doing it—**PROFIT**. They could set this up altruistically with a zero-interest payback—5 percent of the principal until the $50,000 is paid off. Instead, they load it to their benefit and sell it to college students who are not yet educated in these financial differences. Once devised, this profit-generating plan was put in the hands of financial assistance personnel who may or may not explain the differences between a loan and income sharing. Criminal? I think so!

You might think, "Gosh, Renée, 'criminal' is harsh." Maybe it is—I'm an Italian born in New Jersey. I tend to be bold. Criminals steal with intent, knowing full well that what they do will have a negative consequence for those they rob. That is precisely what I believed happened here, and from an institution that our young people and their parents should be able to trust. It seems to fit the definition of "criminal" to me.

In discussing this sort of thing with people in class or with successful businesspeople and entrepreneurs, I will frequently hear, "Good for them." 'Good' for the people who found a way to capitalize on the vulnerability of others and make a few bucks. Really? That's 'good'? I couldn't disagree more. Calling this 'good' gives us a pass on immoral behavior simply because it is legal.

Consider a different business model—Ben & Jerry's Ice Cream (B&J). The company's philosophy is to better their community and the world by selling sweet treats. While I don't know everything about their business, I know they made everyone in the community stockholders in the early days. Even though the company was sold to Unilever, B&J kept its board of directors. They have a sustainable business model that relies on helping family farms. To help the environment, the factory uses renewable energy through solar panels in a neighboring field. As two white men, they progressively advocated for social justice and used their power to elevate marginalized groups. It's fun there—the staff is terrific, and the ice cream is exquisite.

Are the founders of Ben & Jerry's comfortable financially? I hope so—anyone who creates something out of nothing that benefits others should be compensated. Even more than that, these two entrepreneurs ensured that those who helped them were financially rewarded. They did what they could to minimize their negative footprint while using their influence to make the world better for many marginalized people. Wow—now that's moral money.

Do they keep more than they need? I have no idea—that is not for me to answer or to care about. We all must live with our choices of how generous or frugal we are with our financial blessings. Does it seem that they have enriched the lives of countless others? Without a doubt—and they seemed to have done it without harm to others. GOOD FOR THEM.

GOOD FOR WHO?

"Not all of us can do great things.
But we can do small things with great love." —Mother Teresa

In an earlier chapter, I mentioned working with a business consultant. For those that might not recall, when I followed up with a friend to help build my resume, I ended up with a free business consultant.

At this point in the story, you might think, "So, that's the morality of money? Offer services to people for free." That is a fantastic miracle, which may be what you are called to do. That isn't the illustration I was shooting for.

Upon announcing that she was willing to assist me in developing my business, my newfound friend and business consultant asked me, "Would you like to make a million dollars a year?"

Most people wouldn't think twice about answering this question. The response would be, "Yes. Yes, please. Where do I sign up?"

But GOD had changed me, and that reorganization included a greater responsibility to others. The lens through which I view the world is altered—not wholly—nope. I am as selfish and self-absorbed as the next person, yet a change has started that breaks through often enough that I realize these altruistic thoughts originated via a Divine source.

The first thought surrounding this million-dollar question was, "I do not want to be responsible for that." It is partially fear-based. Managing a million dollars of personal income each year is intimidating, but that was not the totality of my consideration. This was the fundamental consideration: "How will I decide what to do with the parts I don't need? Who will I give it to? How will I decide, and can I manage that responsibility?" That was my genuine concern.

I wouldn't feel right about keeping all of it. I just wouldn't—and if you'd be okay with it, or if that sort of income is your goal, that is okay. I do not tell you this to make you feel guilty or ashamed, or to say you should react the same way. As stated earlier, and again many times in this book, financial strategies and life goals are not one-size-fits-all. For me, only living on what I need is what I am called to do.

Figuring out what I 'need' is challenging. I can easily fall victim to the belief that I 'need' more and more. In this book, we'll spend some time considering our long-term financial goals and gaining perspective on how wealthy we are compared to our neighbors and the world.

When I've shared the idea of only living on what I need, many automatically say, "I bet your kids would appreciate it." I bet they would, but we learn the best financial lessons when we do it ourselves. Besides, there are so many people in the world who need it more, and again, I'm back to, "How do I decide? Am I up for that task? Can I be trusted to share it?" Thank GOD I don't need to decide any of that right now.

You might be a little concerned, thinking, "Is this lady going to suggest I give all my money away and live in a commune? Is that what she did?" The answer flatly is, "No, that is not the strategy." In the end, you might decide to manage your finances differently. Your view of money and priorities might change, but that is ultimately between you and the Flow around you on which you choose to rely.

MUTUALLY BENEFICIAL = GREATER MORALITY

"In the long run, if it isn't a win for both of us, we both lose. That's why win-win is the only real alternative in interdependent realities."
—Dr. Stephen R. Covey

Part of the strategy for my new business consultant was to rebrand my products by raising my prices significantly. The theory was that this boost would increase sales revenue and that other BIG BUCK clients would think my courses were elite and prestigious—worth all this extra money because they were that much better than my competitors. I would rebrand to become the Harvard, Versace, and Mercedes-Benz of continuing education.

At this suggestion, all I knew about sales and marketing was creating a quiet storm inside me—this may have been part of why I cried during those sessions. Even if this method worked, which I didn't fully believe it would, it meant much work building client relationships with the right (rich) people, and it also meant I would lose some of my existing customers. With more than twenty years of experience doing this, I had come to know and love many of the people who sat in the chairs of my classes. I didn't want to see any of them go.

The consultant asked me, "What sets you apart from your competition?" The response was simple: I have a knack for connecting with the group and getting them involved in the discussion. This is how I've built lasting relationships with them, and my clients have become family. Harvard, Versace, Mercedes-Benz, or anything in the elite and prestigious world does not ring "family." I desire to have my clients feel valued and cared about, and enormous price increases didn't seem to fit.

Each time two or more people come together, we enter an exchange. One party may give more than the other, or one person may gain more than another, but we are exchanging our time, effort, energy, and attention every moment. We can give more than we get or get more than we give. We seek a mutually beneficial exchange.

My customers know me, they know my classes, and there is an expectation for a specific exchange. I've had price increases—most gladly pay them. Many of my clients would pay me more than I charge, and some have found creative ways to get those extra amounts my way. I appreciate that, and I am grateful for them. That is how a family works best.

But to take the same classes and claim they are worth twice as much is a tough sell. Here's why: I don't always believe those "big buck" elite purchases are worth it.

A few years ago, I bought a scooter. While in Italy, I fell in love with how they scooted around town, and I wanted to scoot around my city. I thought I'd get myself a Vespa until I found that I could buy a highly rated, brand-new, warranted scooter for the price I would pay for a used Vespa. The used Vespa could cost me more in repairs and reduce drive time. It did not take me long to decide that the non-elite brand was best for me. There may be a billion reasons Vespa is superior that I don't know, but I think we can all agree that many price markups are based solely on greed.

Let's take insulin as another example. Insulin was discovered in 1921 by Sir Frederick G. Banting, Charles H. Best, and J.J.R. Macleod, who believed it unethical to profit from something that saves lives, so they sold the patent rights for a dollar. In 1972, the cost of insulin was $9 per vial—by 1996, it was $33, but by 2017, the same vial cost $275 in the U.S.. People died because they rationed this life-saving method to control blood sugar levels. They could not afford it. A very ethical stance became corrupt because someone saw an opportunity to make more money.

In 1996, when each vial of insulin was $33, pharmaceutical companies would profit from the sale. They had to have been, or they would have shifted prices. That's how business works. Lifesaving products have inelastic demand. The buyer's need for the product does not change as the price increases. Fuel and food also have inelastic demand.

Since continuing education is required, demand is also inelastic. This is where competition comes in. Other companies offering the same or similar products can help keep prices down and provide consumers with variety. When entire industries, such as the pharmaceutical or oil industry, collaborate with their competitors, it is referred to as collusion. There are laws against this sort of activity, but the typical outcome is that the consumer suffers the byproduct of inelastic demand and greed. I was not interested in becoming the 'insulin' of the continuing education industry.

THE BOOM & BUST BUSINESS CYCLE

"I wonder, sometimes, whether men and women in fact are capable of learning from history whether we progress from one stage to the next in an upward course or whether we just ride the cycles of boom and bust, war and peace, ascent and decline."
—Barack Obama

Let's face it: Greed, like fear, isn't going anywhere. We are all tied to it to varying degrees and in various ways. These two motivating forces are profoundly intertwined and hyperconnected to the human experience. The world has enough wealth to provide for everyone, but we seem unable to shed enough fear and greed to create the necessary equity to share it fairly. Looking back on history, it appears that this has always been the case. Two thousand years ago, during the Roman Empire, Jesus flipped the tables at the temple because the greed of the religious elite so incensed him. (Matthew 21:12-13, Mark 11:15-18) The version in Mark has an interesting twist in verse 11. Jesus arrives at the temple late in the day, after the crowds were gone, and chooses to leave with the disciples, returning during the busy time the next day, thus ensuring the largest audience and maximizing the effect. I believe He wanted the message of profound harm because of greed to resonate.

Yet, a few chapters later, Jesus tells us we will always have the poor. (Matthew 26:11) Our Social Justice warrior tried, but He knew the trappings of greed were too strong for any number of tables flipped or people who witnessed it. The desire for power and wealth was so alluring among the religious elite that Jesus' message of love, community, and compassion ultimately got Him killed. That's corruption. Their greed was more important than a message of fairness and empathy.

These financial choices—generosity, contentment, and greed—are often at odds within us as we strive to manage our resources. Let me illustrate this with a story involving a thoughtful and generous 12-year-old. While chatting about his plans as a YouTube content creator, he told me he wants to get a Bugatti when he grows up. If you have no idea what that is, please do not feel alone. Neither did I, so I did a quick internet search. It is a crazy expensive car from a French manufacturer. I asked this adorable little person why he would want such a thing. His response was, "It would be so cool." I'm sure it would be for him. Not me—I was thinking of every ding, dent, and dust speck—it would be too much pressure.

I had another thought regarding such a desire, which brings us to the heart of the matter. I asked my brilliant companion, "Would Jesus drive a Bugatti?" Without batting an eye, his response was, "No." Interesting—he seemed to know that answer without having to contemplate, and I decided to fish for something profound, "Why?" This took a few more seconds to answer, but he said, "There is so much more He could do with that money, like feed and house the poor. Jesus would likely give it away." Yes, young man, that is precisely it.

Jesus had nothing. Several people in the Bible said they wanted to follow Him. He told them, "Foxes have dens and birds have nests, but the Son of Man has no place to lay his head." (Matthew 8:20 and Luke 9:58) Yet, each of these possible disciples is tied to something that stops them from giving it up to pursue the more altruistic, sacrificial journey.

I am generally not a gambling person, but I am willing to bet you are not in the Bugatti market. Conversely, you are likely not prepared to give up everything to pursue only the Spiritual as Jesus did. The middle ground leaves us in a space where it is difficult to decide what to do with our financial resources. This is where reliance on the Flow becomes our guide. A little like Jesus walking into the temple the evening before the table tipping. I imagine He sensed that now was not the time. Better to come back tomorrow. Jesus was—and is —always in the Flow, and our willingness to do the same, especially when we make important decisions, is paramount. The Flow will help us see people and the needs of the planet before the pennies are in our pocket. That doesn't mean, however, we should give it all away. I've found there are a few big picture ideas that have given me perspective and helped to develop my morality around money:

Equity—As I consider several effects of greed, like the unfairness of increasing the price of insulin tenfold in three decades, I would like to see the government pass legislation that puts forward cost containment protections—and heck, while we are at it, let's levy some fines or limit market access for various shenanigans. While I support this idea and would love to see better equity in multiple areas of our social structure and economy, it is essential to remember that this does not happen in a vacuum.

For every action, there is an equal and opposite reaction, and those reactions typically create a negative impact. Let's take this big picture and say the United States moves to socialized medicine—like the Medicare for All proposal—and in that, the government now dictates pricing for all medical care, including pharmaceuticals. Those drug companies now know their profit margins are slimmer, and so do the investors who own stock in any facet of healthcare. Stock prices will likely fall, reducing the wealth of millions.

At least on paper, we've lost value, but things will turn around if we don't react in fear. Every company has a desire to thrive. Not all of them will make it through this, but most will, and, in the process, they'll find new ways to generate profits. Nothing stays the same—and resilience is paramount to survival for you, me, the planet, companies, countries—everything.

Most pharmaceutical companies are likely to react by allocating more funds to government officials in exchange for preferential treatment. They'll seek loopholes in the law that allow for profiteering on other products, or they'll work hard to gain more contracts globally to access new markets. Whatever the strategy, eventually a new balance in the marketplace will be found. These companies will continue to seek profit, and we will need elected officials to push back for the greater good of all.

The most important thing for us to remember is that whenever there is a significant change toward equity, it will disrupt things. We can ride the wave without fear if we know what to expect and trust that it will eventually balance to the betterment of the majority.

Prosperity—Since every person, company, and country desires to thrive, whatever BUST cycle we are in will eventually become a BOOM. A BUST is a contraction stage of the business cycle. We would typically refer to this as a recession. It occurs when the stock market declines, unemployment rises, and wages remain stagnant. The BOOM is the opposite. It indicates a growing and prosperous economy, with stock and home values rising, as well as employment and wages increasing.

Looking back over the last 100 years, since the Great Depression, we'll see that the business cycle keeps rolling. Constriction, or BUST, is frequently caused by the bursting of a speculative bubble—the stock market in 1929, the Savings & Loan crisis in 1989, the tech market crash in 2001, or the housing market crash in 2008. It's okay, though—this correction is necessary. It gets us back on track for the next BOOM.

The government steps in with monetary and fiscal policy to cushion the blow of a BUST or to rejuvenate the BOOM. A little like the Wizard of Oz behind the curtain, the US government has several levers to influence the economy. They can increase or decrease interest rates or tax rates. They can pass laws to inject money into specific industries or infrastructure. They can assist us with business loans, education reimbursement, healthcare coverage, housing credits, and more. If they can find a way to agree, and even when they can't, there are numerous things the government can do to help at any stage of the business cycle. There are multiple options, and I could write a book on the pros and cons of each method within a historical context. That thought brings us to the next point.

Knowledge—When Sir Francis Bacon said, "Knowledge itself is power" (Meditationes Sacrae 1597), I wonder if he understood the full scope of all facets of life, including our finances. As I've been writing this section, I've been reminded of how fortunate I am in my career path, particularly in terms of gaining a deeper understanding of finances, legislation, taxes, government programs, the federal structure, history, and politics. It all started with an economics class back in college, and I ended up there by happenstance.

I was college-bound in high school, taking all the required classes to attend a good school and performing well in them. Then, due to a medical issue, I had to take a two-month leave. When I tried to resume, I was so far behind in the accelerated classes that I took a new path—graduating early. I enrolled in the local vocational school to earn high school credit, attend regular high school classes, and participate in a program called "on-the-job training" (OJT), which allowed me to work and earn education credits.

This all lined up nicely for the professional track I was on when I graduated. The OJT placements were in offices doing administrative work, so I gained that experience during high school. I also learned valuable skills in accounting, administration, and management at the vocational school. This all worked so well that when I graduated high school at age 17, I only continued vocational school for a few more months, figuring I could land a full-time professional job, and I did. By the age of 19, I was the Office Manager in a regional office for a national insurance carrier. At 21, I was promoted to Brokerage Manager, and then at age 23, I was their Regional Sales Director.

The most important through line here is education, the acquisition of knowledge. If you follow this storyline, you will notice that I didn't obtain a college degree. Even now, thirty years later, I am not a college graduate. I am grateful that my career developed in an era when a degree wasn't necessary, because even today, and certainly then too, most people would never guess, or even think for a moment, that I didn't have a degree. Although I didn't have a degree, I did attend college.

My employer would pay 100 percent of my college costs—tuition, books, fees—provided I earned a B or better in the class. What a perk! I did better than that; I had a steady 4.0. I initially aspired to be a Clinical Psychologist, but that quickly shifted to a Research Psychologist. Once again, GOD stepped in. My employer changed the rules—they would only pay for classes that directly benefited my job and contributed toward a degree relevant to my position. Shucks, I'm a persuasive salesperson, but I knew I would never convince anyone that a Research Psychology degree would help someone in brokerage marketing. This is when I took my first economics course and realized economics is the psychology of money, and I fell in love.

I understand that would not be everyone's experience in economics. Most of you would be bored to tears in that class, along with many of the professional licensure courses I took. Much of my financial knowledge didn't come from college courses. It came from experience and personal research. Indeed, my career helped. Insurance companies, investment firms, state regulators, and all the people who work for them shared valuable information with me, but when it came to creating our insurance continuing education courses, I had the latitude to research a whole variety of things that are impactful to a better understanding of all levels of our global financial system.

Another thought—I realize any research you might take on regarding the financial world is probably outside the scope of your responsibilities. In essence, this will be "other work" for you, and you, unlike me, might not have a dramatic interest in all this money stuff. I get it—I do. I am at a stage in my life where I am trying to have less work and "must-do" tasks, but we are in the digital age. There are so many options to gain financial knowledge out there that you might have fun doing it. Podcasts, YouTube channels, and documentaries—the list is endless, and this is where I find much of my information and utilize these platforms to create the content for the classes I instruct.

Do you want to know more about Social Security, Medicare, College Funding, High-Interest Savings, Asset Allocation, etc.? Go to YouTube and type in a few searches. Open your favorite streaming service and search for healthcare, investments, retirement, inflation, the Federal Reserve, or anything you might have some interest in. There are numerous documentaries and news segments about these topics and others. You can try the same in your podcast service. I would list my favorites, but the list is long, and I don't want to ruin the fun of you finding your own valuable nuggets of entertaining education. Even searches for finances, economics, and investing can bring good results.

JUST THE FACTS, PLEASE

"Get your facts first, and then you can distort them as much as you please."
—Mark Twain

I am hesitant to send you out to conduct independent research without providing more insight. There is a great deal of misinformation circulating. As it relates to government policy, in my experience, there are more lies than truths. There is also a significant amount of misleading information about product-specific details in the financial world. However, if you are on a specific company site, they generally have strict compliance and disclosure. Not everyone is trying to mislead you, but many of us are in our silo and have created a singular belief. Pundits attempting to get more views or likes try to persuade you they're right instead of developing a better-informed audience.

We should also be aware of our tendency to stick with what we know and believe and try to remain open-minded. The strategies discussed in the earlier chapters are fundamental here to stay in the Flow. This is important as you seek the information that will most benefit you and help you avoid things that are not helpful or even toxic. Check your list of areas you are working on and ask GOD to guide you.

Here are a few things that I have learned over the years to help me navigate the research field:

Source—If you are researching Social Security or Medicare, it's best to visit their website to see what you can find. Most government websites have a wealth of information, so the same would hold for the Federal Reserve, Bureau of Labor

Statistics, Internal Revenue Service, Security Exchange Commission, and Federal Trade Commission. You'll find similar information at state regulatory bodies.

Believe it or not, they've made them easy to navigate and added interesting historical information, as well as other relevant and engaging data. Contrary to the opinion of some pundits, these entities aim to educate Americans about policies, procedures, and benefits. Better-informed voters make better election choices. It's a win for all concerned.

Verify the accuracy of the information based on the credibility of the news source, considering highly reputable sources versus lesser-known ones. Unfortunately, we can't all agree on what might be a quality source, so if you are uncertain, run it through the acid test. You're on the right track if several other resources have similar or identical stories. If this site offers information not duplicated elsewhere, it should not be considered legitimate.

Once again, if it is a documentary or a YouTube channel, consider who published it and try to determine their motivation. Is it primarily to inform or educate? Or are they trying to sway you or sensationalize something? For example, two of my favorites are PBS Frontline and 60 Minutes. They offer educational documentaries on various financial topics, including mortgage lending, investment fees, retirement plans, and healthcare.

One YouTuber I like to use for course creation is Heimler's History, a history professor for Advanced Placement (AP) high school students. AP is a standard college-level history curriculum instructed by someone who can keep teenagers engaged. It works perfectly for me and is fun for our audiences in our continuing education classes. There are many resources like this available.

Another one I like is Vlogbrothers. John and Hank Greene create video content on a wide range of topics, from the cost of medical care to paying for college tuition. They are fun and engaging and pack a lot of information in a short video. They also list the resources they used for the content in their description, the area they sometimes refer to as the "doobaly-doo." This is another key to distinguishing a genuine educational video from one that is not: They offer proof sources and encourage you to conduct further research.

Emotion—Besides determining the source's motivation, pay attention to how the content makes you feel. Many aspects of the financial realm can cause anxiety. Stock prices fall, wages decline, and security can be hard to find. Reviewing these things in our classes every month has kept me on the straight-and-narrow objective of saving consistently to counteract this anxiety. However, if the resource you are reviewing is pushing fear, I think it's best to avoid it.

At this point, you might wonder, "Renée, if financial research can make me anxious, how do I avoid the ones pushing fear? Wouldn't that be all of them?" The ones I am primarily concerned about fall into the "all or nothing" category. Their stories are often linear and binary.

The story might be cataclysmic: "If you don't do this right now or stop doing that right now, your financial world will fall." Or it could be government or world-related: "The national debt is sure to blow everything up." Or "China is going to destroy America."

Point one: In my experience, there is recovery from everything. There's no need to fret—this is why considerations of Faith were our starting point. There is nothing we can't do or overcome when we steadily keep seeking. That is why anyone pushing this sort of fear does not work well in the Flow.

Point two is that anyone predicting anything with certainty in the financial world should not be trusted. PERIOD. There are trends, there is likelihood—there is NO certainty on the outcome, and anyone trying to tell you they know with certainty what the future will bring lacks the common sense you are looking for in someone offering financial advice.

The cryptocurrency craze fell into this category. You might not think this was fear-based, but it was. The main storyline was, "If you don't do this, you will miss out." Part of the fear in this message centered on the regulations in other forms of trading and on long-term issues with the U.S. Monetary system in the global market. All of this contains some truth—these are not entirely false. We'll discuss crypto further later in the book, but this message is one-sided—it's unbalanced. People offering good advice will tell us both sides of the story. If a resource does not provide that balance, seek other sources that offer the counter position.

Balance—No one product or idea is good or bad. They are both. They are tools. Each has a purpose; if used correctly and at the proper time, they help us build something great. However, when misused or at the wrong time, that same tool could produce disastrous results.

It would be ridiculous to say that a screwdriver is a horrible tool and that no one should ever own one. That is silly. Anyone trying to construct or repair anything knows that a screwdriver is helpful and sometimes necessary. I wouldn't use one to cut a piece of wood, however. That would be a mess, so for that, I would select a different tool—a saw would do a better job to cut wood, but I am not pulling out a saw when I need to tighten a screw. Taking a saw to the screw could have dire results.

The same principle applies to everything in the financial world. Anyone telling you that any financial product is good or bad is stuck in a linear, binary view. To be effective in financial planning, and perhaps in life more broadly, we must strive not to become entrenched in rigid beliefs and to find the good and the bad in everything. From there, we can make better decisions about our plan because we're using a more accurate and realistic representation.

It is also essential to find this same balance in our financial plans. We cannot build a house with just a screwdriver. We might need it later, but to construct a good and sturdy house, we will use many tools and materials at different stages throughout the process. Our financial plan is the same. This means we'll use various assets and asset classes to maintain a strong plan.

When building a house, we start with a strong foundation, which is true of our financial plan. We add other tools and materials as our building progresses, sometimes getting more intricate and detailed. We'll have plumbing, electrical, sheetrock and flooring, windows, doors, and a roof. We can choose between expensive lights and something more standard—we have colors to pick from too, but we don't do all this in a day. We steadily work on our build, acquiring new tools and materials as needed.

The same is true of our financial plan. We steadily work on it, and just as no two houses are identical, no two financial strategies are the same. We all start this process with different preferences and needs, and as a result, the outcomes will vary.

If a resource you are using does not offer a balanced approach—telling you the good and bad of each tool as well as how to use them—but instead uses a blanket approach, I would seek out other resources that will allow you to learn how to build a sturdy financial plan.

THE ANTIDOTE TO ABUSE

"Secrecy is the linchpin of abuse of power. Transparency is the only real antidote."
—Glenn Greenwald

Our financial wealth is a commodity that reflects the investment we made with our time, effort, energy, and attention. How we gain our financial resources and what we choose to do with our money illustrates our ethics, morals, and priorities. When we enter a transaction, full transparency is critical to fairness.

This is why insider trading is illegal. The "insider" has information that other traders do not, and this undisclosed information gives insiders an advantage. Suppose our insider learns that XYZ Company will file for bankruptcy at year's end, but this information is not yet public. The insider sells all their stock at the current market price of $90 per share. Those buying these shares are unaware of the bankruptcy, so they are willing to pay this price. The day the bankruptcy news breaks, the stock plummets to $20 per share. This $20 price is the "fair market value" because it's what the market will bear when all investors know the same information.

I want to think about this another way: Our insider stole $70 per share from these investors. (The $90 trade price minus the $20 price with transparency equals $70 per share.) Had they traded in a market where everyone knew the same information, they would have received a $20 sale price. Instead, unaware of the inside information, the buyers paid $90 per share and suffered a loss when the price fell.

This occurs in various situations, and most of them are not illegal. It happened to our university graduate. It affected many homeowners in 2008. In numerous transactions occurring worldwide at this very moment, individuals or entities engage in trade without having complete information about the circumstances. While I would like to think that most of these trades are happening with full transparency, I believe there are far too many people who prioritize financial gains over integrity.

A LOSS OF INTEGRITY

"There is never enough money to be made or lost on a deal to warrant a lack of integrity."—Dave Ramsey, Financial Peace University

Part of the inspiration for this book was Dave Ramsey's *Financial Peace University*. My original title was going to be "What Dave Ramsey Got Wrong," and believe me, my list is LONG—I could fill chapters, but instead, I'll give you a few ideas to illustrate the concepts contained in this book.

For those unfamiliar with his work, the central idea is that debt is detrimental, and his philosophy is often promoted in churches. These two points alone could fill volumes. I even created an ethics question in one of our classes about marketing financial advice in a church. A few pages ago, we illustrated why Jesus overturned tables in response to something like this. (Matthew 21:12-13, Mark 11:15-18)

You might also be thinking, "No financial tool is good or bad, but he tells his readers debt is bad." Right—and Dave Ramsey further goes on in his book, providing judgments about various financial products, deeming some good and some bad in a one-size-fits-all strategy. You can likely see why I disagree with

Mr. Dave Ramsey, and I think it's essential to acknowledge his book as one of the resources that breaks the balanced approach.

As much as I could go on, I want to discuss his chapter, "Buy Only Big, Big Bargains". When I first read that section title, I thought, "That's not right. There are times it makes sense to avoid the bargain." Like how many of you tipped extra for takeout during COVID, knowing the restaurant workers needed it? During that same time, did you shop locally, maybe paying more, to ensure those businesses survived? Sometimes there are very good reasons to avoid the bargain and pay a little more. That is the "Heart of the Matter".

You're probably thinking, "Of all the things to take issue with Renée, BIG BARGAINS, is it?" I hear you. Let me explain—bargains are good. Saving pennies helps our plan. I am not against reducing expenses, but remember our earlier discussion on binary theory—things are either good or bad, right or wrong? <u>ONLY</u> Big Bargains can get us trapped there. You will find lots of this all-or-nothing thinking in Dave Ramsey's book.

Here's another thought: Remember that our money reflects the time, effort, energy, and attention we invest, and what we choose to do with our money reveals our ethics, morals, and priorities. There are times when each one of these conflicts with the lowest price, and as a result, I pay more because I believe it's the right thing to do at that moment. I just bought three reams of recycled paper at twice the price of the stuff from the trees. I also ordered it from a delivery service because I didn't have time to run to the store. It wasn't the best bargain, but this purchase reflects my time, effort, energy, attention, ethics, morals, and priorities. This is what we do every time we enter an exchange.

In "Buy Only Big, Big Bargains", Dave Ramsey has a section where he discusses a seven-point process to find the best deals. There is something else in this section that is really over the top.

The first point, "Always Tell the Truth: There is never enough money to be made or lost on a deal to warrant a lack of integrity. As a society, we seem to have lost this simple and yet far-reaching and profound principle."

Sounds good to me. I read this in my classes. I have yet to have anyone disagree with this statement, and you probably think, "Renée, come on, you have to agree with that?" You're right, I do. I agree with it word for word without exception. That's morality with our money, and if everyone practiced it, the world would be a better and more equitable place.

The chapter then goes through four other points about capturing BIG BARGAINS, and then we get to point number six, "Good Guy—Bad Guy." Looking past the gender bias of the overuse of the male lens, Dave Ramsey suggests that even if your spouse or partner is not present, you should consider using them in the negotiation to secure a better deal. Two examples he uses are "My wife would kill me if I took that price" and "My husband doesn't like it if I come home with a new dress unless I got an excellent buy." He states, "You should **always** use this…" even if these statements are false—even if the person mentioned never said these things.

Isn't this a lie? What happened to "Always Tell the Truth"? Mr. Dave Ramsey, aren't you suggesting we trade our integrity for a better deal? I am sorry, Dave, but it seems you have lost sight of this simple yet far-reaching and profound principle in less than two pages of your book. Worse, you are so comfortable with this idea, you recommend it to your readers—and not one of your editors caught this? What does that say about how fuzzy our morality is around full transparency when entering an exchange?

Remember, *Financial Peace University* is marketed through many churches. Congregations hold workshops where parishioners go through this book and apply the strategies. I wonder if some pastor or parishioner caught this hypocrisy? Did they call it out? Or, like Dave, his editors, and many readers, they choose to ignore it. This does not seem to align with Christian values, at least not my values.

I have had agents in class say to me, "Renée, who cares? It's a little white lie. What's the harm?" Or sometimes, the objection is, "People do this sort of thing all the time. It's customary and practically expected." This second objection is part of Dave Ramsey's rationale for using this practice: "…and you should also be very aware that it is used against you by retailers."

Let's address the second comment first: "It's customary."

When someone in class says this, I am confident they heard the phrase, "Two wrongs don't make a right." Most times, the person appears middle-aged or older, and I think, "This person probably told their kids—just because your friend is jumping off a bridge, would you do it?"

We know most of us would not encourage a child to do something wrong, harmful, or hurtful. Parents and other loving adults work hard to raise little people into big people with a healthy moral compass. We also encourage young people to stand up for what is right and to protect others, even when it's not popular. If a child saw someone getting hurt, would we accept an excuse from a child that others were doing it too? Instead, we encourage them to rise above by doing the right, helpful, caring thing even when others don't. Shouldn't we, as mature adults, set an example and strive to be helpful and caring? Wouldn't that logic bring us to obeying Dave's first point, "Always Tell the Truth," even if others are not?

To the first point, on some barometer of "the worst thing to do," I am sure this lie would not rank highly. However, that is not the issue. Dave Ramsey says, "There is never enough money…to warrant a lack of integrity." No exception—no reduction of merit—NEVER.

Do I apply this perfectly? No, do I expect you to? Certainly not. Do I take exception with Dave Ramsey ranting about integrity and then encouraging people to lie to get a better deal? You had better believe it. He is so comfortable with this idea that he says it out loud, and since churches advocate for this book, it makes me wonder: Are they practicing what they preach?

I disagree with this part of the quote: "As a society, we seem to have lost this simple yet far-reaching and profound principle." I don't think we lost anything. Greed and all its forms of deception have been around since people realized they needed things to survive. I believe every society in every era has had those who lack integrity. This is not something new.

While Dave Ramsey is searching for the right ideal, he misses it, and that is not uncommon either. Anyone can start at point one with integrity, then wander on down to point six and believe the notion that lying in a negotiation doesn't affect number one. But when we do, we reveal that those few pennies are more valuable than our ethics, morals, and principles. Using a lie to get a better deal puts our financial gain above another person's needs. From that perspective, the moral failure is harder to bear—which is why I believe it's essential to keep GOD at the center of everything, including my finances.

CHAPTER FOUR

DEBT IS NOT BAD

IT'S A TOOL

"This is no unsolvable problem if we face it wisely and courageously."
—Franklin D. Roosevelt

NOTHING SCARY HERE

During his first inauguration speech on March 4, 1933, Franklin D. Roosevelt (FDR) said to a great nation, "The only thing we have to fear is fear itself." That line is famous. It's rephrased in many ways and is very important to our initial discussion of personal finances, as we also have nothing to fear.

Let's put FDR's comment in context. It's about two and a half years into the Great Depression. People have lost their savings, unemployment was at an all-time high, taxes were increasing, and the federal budget was in a record deficit. Hoover, the former president, had done little to help, and all hope for recovery rested with FDR.

In this very eloquent speech, FDR is about to tell the American people that we must take on more debt. He doesn't come right out and say it, but he begins to build a story about putting people to work for the government, which he subsequently did with the help of Congress. These Americans would build roads, bridges, highways, and buildings throughout the land, creating an infrastructure that would propel America to prosperous heights for decades. When you have no money and are already running deficits, debt is the only way to finance this plan.

Granted, if you look back, there were some hefty tax increases on the rich. By the height of World War II, and shortly before FDR died in 1945, the maximum tax rate was 94 percent. This was applied to those making $200,000 annually, equivalent to about $3.5 million in 2023. Even with these significant tax rates, the federal government took on more debt every year of FDR's presidential term. It was not until the end of World War II that we transitioned to surpluses.

Also important, the zealous overspending in the 1930s, heightened by the funding of a significant war in the 1940s, created a prosperous boom in the U.S.A. throughout the 1950s and 1960s. Believe it or not, the 90 percent maximum tax rate continued until President Kennedy convinced Congress to lower it to 70 percent in 1961. It wasn't until Reagan in 1985 that it approached the range of the high 30 percent we see today.

All of this gives us three valuable financial lessons:

1. Imposing higher taxes on the rich does not diminish the economic prosperity of the masses. If done right, it can enhance wealth through a more equitable distribution.
2. We cannot balance budgets by only increasing tax rates (or, in our finances, increasing our income). It's about managing our money.
3. If used appropriately, debt can help us achieve specific goals. Some goals could be financial, while others might be social, emotional, or relational.

UNJUSTIFIED TERROR

"—nameless, unreasoning, unjustified terror which paralyzes needed efforts to convert retreat into advance."—Franklin D. Roosevelt, 1933

FDR knew people wanted a solution to this financial crisis, but "unjustified terror, which paralyzes needed efforts," would prevent a good plan from happening. He understood that fear is the enemy in all sorts of plans GOD may have for us. FDR had a vision. His job now was to help the American people better understand the plan so they could feel more confident in it. We are at the same point when considering our future financial goals. As our understanding increases, we will also feel more confident.

Debt isn't bad. It isn't good either. It is a tool. Once we understand how this tool works, we will know when to use it and how to utilize it to our advantage. If we don't figure out how to use a tool properly, we might hurt ourselves or damage the project. The same principle applies to using debt; before employing any tool, we should have a plan. Without a plan, we cannot be sure this is the right tool for the job.

If debt isn't bad, why do some people think it is? Because things didn't work well when they used it. Take Dave Ramsey as an example. He over-leveraged himself in the 1980s, had to file for bankruptcy, and now tells people there is "NO GOOD DEBT". Most wealthy people disagree. They frequently use debt to expand their holdings and ventures while keeping their money safe from that risk. We'll explore this idea in the chapter, "A Money Maker."

I believe that author Dave Ramsey didn't fully understand the use of debt in his business decisions. As he recounts the story in his book, it seems as if greed overtook a solid plan, and honestly, that could happen to anyone. I'll share some stories of my own about financial loss with you. One of them includes the foreclosure of our family home. While it didn't turn out as I had hoped, and I suffered a financial loss, I stand behind the reasons for my choices.

Most importantly, I will never say mortgages are bad. That would be ridiculous. Do you know how long it would take you to save enough money to buy a house with cash while paying rent somewhere else or living in someone's basement? There might be exceptions, but when someone says, "NO GOOD DEBT," we are back to those linear, binary ideas that keep us stuck and limit our possibilities.

Using debt wisely can help us make informed investments for our future, just as FDR did for Americans in the 1930s. Proper use of debt can even help us keep and make more pennies. Debt instruments can pay you. Debt can help make us more prosperous if we consider it through a cost-benefit analysis. The key to this is first releasing the fear.

3 COST-BENEFIT ANALYSES

"A good tool improves the way you work. A great tool improves the way you think."
—Jeff Duntemann

1. Debt Exchange—I recently secured a small business loan of $5,000 at an interest rate of 4 percent. It would cost me about $200 in interest each year, which would reduce over time. Not bad, but one of my business credit cards sent me an offer for a 0 percent interest cash advance for 18 months. This is where it's essential to read the fine print. This was NOT free. There was a 2 percent transaction fee. When considering any loan, the fees are also crucial. It might be 0 percent, so there is no interest for this term, but there is still a cost to the loan—$100 for 18 months. Since I would have paid more than $200 in interest during those 18 months with the original loan, I would save at least $100 the following year if I made a move. Many would consider this nominal, which it probably is, but remember Ben from our first chapter? "A penny saved is two pence clear." That $100 is 10,000 pennies, and each is worth more in my pocket than paying them to the bank—two pence clear and all that.

To make all this work, I need to adhere to the terms and either pay it off or move it elsewhere before the 18 months expire, because when the 18 percent, 22 percent (or whatever insane rate the credit card charges kicks in) it will negate any potential savings I receive.

If I had the money to pay this off, and I do, why would I mess with any of this? Why not just pay off the $5,000? Because I hope, and it's usually true, that the money I have saved elsewhere will earn enough to cover the $100 fee and give me a few extra pennies. I decided that this idea was so good that I borrowed the entire $15,000 I was allowed and invested the other $10,000 in a money market account.

A money market account generally pays higher interest rates than a standard savings account because it invests in short-term treasury notes. This means they are highly liquid, and although the FDIC (Federal Deposit Insurance Corporation) doesn't insure them, they may be eligible for $500,000 coverage under SIPC (Securities Investor Protection Corporation) when held in a brokerage account.

You might also wonder why I would borrow more than I need. Two reasons:

1. By borrowing the additional $10,000 and depositing it into an interest-bearing account where my principal is guaranteed, I might earn the $300 it costs to borrow it all, making my $5,000 loan effectively zero-cost.
2. With more cash on hand during the 18-month term, I have the flexibility to pay off other balances or use it short-term for emergencies while deciding whether to use my income or another account to pay for it.

Ultimately, this worked well—I took this loan early in 2022. The Federal Reserve increased interest rates several times that year to curb inflation. The $10,000 in the money market was earning more than $40 per month by the time I had to pay off the remaining balance of $12,000.

Here's the real kicker: I received an offer a few weeks before my payoff date that included a balance transfer at 0% interest with no transaction fees. This meant I could borrow the $12,000 I needed to pay off the other loan balance at no cost. It also meant I could keep the extra cash in my money market account, which would continue to earn more pennies for another 15 months. By making regular payments over the term, the original $5,000 loan would be paid off. Amazing!

IMPORTANT CONSIDERATIONS:

- **Calculated Risk—**This scenario is not typical. It could have gone the other way just as quickly, with interest rates falling. This was a calculated risk that paid off.
- **Be Responsible**—This plan does not work if I don't follow the loan terms by making the required payments or paying off the loan balance by the deadline. It also doesn't work if (and this one is the worst of all) I spend the extra $10,000 I borrowed on a bunch of junk.
- **Credit Score**—This sort of plan does not work without a good credit score. It's why I receive offers like these, and it provides me with enhanced flexibility and the best terms from creditors. We'll talk more about this later.
- **GOD Guidance**—I started to worry toward the end of the 18-month term. The original $5,000 loan wasn't fully paid off, and I was unsure whether I should make a withdrawal from my savings to cover the remaining balance. Then, this second loan offer gave me the exact $12,000 I needed to keep this plan running. I cannot boldly claim GOD did it, yet it is far too coincidental not to be grateful for the Flow.

2. Bait and Switch—When I decided to write this book, I knew biking would help stimulate my creative juices. I used this story earlier to illustrate finding joy in our plans in the "Let Your Heart Sing" section. Although this motorized pedaling two-wheeler has more problems than I can name, riding it has brought me much joy.

You may also recall that my finances were in a difficult situation. My business was not generating the same income as before, yet I had been pricing new e-bikes. I wanted one for over a year, but the timing was wrong. Once I decided on a particular model, they had a special sale, but the price was still a bit more than I wanted to spend from my savings. Then, they offered 0% financing. I felt like I won the lottery. It was March, and I'd have this new bike by spring.

I filled out the online credit application and was informed that I qualified for an interest rate of 4.99 percent for 18 months. I was upset. Nothing I read that day mentioned varying rates or the criteria for different interest rates. They may have mentioned something about this elsewhere, but it should be more clear than that if they operate transparently. This circles back to honesty and fairness and the fact that many people and entities may not continuously operate under these guiding principles. Given that I have excellent credit, there seemed to be no reason for this change from their original 0 percent financing offer.

When others do not readily provide the proper disclosure, I approach this dilemma objectively, seeking the facts I need to make an informed decision. Was I mad and sad about the thought that I still might need to wait for the bike? Yes, I was, but it's also better to wait than to jump into a deal that I will pay for in multiple ways if it's not in my best interest. Our university graduate suffered that fate—it's best to resist the temptation to make rash financial decisions.

My monthly payment would be approximately $83. If I were to make these minimum payments over the term, my total interest cost would be $60 for the loan term. The seller provided me with a $75 coupon off the bike's cost, and since the seller is overseas, there was no sales tax on the purchase. In my home state, that is a 7 percent savings right there.

Although I felt this was a bait-and-switch, when I considered all the terms, I decided to buy it. A bait-and-switch is when someone 'lures' you in with one offer (bait) and then changes the terms (switch). That summer, gas prices were steadily coasting above $4 per gallon, and this bike allowed me to do most of my daily running around town, saving me countless dollars in fuel. I am forever grateful I bought that little beauty. I felt healthier, and so did the planet.

Ultimately, I was unhappy with the lender and paid off the loan early. The interest rate switch was just the beginning of the issues. I couldn't pay them through the bill pay system on my checking account, so I put my checking information into their system for automatic payments. The first couple of payments worked great. The $83 draft went through automatically as expected, but I then started receiving notices each month stating that no account was set up for auto payments. This required me to go back into their system. I would see the same checking information, yet I would still have to process the payment manually each month. I don't believe I was charged any late fees, but after dealing with this for a couple of months, I decided the hassle was not worth the savings and paid off the balance.

IMPORTANT CONSIDERATIONS:

- **Stick to the Facts**—If the rules keep changing or the value of the purchase diminishes, it's best to stick to the facts and not let the emotions take over.
- **Think About It**—Carefully consider all the information—payment terms, interest rates, rebates, taxes—before proceeding with any plan. If the variables change, we can make other choices.
- **The Full Savings or Expense**—When making purchase decisions, the cost of the item and the debt are crucial, but so are other expenses, such as insurance costs, a healthier lifestyle, or savings, like reducing fuel consumption.
- **Multiplying Problems**—Entities (and people) will tell us who they are. Sometimes accidents happen, or the company is an accident waiting to happen. If there are too many negatives, it may be best to stay clear.

3. No Cash at Closing—I bought my house in 2019 as real estate housing prices were skyrocketing and before the extremely low lending rates of 2021. Like any lender seeking to maximize profits, my mortgage company continued to send offers to refinance. However, I had just paid thousands of dollars in closing costs and other fees to get into this mortgage. I was not interested in paying for that again, especially since I had not yet decided how long I wanted to stay in that home. I love the house. I love the area, but my kids are in different parts of North America—one in Canada, the other on the East Coast of the U.S.—and I feel a draw to be closer to them. I knew I might not stay in that home long enough for a refinance to pay off.

This is why all the variables are critical to consider when answering the question, "What will that loan cost you?" (Or "save you.") To answer this, I needed the bank to provide answers to the following questions: "What are the closing costs and other fees?" and "What is the interest rate?"

In normal circumstances, one might add, "What is the term?" The number of payments would help me arrive at the total cost of this loan. For a mortgage, though, I don't worry too much about that. If I'm doing this right, I can always choose to pay this off. We'll talk more about that later.

For the interest rate question, the staff member stated that I would receive a 2.3 percent APR (Annual Percentage Rate). Since my mortgage was at 4 percent, this would save me a significant sum—close to half the interest cost. When asked, "What are the closing costs?" He replied, "You won't need to bring cash to closing."

Gosh darn, wasn't that sly? Instead of answering my question, he addressed a different one and never really got to the point I wanted to make. The thought screaming in my head, "This is one of the many ways people get ripped off."

I reply, "Yes, I may not need to bring cash to closing, but what fees are bundled into the loan?" His reply was, "There's nothing due at closing time." Oh my gosh, now I'm agitated. Not for me. I understand this game, but I am enraged on behalf of the homeowners in their first house who don't see the deception, as well as the whole host of people who think he's answering the question when he isn't.

I try a different tactic: "You still are not answering my question." I say, "I'd like you to email me a Good Faith Estimate. A "Good Faith Estimate" (GFE) outlines what the lender believes the terms of your mortgage will be—any fees, closing costs, escrow amounts, payment, and the cost of interest over the term. This is an estimate of the loan made in good faith. In 2015, GFE was replaced by the Loan Estimate (LE), but the idea is the same.

His initial response was, "We don't do those." Now I'm jacked up. These are very common and required by law in most states. I wonder what the Consumer Financial Protection Bureau (CFPB—the U.S. federal agency overseeing banks, lenders, and other financial institutions) would think of this response. At this moment, I want to run as fast and far as possible from this mortgage lender. A thought screams, "Even if they give me the sweetest deal, I do not want them to profit from me." Here's the rub, though: Typically, companies with the most significant volume offer the best deals.

I say, "Are you new there? An estimate is common and usually required by law." He says something else, but I'm not sure what because, to be honest, I stopped listening to him. I decided right around question two that I did not want to work with this person, and right about now, I'd decided I'd not take a loan from this company, but I did want to see what he refused to say out loud—the cost of securing this loan.

I again asked for the Good Faith Estimate and gave him my email address. I also said, "I figure the company you work for trained you to handle the question of fees as you did, but it is not cool to make it difficult for a customer to get important financial information. Many people are not as financially savvy as you are, and the kind and gracious thing to do is help them understand more, not less."

Wouldn't the world be a better place if we all did that? The costs associated with the loan should be transparent, questions should be answered, and anyone entering this exchange should know all the terms. I do not believe this is the salesperson's fault. I think they were trained to handle questions just this way, but this cat-and-mouse game of running things around so the company wins is part of the problem with this snowball of corporate greed. One would think that after the 2008 financial crisis, issues like this would be cleaned up due to many failures in mortgage lending, but it seems they were not.

Let's go back to deciding the loan's value or whether refinancing makes good financial sense. When I finally received the LE, it listed my closing costs as $5,500. My current mortgage balance is around $170,000. This means I would pay about $6,800 in interest over the next year if I stayed at the 4 percent rate.

If I refinanced and bundled the $5,500 cost at closing, my new mortgage balance would be $175,500, with a 2.3 percent interest rate and a cost of interest of about $4,000, which is $2,800 less than my current mortgage, or a monthly savings of a little more than $230 per month. I would need to stay in the house for over two years to recoup the cost of the loan. ($2,800 annual interest savings for two years is $5,600.) When we bundle the closing cost into the mortgage, we are also paying interest on it over the term.

Another thought to consider is that if we take the $5,500 in closing costs and bundle them into the mortgage, then make only minimum payments, the $5,500 becomes $7,619 because of $2,119 in interest at the end of thirty years. I would have bundled in the costs because the rate was so low, but it also means it is now closer to three years to break even—$7,619 divided by $230 is about 33 months.

This makes me feel slightly better because I didn't take the deal. I still own that home two years later and am planning to keep it and the mortgage until at least June 2029. Right now, the $230 per month savings sounds pretty good, but at the time, I did not want to lay out all those extra thousands after just having paid a bundle at closing, especially since I was not committed to staying in this house at least two to three years. Had I moved, those thousands would have been a loss. My consolation is that 4 percent is still an excellent rate, and I am blessed to be able to afford my payment.

IMPORTANT CONSIDERATIONS:

- **Get All the Information**—Before deciding on any big money move, get all the information to make the most informed decision. A lower interest rate is less valuable if it comes with high fees.
- **Listen Carefully**—Too often, salespeople are trained to position information in the most favorable light. This isn't bad if they are giving you full disclosure, but, as the example above shows, too often the intent is to keep important information from the buyer.
- **Written Confirmation**—Before proceeding with any application, it is a good idea to have the terms in writing. Even an email to confirm the facts is better than nothing. Memories can fade, and written confirmation ensures clarity for both seller and buyer.
- **Know the Law**—It helps you to do some research and learn the laws in your area. If something doesn't sound correct or fair to the consumer, do a few internet searches to find the government entity or department that can assist.

MORTGAGE MADNESS

"Greed is a bottomless pit which exhausts the person in an endless effort to satisfy the need without ever reaching satisfaction." —Erich Fromm

Part of my reluctance to refinance was due to the numerous refinances I made on my first home, and how more than one of them hindered my long-term financial goals. That home and my use of debt around it taught me a valuable life lesson about the use of debt and the drawbacks of paying extra on long-term debt. I'll start at the beginning to offer you the best perspective on all my choices and the educational value of historical interest rate trends.

I bought my first home in 1990, when I was married. The home was more his dream than mine. It was a new construction. For two acres on the lake, we got it for a steal at about $130,000. I realize this seems like an incredible deal compared to today's prices. Still, at the time, median home prices in Minnesota were around $75,000, so this price reflected the elevated market value of lakeshore properties.

Our first mortgage was at 10 percent. Believe it or not, this was considered a reasonable rate. To provide historical context, the 1970s and early 1980s were marked by high inflation. The Federal Reserve increased interest rates to reduce inflation, as it did in 2021 and 2022. Because the earlier inflation was even more dramatic, the increase in interest rates was grander, too. This was great for people investing money. One could get guaranteed returns in the double digits. Higher interest rates are not a friend to the borrower, however.

My husband and I decided to pay extra each month to reduce our interest costs. I would send an additional $100, $200, or even $300 or more each month. At the time, I was earning a good salary, plus bonuses, and had exceeded the Social Security tax income limit more than once, so we could afford it. (For those unaware, the Social Security tax has "maximum taxable earnings," which increases annually according to the Consumer Price Index (CPI). In 2023, when this section was written, one pays this tax up to $160,200 annual earnings. In 1990, this limit was $51,300.)

We also refinanced more than once. I don't have all the details on these transactions, but interest rates steadily decreased over the next two decades. First, dropping to the 9 percent range. Then continued to go down to the 7 percent range. Seeking lower rates, we would refinance and typically take out some of our equity for home improvements or business plans.

Fast-forward to 2007. I got divorced and decided to buy out my ex-husband from the home. The original $130,000 mortgage has now increased to $190,000, and the house is appraised at $450,000. Triple gain from the 1990 purchase price was a nice return, but I also realized that home prices in 2007 were incredibly inflated. This was just before the 2008 housing market crash. At the time, I had no idea how bad it would get or how long it would last.

What I did know was that I wanted to keep my kids in our family home. They had been through a lot, and I needed to maintain as much stability as possible. The decision to proceed with this purchase echoes the earlier philosophy that sometimes we don't opt for the big bargain because there are other considerations beyond saving pennies. My children's well-being is worth more than a pile of pennies every day.

I proceeded with a refinance late in 2007 at a rate of around 7 percent—some of this is fuzzy. I was going through a lot emotionally, working hard on other priorities with my kids, and trying to keep my business afloat. I clearly remember this part, though—my new mortgage was for more than $300,000. At the mortgage closing, my ex-husband received his equity, about $125,000, and a year later, during the 2008 housing market crash, I would lose mine.

In 2008, it was devastating to me to think that my ex-husband didn't suffer the same financial loss that I had, but I still had the income to make the $2,200 monthly payment, which was a blessing. I also figured it would turn around, but regardless, my kids and I were okay at that moment. I continued making those payments and paid extra to the bank every month.

By 2010, I had lived in that house for 20 years and had paid the bank tens of thousands of dollars in interest. These payments also included at least $100 in extra principal (often $200 or $300 per month). After all this time, this also meant thousands of extra dollars to the bank. Additionally, 2010 was the year in which pivotal changes to the regulations governing my business were enacted. Within two years, my annual income was reduced to one-sixth of what it had been.

I think it's essential to pause and consider this reduction in income for a moment. We can quickly read 'a sixth' without sensing the gravity of how this changed my ability to afford my current expenses and lifestyle. Please imagine any modest six-figure income you wish. Let's keep this a nice, round number for ease of calculation —$100,000. To arrive at one-sixth, we divide this in half, which equals $50,000. Then we do that again, $25,000, but we are still not done; that's 25 percent. To reach one-sixth, we nearly halved it again, arriving at a figure around $16,700. It's almost impossible for even a single person in 2012 to live on that, even with a house paid off. However, you already know that my mortgage payment was $2,200, and I was raising two children with no assistance.

While I was aware of the legislative change, I had no idea how much it would impact my income, so I jumped at the opportunity when I received an offer from my bank to refinance at a lower interest rate with no closing costs. Little did I know that accepting this offer would have profound financial implications.

It was part of the Making Homes Affordable Act, and adopting this loan meant I was no longer eligible for other hardship programs under the law. I later argued that this was not made clear when my family required additional assistance to remain in our home, and I hoped the bank would allow me into those other programs. This is where I learned that when we raise legitimate legal arguments against a big player, we rarely win.

At this time, I was running on my own steam. I claimed an agnostic posture in 2005 when I left my husband because I found GOD's way of helping me lacking. I could see GOD's Hand in many areas of my life, and I certainly felt nudges to various choices, but there was no fundamental reliance or relationship development. I also inherently knew and would acknowledge that many of the blessings in my life were Gifts. Expressions of gratitude were perfunctory and lacked genuine heartfelt sincerity. I used GOD as a vending machine. I'd drop in a few prayers like they were quarters and push what I thought were the proper buttons to get what I wanted. I went to church and read the Bible when things got bad. My faith then, and even in the early stages of my renewed commitment, was nothing like the Spirit-guided, GOD-centered faith I practice today. Even now, it is nowhere near perfect. I expect my faith and relationship with GOD will continue to renew and develop if I tap the Flow.

As my income declined, I did the customary things that generally brought in business—expensive mailings, enhancements to our classes, and price reductions for our online courses —but nothing worked. All it did was increase my expenses or decrease my revenue, leaving me with less money. Things weren't great in my personal life either. Changes in friendships, loss of a relationship, and various challenges raising two kids alone had my emotional health in shambles.

By the end of 2012, not only was I back in church seeking a Spiritual solution, but I had also decided to stop paying my mortgage and seek relief from the bank. I had borrowed the money to make the payment more than once that year, and that choice was unsustainable. I made so many mistakes at this time. A friend suggested that I hire someone to file the papers with the bank, which they claimed would increase my chances of success in negotiating hardship. This did nothing to help me. It only cost me thousands of dollars, which I did not have. There were numerous scams taking advantage of the widespread fear and panic. All of this taught me valuable lessons about fear and faith.

I was shocked when I received my first modification. To someone who had been a loyal customer for more than two decades, they increased my term to 40 years and dropped my interest rate by a quarter of a percentage point. Lending rates at that time were about 2 percent lower than the offer, which meant I would pay tens of thousands of dollars more in interest than I had with my original mortgage. I was dumbfounded to understand how this offer would "really" help someone in a real financial crisis.

In this offer, my payment would decrease by a couple of hundred dollars, approximately 20 percent savings from my previous payment. This didn't seem right when my income was down 80 percent. Besides, it's not as if I were a new customer. I used this bank for every refinance. They had received many pennies from me over the years, but whenever I pointed that out, I was told, "Your loan is less than two years old." The acceptance of their refinance offers even erased the history of the home buyout from my ex-husband.

I filed for two other modifications; both were accepted, and both offers were worse than the first. I contacted every elected official who represented me, the attorney general of my state, and any federal entity I could think of that oversees banking. While somewere more helpful than others, none of it changed my circumstances.

I tried to sell my property short—a Short Sale is when the lender will accept a purchase price 'short' of the debt owed—but a home that appraised at $450,000 in 2007 wouldn't even sell for $180,000 in 2013. The one offer I received wanted me to include my items, including furniture, in the sale. It was too much to consider—it was heartless

If you have not yet hit a place of shock and awe, this story isn't entirely done. My final attempt to rectify this to some degree was an application for a Deed in Lieu. With this arrangement, the mortgage lender will accept the deed "in lieu" of debt forgiveness. I heard that this is less costly for the lender than a foreclosure, so they sometimes include a cash allowance in the offer to help the person move. Many homeowners would receive a $10,000 check to sign over the deed.

Not me. Oh no, they would accept my deed in place of "partial" debt forgiveness. They expected a single mom who had paid them for more than 20 years, kicking in lots of extra pennies with each payment, who was now suffering a substantial financial hardship, to cough up an additional $17,000 for the luxury of leaving my home. You read that right—the lender wanted me to pay them to leave my home.

Believe it or not, the letter with this offer was attached to letters for homeowners in Tennessee and Alabama who were offered $10,000 cash to vacate their houses for a Deed in Lieu. I still don't know why these were in my envelope. I know it was an accident on the company's part, but it was as if the Universe wanted me to know that those offers existed, yet I couldn't have one. I worked hard all my life, trying to do what I thought was right, but I couldn't catch a break.

You might also wonder where my ex-husband was in this mess—nowhere. When we divorced, he wanted joint custody. I figured it was because he didn't want to pay for child support, but I didn't want to argue about caring for our children. I gave it to him. He never paid and barely took them. I could have played this differently, and as I was going broke, I wish I had. However, I still stand by my choice not to argue about the care of our children. Although I would have preferred that my ex-husband willingly help, I was happy to provide for them, and they have been my greatest joy.

When I shared this story in a class, a gentleman said, "Didn't the father offer assistance?" It is reassuring to know that some men consider this in terms of what is best for the children. I did contact my ex-husband as things were spiraling out of control. He declined any assistance until we were forced to leave our home. Then he said, "You can move in here." As you'd imagine, there was no way I was going back there. I knew GOD would provide for us.

Since my son was in college, my daughter and I moved out of our house in the spring of 2015. The house was not foreclosed upon until well into 2016. Some parts of me wish I had taken advantage of that final year to save a few more pennies instead of paying rent elsewhere, but those twelve months away from that family home taught us many valuable life lessons. Staying there might have been practical, but I believe it would have been emotionally draining. GOD had shown me in every possible way that it was time to move on.

THE MORAL

"Everything's got a moral, if only you can find it."
— The Duchess, in Lewis Carroll's Alice's Adventures in Wonderland

You might think, "Dave Ramsey is right—we should all work to pay off debt. If Renée had just paid that off, she could have kept that house." While that might be true, I am uncertain how I would have paid off $300,000 in five years. Given my income, even the modest six-figure one I had before 2010, a total payoff in two years was impossible. Granted, I didn't need to buy that home. We could have sold it, and I could have taken my share of the gain, $125,000 (if it sold for that amount), and put it towards another house. My payment might have been less, but I would face the same challenges—a loss of equity and difficulty making the payments.

My Lesson: Don't Give Extra Pennies to a Lender. I found that when I gave a lender extra money, I effectively gave them my power, options, and control. When I count on a lender to do the right thing, they have control, and since their primary objective is to create profit, the needs of my family and me, or even a consideration of fairness, do not figure into the mix. As you can see from my example, my reliance on their goodwill failed.

But when I save my pennies, those pennies make more pennies, and I have greater control over my destiny. My kids and I would have had something if I had saved all those extra pennies—every extra hundred dollars I gave the bank was a waste, and I gave them many. If I'd saved all that, I would have had something to rely on for my kids and myself. Instead, I walked away with absolutely nothing from a home I had come close to paying for.

Today, I have enough savings to pay all my debts if I choose to, which is a form of freedom. Even if I had no debt, a fully paid-off home, and no savings, I would still be at high risk of losing everything if I couldn't afford taxes, insurance, and other essentials. When we have investments that generate a steady stream of income, which in turn generates more income, we have a cash flow that sustains us.

This strategy of taking any extra amounts I might have paid toward the mortgage and saving them instead only works if I let the money grow. For some, it might take discipline not to spend what we are working to save. Now, when I see my account values grow, I don't want to spend any of it. I've experienced the value of compounding gains and want to continue that momentum.

While writing this, I thought, "Renée, how many pennies did your pennies make this month?" It was three weeks ago that I last logged into my accounts.

In that time, my pennies created an additional $17,000. That's $800 a day—granted, there are times I've logged in, and I could be down $17,000 in the same three-week period. I don't let that bother me. Those losses are a typical part of the cycle. However, many wealthy individuals have a vested interest in ensuring their investments generate substantial returns. When I take advantage of that side of greed, I win, too.

CHAPTER FIVE

TOOLS AND THE TRADE-OFF

Save or Pay Off Debt

"Technology and tools are useful and powerful when they are your servant and not your master." —Stephen Covey

TOOL MASTERY

I am not saying that we should borrow money for everything we want. That is financial suicide. If that is the message you've received thus far, I want to clarify that it is not prudent at any time, and certainly not when trying to accumulate wealth. Spending, even with debt, means we are not saving those pennies. We cannot meet our long-term financial goals if we aren't saving as many pennies as possible; however, mastering financial tools, including debt management, can help us build more wealth.

Have you ever heard that many billionaires pay no tax? Ever wonder how they can do that all while maintaining a lavish lifestyle? It's simple: They borrow large sums to avoid taxes—borrowing all they need to live on—and use their assets as collateral. Since the debt is not considered income and they didn't have to sell any assets for a gain, they pay no tax. When it comes to paying off the loans, individuals can do so by selling a significant asset or, even better, passing it on to their heirs upon death. When their heirs receive the assets, they get a stepped-up basis in value, so no capital gains are due should they sell some of the assets to pay off the debt. There are other loopholes to avoid the estate taxes, and there you go, an extravagant lifestyle at lower tax rates than the average American pays.

If you could reduce your tax liability to zero this year, what would that mean to your budget and your ability to create more wealth? It would be a game-changer for most people. This billionaire tax strategy may not be suitable for the typical American. Still, it effectively illustrates the importance of mastering all financial tools, including those that may have received some negative press.

I am asking you to objectively examine debt and savings instruments, setting aside emotions and viewing them through factual lenses. That can be hard to do when there is uncertainty in one's future and so much is at stake. In my experience, there is a direct correlation between the degree to which we tap into the Flow while allowing solid financial principles to guide us, and our confidence in the reality of our safety and security.

Consider again the people above who are paying no tax and have access to many billions of dollars. Their concerns are not about how they will pay for that—their objective is how they keep this magnificent asset snowballing. One can lose or make millions (or billions) a day in this arena.

Our goal is to get you there on a less grand scale. If applied consistently, this strategy will help you accumulate sufficient savings to feel secure and confident about your future. You'll rest knowing the Universe and the Flow are working for you, and you'll have fewer concerns about what the future will bring. With every changing tide, you'll sense the next direction in each step, and your GOD will guide you.

SNOWBALLS ARE TOOLS

"If the only tool you have is a hammer, it's hard to eat spaghetti."
—David Allen

In Dave Ramsey's *Financial Peace University*, he uses the "Debt Snowball" method to pay off debt. You start with your lowest balance debt first, putting as much money as possible toward it each month. Once it's paid off, you take all you were paying toward that loan and start paying down the next lowest balance debt. All the while you are doing this, Mr. Ramsey's "Baby Steps" plan suggests you have only $1,000 in savings. Yes, just $1,000.

Imagine you're following this plan, and your furnace breaks down. Can you get a new one for $1,000? Or your spouse gets cancer, and your health insurance has a $2,500 deductible. Or you lose your job…You get the idea —$1,000 in an emergency fund is not enough to offer security while giving all your extra pennies to a lender. As illustrated by the financial tragedy of losing my home, when we give our extra pennies to a bank or credit card company, we surrender our power and security to an entity whose primary objective is profit. That is not a secure financial strategy.

When discussing this in our classes, agents frequently say, "Dave Ramsey's plan is good for people with out-of-control spending and debt." Yup, that very well may be. If I have out-of-control spending and use credit to finance it, that is a vicious cycle with a disastrous end. One must get their spending under control if any financial plan is going to work—PERIOD. If spending is the issue, it must be dealt with first.

We must align our emotional, spiritual, and physical house properly to successfully apply any financial strategy. Suppose I have zealous overspending that I cannot control, or even spending that gets in the way of other financial priorities. That suggests other issues I need to address as I consider a new monetary policy in my home.

Out-of-control spending does not mean we should use all our extra pennies to pay off debt. It simply means we should spend less and gain better control of our financial future. We reduce our spending and expenses, putting those pennies in savings while making reasonable payments on our debts. What's reasonable? The payment. Whatever it is, just the minimum payment. We'll discuss this strategy and ways to reduce the cost of our debt in the coming pages, but first, we must understand the facts behind putting those extra pennies in our pockets so they can grow. We get the biggest and best snowball by using the most straightforward tools—compounding and time.

USING THE RIGHT TOOL

"It is essential to have good tools, but it is also essential that the tools should be used in the right way." —Wallace Wattles

Imagine, if you will, you have an extra $250 per month coming in—you got a raise! You also recently bought a car and have a $20,000 car loan at 6 percent for a five-year term. The minimum payment is $387 per month. If you make only minimum payments, the total interest paid over the term is $3,200.

LOAN VALUE	MONTHLY PAYMENTS	INTEREST - TERM	INTEREST COST
$20,000	$386.66	6 percent — 5 yrs (or 60 mos.)	$3,200

If you take the extra $250 per month and apply it to this loan, you'll pay it off in just under three years and save about $1,400 in interest. Not bad.

LOAN VALUE	MONTHLY PAYMENTS	INTEREST - TERM	INTEREST COST
$20,000	$636.66	6 percent — 2 yrs & 11 mos.	$1,800

However, if you put the same $250 in an account earning 6 percent, the account is valued at $9,858 at the end of three years. This is more than enough to pay off the loan balance if you choose. This is our breakeven point. We can now decide—will we pay this off or keep going? In this instance, we have control—we have choices. We have the security of knowing that although we *have* debt, we are not *in* debt.

Where did I get 6 percent interest? Most stock indices grow above this on average over the long term. While not guaranteed, this is not an uncommon return for a stock portfolio; some might consider it conservative. The S&P 500 has returned a historic annualized average return of around 11.88 percent from its 1957 inception through the end of 2021. If we adjust the value for inflation, the average return would be in the single digits, but still well above the 6 percent we used above.

As I type this in August 2023, money market rates are around 5 percent, and bank CD (Certificate of Deposit) rates are slightly better. Both guarantee the principal in the account, and a money market account with most companies is fully liquid. "Liquidity" is a term used to describe the ability to access funds in an account without penalty.

This is precisely why we discussed various cost-benefit analyses in the last chapter. Interest rates will change over time. New financial products will come on the market. The economy might be in a boom or a bust—or we could have another pandemic. When any of these things happen, and they will, it will be vital for us to make sound decisions based on the current market and to feel the security of having money saved.

JUST STAY PUT

"If you thought of yourself as having a card with only twenty punches in a lifetime, and every financial decision used up one punch. You'd resist the temptation to dabble. You'd make more good decisions."

—Warren Buffett, quoted in The Snowball, by Alice Schroeder

It is costly and time-consuming to keep switching plans. As illustrated in earlier examples, sometimes it is best to use savings to pay off debt, but what is more important is to keep adding to our savings, and to allow time to create

FREE pennies. From our earlier example, the real magic begins if we keep our savings snowball going.

If we continue to add $250 per month to savings for the full five years while making only minimum payments on the car, we will have an account balance of almost $17,500. If you drove this now 5-year-old car for another five years and put the $637 (the original $387 car payment plus the $250) into the savings account, you'd have $67,680 at the end of the ten years. Granted, you're driving around a ten-year-old car. You might have had to dip into that for some repairs, but you would still have a beautiful chunk of change even with those expenses.

MONTHLY PAYMENT	TIME PERIOD	INTEREST RATE	SAVINGS BALANCE
$250	3 years	6 percent	$9,860
$250	5 years	6 percent	$17,456
$637 ($250 plus $387)	10 years (5 years at $250, then 5 years at $637)	6 percent	$67,680

The beauty of this plan, and the security it offers, is that if you decide the repairs are too much, you can get a new car and use some of the savings you've created. Or, if you like how this snowball is growing (and you will), you can fix up the older car, or take out another loan for a newer model, and do it again.

People in my classes frequently say, "But Renée, we could pay off the car in three years with the $250 and start saving the $637 per month for the remaining two years of the five-year loan period." Yes—if you select that option, the account is valued at $16,200 at the end of the initial five-year period, $1,300 less than our savings alternative above. To make this example fair, we should add back the $1,400 in interest we saved with the early payoff, so the difference is a wash.

We have this result because we used 6 percent in both calculations—the loan and the savings. If you can secure a loan rate lower or higher than this, then considering variables regarding the savings return changes the outcome. This is why reevaluating, making wise financial decisions, and trusting the process are essential.

Let's return this discussion to the most critical point: three years into either alternative. If I choose savings, I will likely have over $9,000 in an account with my name on it. At this moment, I have a car to drive around, and I have security. If something happens to me, my family, my job, or my car, I have some extra cash to back me up. I don't know about you, but right now, I envision myself in a snazzy red convertible, wind in my hair, sun on my face, and feeling free. Sure—I have debt on the car, but I have a means to pay for it. I am in control, and I have options. It feels good.

If I give that same $250 to a bank for three years, I have a car title, and if I need a furnace, get cancer, or lose my job, I cannot use that car title to bail me out of those problems. If anything happens, I will go back into debt to cover these life events. Since I am seeking alternatives under the stress of these other concerns, I may not have enough time and attention to consider the best solution. When contemplating this option, I imagine myself driving around in a small, boxy hatchback, feeling like the car is closing in on me. Sure, I can sell this car, downsize it, and get some cash, but is that something we want to do while dealing with a furnace issue, cancer, or a job loss?

Whichever way we look at it, $9,000 cash offers us more security, opportunity, and alternatives than a car title—PERIOD.

BIGGER IS SOMETIMES BETTER

"Worry about being better; bigger will take care of itself." —Gary Comer

Let's take this car example and snowball the concept to make it bigger. We'll consider a mortgage instead—$100,000 at 6 percent for a 30-year term. The payment of principal and interest is $599 per month. If we make only minimum payments, we will have paid $115,838 in interest over the term, bringing the total cost of this loan (excluding closing costs and other fees) to almost $216,000.

If, on the other hand, we pay an extra $50 each month, we would have this paid off in 24 years and save ourselves $24,000 in interest. If we can increase that by an additional $100 per month, it will pay off in 21 years, and we will have saved $39,000 in interest. If we can make it to $200 every month, we will have it paid off in 16 years and save ourselves $58,000 in interest. The interest we are saving is substantial, and I've noted the amounts in the outline below.

LOAN VALUE	MONTHLY PAYMENT	PAYOFF TIME	INTEREST COST / SAVINGS
$100,000 at 6% interest rate	$599	30 years	$115,838.19 interest
+$50/mo.	$649	24 years	$91,268.98 interest $24,000 savings
+$100/mo.	$699	21 years	$75,937.94 interest $39,000 savings
+$200/mo.	$799	16 years	$57,386.83 interest $58,000 savings

P&I = principal and interest. Figures rounded.

This example has been used in our continuing education classes for over a decade. That was it for the first few years—this is how much interest you can save by paying off debt early. Then, one November, as I was prepping courses for the coming year, I thought, "I wonder what would happen if someone saved those amounts instead." This was the beginning of my shift in thinking about saving versus paying off debt, and the overview is below.

If we were to take the same $50 and put it into savings instead of paying extra on the mortgage over the same 24-year period, we would have accumulated $32,319 rather than saving $24,000 of interest. The $100 principal payment in an account over 21 years grows to almost $51,000, rather than reducing the interest cost by $39,000, and the $200 saved over 16 years grows to $65,000, versus a reduction of $58,000 in mortgage interest. By comparison, the savings column is larger.

SCENARIO	MORTGAGE PAYOFF	MORTGAGE SAVINGS	INVESTMENT ACCUMULATION	INVESTMENT VALUE 30 YRS
+$50/mo.	24 years	$24,000	$32,381	$50,281
+$100/mo.	21 years	$39,000	$50,870	$100,562
+$200/mo.	16 years	$58,000	$65,310	$201,124

Assumes 6 percent return. Figures rounded.

Our work still isn't done yet. There are other variables to consider, like taxation. As we pay down our mortgage, we may be sacrificing a tax deduction for the interest, which reduces the value of the "Mortgage Savings" column. Depending on where we saved these pennies, the earnings could be taxable, reducing the two "Investment" columns in the comparison above. Moreover, the investment accumulation is only valuable if we leave the money in the account to grow. If one is not disciplined enough to do so, one may get more value by paying off the debt. There may also be additional variables specific to your situation.

In our classes, insurance agents sometimes say, "Where will you get that 6 percent savings rate?" The response I provide to these participants has already been discussed—stock market averages are above this value. No need to belabor the point. When I first created this, a 6 percent mortgage lending rate was expected, and I matched it on the savings side. What I find most interesting about this routine question is that it ultimately raises an objection to the value of retaining debt and instead saving. Class participants never comment on the 6 percent mortgage lending rate.

After the housing bubble burst in 2008, mortgage lending rates were well below 6 percent until the interest rate increased beginning in 2022. This means that for nearly 15 years, people could borrow money well below the costs described in this example. This reduces the value of interest savings from paying off debt early and increases the value of saving that money each month instead. Yet, this significant point seems to have escaped the minds of the "pay your debt off first" crowd.

CHANGING TIDES

"The greatest danger in times of turbulence is not the turbulence —it is to act with yesterday's logic." —Peter Drucker

Beginning around the end of 2020, the height of the COVID-19 pandemic, until early 2022, mortgage lending rates for a 30-year term were in the 2.5 percent range. If I wanted a 15-year term, depending on my credit score, I could borrow money at under 2 percent. A seasoned financial professional in one of my classes said, "That is free money." His thought, and that of other savvy-minded money managers, was, "If I can borrow that money at rates that low for that long, I surely can put it just about anywhere and earn more on those pennies." This makes the cost of the debt zero—or FREE.

This man took out a mortgage on a debt-free home to capitalize on this opportunity. Like many others who feel more secure without debt, his wife was worried. Over and over, she asked, "Why would you take out a loan on our house when we worked so hard to pay it off?" And over and over, he replied, "Because this is a historic low. Interest rates will surely increase, and if we put this borrowed money elsewhere, we will make money on their money." Sure enough, just a couple of years later, mortgage lending rates are in the 7 to 8 percent range, and they have their borrowed 2.5 percent money tucked away, earning 5 percent or more. That's FREE money.

Those lucky enough to have a 2 percent mortgage in 2021 who chose to put their pennies in the S&P 500 would have seen a 23 percent return. It is downright silly to give my pretty little pennies to a lender to pay off a 2 percent mortgage early, considering the difference in pennies created by investing it.

I'll also say this—and I am typing all these words because this is the most crucial point in the whole "FREE Money; Two Percent Mortgage" discussion: I think it is morally bankrupt to advocate for people to pay off this low-interest debt without explaining the alternative. The fact that many pundits never changed their tune (Dave Ramsey topping the list) considering these historically low-interest rates, is highly suspect. Can they not admit they're wrong? Do they not care? I'm unsure of their motivation, but I would never take financial advice from someone who does not approach financial education with transparency. This is why it is far better to be informed about money principles and formulate a decision that works well for you than to follow some rote philosophy.

In an earlier chapter, I explained that my first mortgage was at 10 percent in 1990, and to reduce our interest costs, my husband and I decided to pay extra each month. As I wrote that section, I thought, "What did the S&P 500 do over that term?" I lived through it, worked in financial circles, and knew that the 1990s offered a bullish stock market. Bullish is an expectation for gain, and there were many.

When I first looked, I found that 1990 was a year of loss of about -6.5 percent, but that doesn't tell the full story. Pennies I put away in 1990 grow in future years. The next page offers a chart of S&P 500 Index values from the 1990s. Look at all those glorious double-digit gains while we continued to refinance at lower lending rates. Even at a 10 percent mortgage in 1991, those pretty pennies would have gained 26 percent in the market instead.

S&P 500 INDEX

HISTORICAL ANNUAL DATA

YEAR	AVERAGE CLOSING PRICE	YEAR OPEN	YEAR HIGH	YEAR LOW	YEAR CLOSE	ANNUAL % CHANGE
1999	1,327.33	1,228.10	1,469.25	1,212.19	1,469.25	19.53%
1998	1,085.50	975.04	1,241.81	927.69	1,229.23	26.67%
1997	873.43	737.01	983.79	737.01	970.43	31.01%
1996	670.49	620.73	757.03	598.48	740.74	20.26%
1995	541.72	459.11	621.69	459.11	615.93	34.11%
1994	460.42	465.44	482.00	438.92	459.27	-1.54%
1993	451.61	435.38	470.94	429.05	466.45	7.06%
1992	415.75	417.26	441.28	394.50	435.71	4.46%
1991	376.19	326.45	417.09	311.49	417.09	26.31%
1990	334.63	359.69	368.95	295.46	330.22	-6.56%

SOURCE:
https://www.macrotrends.net/2324/sp-500-historical-chart-data

These glorious double-digit gains are not guaranteed, and only happen some of the time. Sometimes, the market has a very long recovery period, or many political or economic things create volatility. For me, the period that comes to mind is the 1930s during the Great Depression or the 1970s, which some have cited as one of the worst bear markets. A bear market produces losses, unlike a bull market, which creates gains. For this discussion, I want to consider something more recent, "The Lost Decade."

"The Lost Decade for Stocks" refers to the ten years from 12/31/1999 through 12/31/2009, when the S&P 500® generated an annualized total return of -0.9 percent. This was only the second time the market had a negative return at the end of a decade. The other period was the Great Depression, which began on Black Monday (October 28, 1929)—this decade, the 1930s, saw a loss of 0.5 percent.

S&P 500 VS. INFLATION

BY DECADE

DECADE	S&P 500 TOTAL RETURN (%)	INFLATION (CPI %)
1930s	-0.5	-18.7
1940s	140.4	69.4
1950s	486.6	24.3
1960s	112.2	28.3
1970s	76.8	103.6
1980s	403.7	64.5
1990s	432.8	33.8
2000s	-9.1	28.3

SOURCE:
Robert J. Shiller, *Stocks for the Long Run (Updated Edition)*.
Yale University Press, 2015.

Having lived through "The Lost Decade," I am not about to sugarcoat it or try to convince you it was great. It was not. When I thought things might turn around, something else made the market tumble. There were the events of September 11, 2001, the tech-stock bubble bursting, the invasion of Iraq, and the housing market crash. It was not pretty. It was not fun, and it was right in the middle of my working years when many of us Gen Xers were trying to secure a solid financial future. I didn't know if I would ever reach my future savings goals. While this period was not as devastating to the typical American as the Great Depression, it was a tough pill to swallow.

In the middle of this decade and most certainly toward the end, I questioned my plan many times. Should I keep saving as much as I had been? Or should I try to save more to catch up? Or throw in the towel and give up. In hindsight, I wish I had stopped giving my mortgage company my extra pennies during this decade. Indeed, questioning that decision seems valid, mainly because I never recovered the cash I put into that mortgage and home due to the later foreclosure, and because of the investment value I would have received if I had saved that extra money instead. Even "The Lost Decade" would have provided a better value investing all my pretty pennies. Let me explain more about that.

RIDE THE WAVE

"The true investor welcomes volatility ... a wildly fluctuating market means that irrationally low prices will periodically be attached to solid businesses."
—Warren Buffett

Depressed markets are a joy to seasoned traders. This means bargain prices, and we don't need to be aggressive or highly involved traders to take advantage of opportunities. We only need to keep our eyes on the prize of future security by remembering the "Four Ds of Investing":

D-1: Dollar-cost averaging tells us that if we invest at regular intervals (weekly, bi-weekly, or monthly), sometimes we'll invest when the market is high, and sometimes we'll invest when the market is low. This "averaging" helps reduce the risk of market volatility. "The Lost Decade" was quite volatile, with two high years in the S&P 500 closing price range of $1,400, followed by three years with average closing price values closer to $900. (Values from the chart on page 109.)

The numbers provided above are also "averages" for the year. During "The Lost Decade," the lowest value was $676 in 2009. Those who were buying routinely got to buy in at or near that price. This means when their pennies purchased at that price hit the end of the following year, December 31, 2010, they nearly doubled to $1,258. Today, August 2023, the value is over $4,400.

By dollar-cost averaging, we don't need to time the market for when we believe it is the lowest buy-in price. We will naturally have some of our money buying in at those prices. The reverse, of course, would also be true. If one is investing routinely, they would also naturally buy in at the decade high of $1,565 in 2007. By dollar-cost averaging, the composite of all our pretty pennies becomes invested at the average value through the entire decade, making a buy at high values less painful.

D-2: Dividends are another part of the investment value that stocks produce. When we own stocks, we own a "share" of the company. When the company makes a profit, the board of directors may choose to pay a portion of the profits to the shareholders. While not required, these dividend payments make the company stock more attractive. Attractive stocks attract more buyers, and when there is an increase in demand with a limited supply, price (or value) normally increases.

A recent U.S. asset manager Hartford Funds analysis found that "The Lost Decade's" negative annual return changed to a 1.8 percent positive return after dividend payouts. Since many investors reinvest the dividend payments, this brings the average return for the S&P 500 from about 9 percent to over 12 percent. Dividends help us turn pennies into dollars, too.

D-3: Diversification: Thus far, I've talked primarily about stocks through the S&P 500 and basic interest-bearing accounts. The S&P 500 is a reasonably diversified stock index representing the top 500 U.S. companies in market capitalization. This would be more diverse than, say, the Dow, which comprises only 30 stocks. Another common one, the Nasdaq, comprises 2,500 equities and is further broadened by including other investment assets like American depositary receipts (ADRs), units of real estate investment trusts (REITs), and publicly traded partnerships.

This is just three of 2,500 U.S. indices. Foreign and international indices, bond investments, leasing equipment contracts, cryptocurrency, precious metals, options, commodities, and more also exist. Anywhere one believes that there is a profit to be made for investments (and investment managers), it can be structured into an investment. During "The Lost Decade", some of these assets performed better than others. We'll talk more about some of these strategies in the chapter "More FREE Pennies."

D-4: DYNAMITE: You might be wondering, "Renée, I'm not super well-versed in the world of investing, but I have never heard of an asset class called 'DYNAMITE'." Yes, you are not alone. There isn't one. I created this category to talk about the most crucial point on this list, and DYNAMITE was the only 'D' word I could think of that would illustrate this vital reason to keep saving no matter what.

Regardless of how the market or any investment performs at any given time, our efforts to keep saving will pay off. In some seasons, the payoff will take longer than it did during "The Lost Decade," but those who put away pretty pennies during the first ten years of the new millennium gained a gross, non-compounded gain of 140 percent or an average of 14 percent per year during the next decade (2010-2020). When you add the compounding for those who left their pretty pennies there, we are discussing an even higher return. This explosion takes little pennies and blows them up into hefty bucks. But if we don't get started now, we cannot take advantage of the explosions when they come.

This brings us to the other tool we must take advantage of—TIME.

S&P 500 — Annual Data Snapshot

2000–2020

Year	Year High	Year Low	Year Close	Annual % Change
2020	3,756.07	2,237.40	3,756.07	**16.26%**
2019	3,240.02	2,447.89	3,230.78	**28.88%**
2018	2,930.75	2,351.10	2,506.85	**-6.24%**
2017	2,690.16	2,257.83	2,673.61	**19.42%**
2016	2,271.72	1,829.08	2,238.83	**9.54%**
2015	2,130.82	1,867.61	2,043.94	**-0.73%**
2014	2,090.57	1,741.89	2,058.90	**11.39%**
2013	1,848.36	1,457.15	1,848.36	**29.60%**
2012	1,465.77	1,277.06	1,426.19	**13.41%**
2011	1,363.61	1,099.23	1,257.60	**0.00%**
2010	1,259.78	1,022.58	1,257.64	**12.78%**
2009	1,127.78	676.53	1,115.10	**23.45%**
2008	1,447.16	752.44	903.25	**-38.49%**
2007	1,565.15	1,374.12	1,468.36	**3.53%**
2006	1,427.09	1,223.69	1,418.30	**13.62%**
2005	1,272.74	1,137.50	1,248.29	**3.00%**
2004	1,213.55	1,063.23	1,211.92	**8.99%**
2003	1,111.92	800.73	1,111.92	**26.38%**
2002	1,172.51	776.76	879.82	**-23.37%**
2001	1,373.73	965.80	1,148.08	**-13.04%**
2000	1,527.46	1,264.74	1,320.28	**-10.14%**

Source: *Macrotrends.net, "S&P 500 Historical Chart Data."*

THE EARLIER WE START

"In youth, we learn; in age, we understand."—Marie von Ebner-Eschenbach

Ben Franklin might have said, "Remember that time is money." But Ben didn't give you the whole story. The truth is, "Time makes money." With it, new money, FREE MONEY, will appear in our account, for which we do nothing but wait. This power tool only works when we put forth the effort to save our pretty pennies.

As one of my favorite YouTubers, John Green of the Vlogbrothers, said in his video, 'How to Turn Your Dumb Summer Job Into $162,000'—"[a savings account] IS A MACHINE THAT MAKES MONEY WITH NOTHING BUT TIME." It's one of my favorite lines ever.

Here's another line I love, which is equally impactful:

As John goes through the title example of how teenagers can accumulate $162,000 by retirement age, starting with only $5,900, he also admits that $6,000 may be tough for the typical teen to save. So, he then tells the audience that even if this teen only scrapes together $2,000 to save, it still becomes $50,000.

John then says—and here comes the other part I love, "But if I do the same as the tottering old man that I am at 33, when I retire in 37 years, it's only worth about $20,000."

The 13-year age difference cost John $30,000. The earlier we start saving, the better off we are financially. PERIOD. That is why the very first chapter was START SAVING NOW. Every day we wait costs us future earnings, and I could not let you wait even one more day: Don't put it off--don't slow it down. Every day that you can, put some pennies away for the future you.

IT'S ALL GONNA BE OKAY

"Success isn't permanent, and failure isn't fatal." —Mike Ditka

When I teach this material in a live class, we never have a 19-year-old in the room, and rarely even have anyone as young as age 33. This means the natural next thought for the person who has not yet saved anything might be, "It's too late for me." I'm inclined to say, "It's never too late." But such platitudes rarely motivate us to change our patterns. I'll tell you a success story instead—MINE.

I've already shared that I lost my home to foreclosure. Over the decades, tens of thousands of dollars have been paid to a mortgage lender, and not one dime of equity gain has been shown for it. Top that off with giving my ex-husband a third of my retirement accounts in the divorce. I also raised our children with very little financial support from him. This means that more than $300,000 of financial gain was moved from my column to his. That is a devastating financial hit, much more than any of the numbers from John Greene in our last example. It makes the $162,000 figure (saving $5,900 as a teen) feel like pocket change, and all of this happened to me after age 40.

Who do you think is doing better financially today, me or my ex-husband? Me—1000 percent me, and it's not because I make so much more money than he does. I think he may earn more money than I do now. It is all because I Flowed these principles, and you can too.

I intended to write "follow," but I accidentally typed "Flowed." I moved to correct it, then thought, "That is truer than anything." I allowed GOD to steer the ship, and things have worked for me. Of course, I am not always in the Flow, and everything has not been perfect, but it worked for my betterment. Certainly, financially, but also emotionally. When things weren't Flowing my way, I was not so prone to fear and anxiety. I had peace, and you can have that, too.

By now, you realize that if you strategically use debt, it can work to your advantage, and there are significant advantages to getting every penny you can into some accumulation account with your name on it. If you are on board with these ideas, it has likely raised several questions. Everything from how much and where to save to what sort of debt makes sense. I aim to answer many of these questions in the coming chapters. First, we start with six easy steps in "Debt Decisions" because reducing the cost of your debt will give you more money to save. Simple as that.

CHAPTER SIX

DEBT DECISIONS

Six-Step Strategy

RULE 1:
MINIMUM PAYMENTS ONLY
MORE PENNIES TO GROW

Earlier, I suggested you make minimum payments only. The intent was to free up money each month to save it. We should be tucking all our extra pennies into an account with our name on it. Those with credit card debt might have thought, "That's crazy. How will I ever get ahead making minimum payments with high interest [18, 20, 28 percent or more] tacked on?"

You won't, but I didn't tell you to keep your credit card debt.

RULE 2:
NEVER KEEP HIGH-INTEREST CREDIT CARD DEBT
GET A LINE OF CREDIT

My father taught me this lesson years ago. I moved out of my parents' home way too early, at age seventeen, and quickly discovered that I could not afford to live independently, even with a roommate. I covered the rent, sure. I paid half of the bills, but I had a credit card I used for food and household supplies. I made payments on it. It didn't go delinquent, but I charged more on the card than I could afford to pay at the end of the month. Before long, I owed the credit card company $1,200 (in 1984)!

I went home to live and asked my father to lend me the money to pay it off. He said he would on one condition—I had to promise to never retain a balance on a high-interest credit card again. I made that promise, and I kept it. I have never carried a balance on a high-interest credit card since. You know what else? I use my credit cards for nearly all my expenses. We'll talk more about this strategy, but I don't always have the income to pay off the balance.

Your first thought probably is, "That's not so revolutionary, Renée. If you are doing all this penny-saving you keep talking about, you probably take the money from your savings." Nope, that's way too precious. I've seen the power of compounding, which gives me FREE pennies when I leave it there. I am reluctant to withdraw that money. I spend my savings on infrequent occasions.

Instead, I suggest you do what I did: Get yourself a line of credit.

USE SOMEONE ELSE'S MONEY

"Don't let your mouth write no check that your tail can't cash."
—Bo Diddley

Ever since I can remember, I have had a personal line of credit on my checking accounts—business and personal. I cannot recall how it started. Maybe a bank offered me one to avoid overdraft charges. I learned precisely how handy this credit line is when avoiding a credit card balance. Tapping into it for a week or more gives me time to figure out how to pay it off.

I don't like to allow a balance on the line of credit from month to month. This is my emergency transition fund, so I prefer to pay it off in a few weeks. There are months when I cannot meet this objective, and part of the balance carries through to the next billing cycle. I say "part" because, throughout the month, I transfer over any extra income, reducing the balance and interest cost.

Interest accumulates on a line of credit differently than on a credit card. Provided I pay off the balance for new purchases on my credit card in the next billing cycle, there will be no interest charge. That is not the case with a line of credit. The interest charges begin from the day I tap into this reserve loan. The same would be true if one made a cash advance on a credit card, which typically has an immediate cost. This is why I will make frequent payments on an outstanding balance on a line of credit but wait until the very last day possible to pay off my credit card.

There are several benefits to having the cushion of a Line of Credit (LOC):

1. I have never had overdraft charges and don't need to worry about them. I am covered if an accounting error in my books or a forgotten autopay comes through.
2. It helps me budget. Financial planning books repeatedly discuss the need for a budget and ask you to stick to it. That is tough for most of us. But my line of credit keeps my spending in line. If I have a balance on the LOC, I watch what I spend until it's paid off.
3. A line of credit has a lower interest rate than credit cards—one of mine is 2 percent above prime. That is about 10.5 percent in the higher interest rate environment of February 2024. When the Federal Reserve had zero rates, this account charged me pennies.
4. If you are a homeowner, having a Home Equity Line of Credit (or HELOC) may also be worthwhile. The interest rate is even lower, typically 1 percent above prime if you have good credit, because the home secures this debt. This option has closing costs, so weigh the total expense. The rate will vary with interest rate fluctuations.
5. If a significant purchase or a financial emergency arises, I can act quickly and determine the long-term payoff options.

WORK THAT DEBT

"Debts are like children - begot with pleasure, but brought forth with pain."
—Moliére

Debt and children are alike in another way: "They're both a lot of work." If we are going to make the most of all our pennies, we need to work on our debt, seeking the lowest-cost solutions. This means using a line of credit to pay off our monthly credit card balance if necessary and refinancing debt at lower interest rates whenever possible. We move balances from our credit cards to lower-cost solutions, but it can also mean other transfers.

A few years ago, a young woman wrapping up her graduate studies asked me for financial advice. The COVID pause on student loan repayment was lapsing, and she would need to resume making payments. As we talked, she told me her interest rate was 9 percent on some of her loans. I thought this was plain crazy. Mortgage lending rates were at 3 percent. I bought a car at that time with a 4.89 percent rate on the loan.

Depending on her credit score, she could qualify for a loan at lower interest rates and refinance that debt. I told her as much. Her response was, "You can do that?" Yes, yes, you can do that. Paying our bills shows lenders we are creditworthy, allowing us to qualify for better rates. A good credit score is a golden ticket to many forms of advancement. We'll discuss more about that later.

I checked in with her a few weeks later to see how the plan worked. Our young graduate student said, "I talked to my mom about it, and she said you can't do that." This was surprising: Mom is not a banker and is not in finance—it was not her area of expertise.

Banks want to lend us money—secured or unsecured, variable or fixed. They can make money from all of it. If BANK B has your loan and you're making steady payments, BANK A would gladly take that over and offer a competitive rate. A 5 percent rate is better for BANK A than nothing, and if BANK B were on the ball, they could have provided a lower rate to keep the money.

I turned to our lovely graduate student and asked, "Did you still research it?" She responded, "No, I wasn't sure." My immediate thought, and I don't believe I said it then, was, "An internet search takes three seconds. You weren't willing to take three seconds to find out if you could cut your costs in half?"

To make sure I was right about any of this because I could have been wrong, I opened my browser and put in, "Can I refinance my student loans?" Bam—in less than two seconds, I had multiple resources: everything from YouTube videos and blogs explaining how it works to lenders and government sources defining current rates and the application process. It's super easy and very slick.

Here's the point: Well-meaning people from everywhere will tell us things. Not all of it is accurate. It is worth the time and effort to check things out. It might be a little work, but it is well worth it.

If this woman could have gotten close to the 5 percent rates I saw in my research, she would have saved hundreds of dollars monthly in interest. This means a lot more pennies in savings. Even more important, I keep a 7 percent average return from the S&P in mind. If I have 9 percent on my debt but earn only 7 percent, it might make more sense to pay it off. But if I can reduce the loan cost to 5 percent, I have a decisive margin for my investment.

RULE 3:
OVERCOME OBSTACLES
SEEK OTHER SOLUTIONS

"Procrastination is like a credit card: it's a lot fun until you get the bill."
—Christopher Parker

You might think, "Renée, all of that is good for some people, but that won't work for me. My {debt or credit score} is out of control, and no lender will help me." I will not minimize that dilemma by sugarcoating it or acting like that isn't a real problem. There are instances when, for whatever reason, it will not work to reorganize your debt.

Some of the causes of our debt problems are under our control, and some (like my dramatic income change causing the foreclosure of my home) are outside the scope of our control. How it happened and why you have found yourself here are less important than what you choose to do about it going forward. You picked up this book for starters, and you read this far. That is the crucial part of a favorable end to your story.

It is also essential to consider ways to heal any behaviors that brought us here. I can give you the following ideas and suggestions to help, which may or may not help immediately. We cannot be assured of success if we don't work through any underlying issues. None of us is perfect at this—all it requires is honest attempts.

Improving one's credit score will be discussed later in this chapter, so let's start with the problem of having a debt that is more significant than your income allows you to pay. By "pay," I mean affording each month's payments or making headway on the debt to pay it off in a reasonable time. Since I am unsure of your situation, I cannot define "reasonable time." However, the resources below can assist you in making that determination and provide various courses of action to get you on track.

- **Debtors Anonymous (DA):** I have never used DA, but two people I respect told me about this organization. DA is very much like AA (Alcoholics Anonymous) and other 12-step programs. There are no dues or fees. The people you meet struggle with the same fears, concerns, and problems with money and debt. They found a way out and want to help others do the same. This organization can also be of value to you as you make future financial decisions. An internet search brought me to this website: DebtorsAnonymous.org. I found everything necessary to learn more and find a nearby meeting to attend.

- **Credit Counselors:** We are now moving into resources that are not wholly altruistic. It is their job to help people find a debt solution. This includes many of the ideas above, such as help with budgeting, debt negotiation, and referrals to other support entities. Here, however, they may ask for fees. Like too many entities offering services to those possibly full of fear, some are prepared to take advantage of you. As a result, I would be cautious of anyone charging fees or using fear to get you to sign up. Look to the Consumer Financial Protection Bureau (CFPB), a U.S. government resource, which offers guidelines for interviewing these services.
- **Bankruptcy:** Sometimes, our debts have gone too far, and the only viable solution is bankruptcy. I would shop around a bit for an attorney. They are not all the same; this will likely be an emotional time. It's worth taking the time to find someone who will help you through this process. In addition to competency, you'll want someone who prioritizes your best interests.
- **Evaluate and Refresh:** The problem could be related to your income, monthly expenses, lifestyle, or something else GOD is nudging toward change. Even if everything is going well, evaluate these things and see if some change could bring relief and help you achieve the next level.
- **Other Solutions:** This list includes a few things that could help, but it is incomplete. GOD may have another plan for you, so write your list and tap the Flow. Keeping connected and open to possibilities will reveal the right door for you.

WINNING THE RACE

"It does not matter how slow you go as long as you do not stop" —Confucius

It's worth repeating—Financial success using these strategies only works if I manage my spending and debt. If I already have out-of-control credit card balances and use a credit line, consolidation, or bankruptcy to spend more, it will only compound the problem.

This does not mean we have to live as if we're destitute. As we have already discussed, our financial plan should bring us some joy now. If we only benefit our future selves by sacrificing everything today, we will not stick with it, and this is not what GOD has designed for us.

Out-of-control spending doesn't bring joy, either. It usually brings fear and dread, especially with mounting credit card balances. That is also not what GOD wants for us. Our goal is to find balance. This is why we discussed tapping the Flow and relying on Spiritual principles as a guide in the earlier chapters.

I selected the quote above—slow and steady wins the race—because this is not a sprint but a marathon. We will sometimes fail to balance these financial principles. What is important is that we are trying and willing to keep going. I have a personal story about the beauty of the journey and the lessons we can learn from the littlest among us.

WRONGWAYLIZZIE.ME

My blog and screen name on many platforms is WrongWayLizzie, and many people ask, "Where'd you get the name?" Lizzie comes from my middle name. Elizabeth was my Italian grandmother's name. I loved her very much, so I carried on the family tradition when my daughter was born and named her Lizzie, too.

Let me tell you about the wrong-way part.

When my daughter was young, she constantly darted off and headed the wrong way. I hate to use the word "constantly". It's so emphatic and rarely accurate, but it's the most fitting here. We'd leave the store, and little Lizzie would run off in the opposite direction from the car. I would stand in the doorway, a bit dumbfounded, and then yell, "Lizzie—this way." Indicating, of course, an area she was nowhere near. This would cause her to turn around and run back the other way.

I'll never forget when we were at a condo in Florida. At the time, Lizzie was about three or four years of age. After a light breakfast each morning, I would take the kids to the pool. When we left the pool, Lizzie would go the wrong way every one of the seven days of our vacation. By the third or fourth day, I was astounded. I turned to her brother, who was six years her senior, and said, "I can't believe she's still going the wrong way!"

It's not as if she lacked intellect. She was and is a bright person, but she was in the moment, full of joy, and the details didn't matter. She was safe to know she would get there, and she knew her mother and brother were there to guide her. Her compass was set on adventure and learning. The right direction was a minor detail that didn't matter.

It was there that the nickname was born. Whenever she would head off, missing where we were going, I would think, "There goes WrongWayLizzie!"

On the remaining days of our vacation, I noticed something else. When I would call out to tell her our direction, she was never mad about it. She'd hear me, accept the direction, and merely turn around. It seemed that she realized she would make mistakes, and it was okay. She almost embraced the error. It gave her more time to run and explore, creating a more remarkable adventure.

This is how children generally handle life's challenges. Their little Buddha bellies stick out, and they don't think they're fat. They know they're adorable. They're trying to walk and fall more than they stand, but they don't sit there telling themselves they're worthless or will never get it. Nope, they try it again—and again—and again until they finally get it.

This is why I graciously accept WrongWayLizzie as my screen name. I've made plenty of mistakes, and I am far from perfect, but I want to face it all with the resilience of a child. It's all okay. I hope you, too, can take a lesson from WrongWayLizzie and the other children around you because no matter how far off track you get or how many times you fall, you will eventually get there. All we need is a willingness to turn around and keep trying. What a beautiful thing it would be if we could truly enjoy our journey regardless of how far off track we might go.

IT'S A NEW LANGUAGE

"Learning is not attained by chance, it must be sought for with ardor and diligence."
—Abigail Adams

Maybe all this financial stuff is like a new language to you. When discussing these matters with some of my friends, I realize how blessed I am to have had a career that allowed me to learn the language of money. It is functional, practical, and helpful to everyone's life, yet it is not readily taught in school. Many people don't know the basics because it might not have been a language your parents could share with you.

I moved to Mexico last year. I'll tell you all about it in the next chapter. It is part of my financial plan and the use of debt. Because I wanted to know the Mexican people better, I decided to learn Spanish. Yup, that's the kind of thing I do. I write a book and run a business involving lots of communication in English, and then I add a whole new language to my schedule. It seems crazy, I know, yet I have the energy for it and sense the Flow.

Learning a new language is hard. During my first week working to soak up Spanish, I invested 20 hours—every day since I have studied for an hour or two. I began six weeks ago. I figure that's at least 75 hours invested in my new language, and here's my status:

My head is packed with random things. For example, I know my numbers, days of the week, months, and other items. I'm fantastic at Spanglish because I use the various Spanish words I know in my English sentences. I was tickled the last two days when I could use two sentences in Spanish to communicate simple requests.

¿Puedo usar el baño? (Can I use the bathroom?)

¿Puedo pagar para mi agua? (Can I pay for my water?)

Yes, I am asking permission for many things, which are elementary sentences. If I think about how long I've been working on this and I made two simple sentences, it will depress me, but you know what? I was super excited that I was able to do it. I've been discouraged. I didn't think I would get there. I made many mistakes and couldn't remember simple items I had been over many times, but finally, I can see progress.

Your process might be similar if this financial stuff is new to you. There are a few things I've learned along the way that might also help you:

Enjoy the Process: I make everything a race. The faster I finish, the better, because my mindset is centered on today's product. In truth, there is also value in the process. I have found many fun ways to learn Spanish, including podcasts, YouTube videos, interactive apps, flashcards, and more.

I have the same challenge writing this book. I sit down to write pages focused on some self-imposed deadline. Rush and worry cramp the Flow. It works better when I think about the time I am investing as an opportunity. When the thought is, "I get to do this," instead of "I have to get this done," wonderful thoughts, considerations, and opportunities can Flow through.

Embrace the Mistakes: This one isn't easy either, but the process takes on a brighter lens when I do it. Mistakes are inevitable. I will make them (and so will you), and if I expect it, the pill is easier to swallow. Every person who has learned Spanish told me up front, "You will make mistakes. We all did. Don't let that stop you."

One evening, I was in an Uber with some friends. I was in the front seat, trying to chat and practice my Spanish with the Mexican driver. When we went to leave, I said, "BUENOS NACHOS." For those unaware, the correct phrase is "BUENOS NOCHES." Noches means "night," and nachos are a tasty treat. Instead of saying GOOD NIGHT to the Uber driver, I said, "GOOD NACHOS."

Everyone burst out laughing. Heck, I'm laughing right now. That's ridiculous and funny, but I wasn't laughing then. My memory tracks failed me. I reverted to the word I was more familiar with instead of the right word I knew I should use. At that moment, I thought, "That was so dumb." I might have told myself, "You are so dumb." (Ouch!)

However, I did not allow myself to stay there. I laughed it off, too, and I've used it as a good joke. I tell the story often. It makes me human. Sharing it allows me to be vulnerable. It also humbles me and hopefully will enable others to feel comfortable sharing their vulnerabilities. People laugh, but who the heck doesn't like a good laugh?

Whatever way you choose to deal with errors, please don't allow yourself to get stuck in the negative messages of "That was dumb." Or worse yet, "You are dumb." Both hold us back, and neither is true.

RULE 4:
KEEP AN EXCELLENT CREDIT SCORE
PAY YOUR BILLS ON TIME—IT'S THAT EASY

"Well done is better than well said." —*Benjamin Franklin*

You've likely heard many things about improving your credit score and several things that can hinder it. We'll discuss many of those ideas here, but this isn't complicated.

Your score will improve if you consistently pay all your obligations on time. If you do this for an extended period, you can come close to a perfect score. There is always some inherent credit risk, so a perfect score is challenging. Statistics say only about 1 percent ever get there, but it doesn't matter. Most lenders consider you a very good credit risk if your score is in the 700 range or above.

The beauty of this is that regardless of where you are on this scale, your score will improve if you pay all your bills on time. It's that simple. You won't jump from 600 to 800 in a couple of months, but slowly and steadily, your score will increase over time. Some little hiccups might create a slight or temporary decline. We'll discuss those, too, but if you pay all your bills on or before the deadline, your score will improve—PERIOD.

THE GOOD, THE BAD, AND THE RIDICULOUS

"In 1973, a woman could not get a credit card without a male signing off on it."
—Billie Jean King

The things women have endured. If you are unaware, women couldn't have a checking account without a male co-signer until the Equal Credit Opportunity Act (ECOA) of 1974. I am unsure of the logic. Did they believe women to be irresponsible, incapable, or both? Or was it all about control?

Whatever the reason, you might find some of the other items listed below that impact your credit score equally as dumbfounding. I provided the rationale for these points as I understood them from prior research, and showed you how to work these variables to your advantage. Most of these items do not significantly impact your overall score, even if you've heard something to the contrary. Remember, lots of well-meaning people give us misinformation. It's worth the time to research the facts. Here are some things I've learned about the credit score process.

Income—Lenders will look at your income and employment history to determine if they will give you a loan, but these variables and others like them are not part of your credit score. The credit scoring entities assume you have the income to meet your obligations if you pay your bills. Personal items you have not released to them, like income, employment, gender, age, and the like, are not included, as these could be considered discriminatory.

Paying Off Your Balance—Lots of people think they get bonus points on their credit score for paying off their balance each month, but there is no such thing. Making the minimum payment, provided it is on time, has the same impact, and if you use the card routinely, it never has a zero balance. If you are like me, you have been making purchases throughout the month, so by the time the payment arrives, which was intended to zero out last month's balance, you've got a new balance for next month. Paying the balance eliminates the cost of interest. That's the bonus.

Fewer Credit Cards Increase a Credit Score—Or the reverse, too many credit cards lower one's credit score. The opposite is more likely true. If I have many sources of credit and I avail myself only of those I know I can afford to pay, it shows I am responsible with my credit use. That is good for one's credit score. At one point, I could have bought a house with credit cards and furnished it too, and my score was nearly perfect because I kept my spending (and the balances) to amounts well under what I could access.

Too Many Credit Checks—This can impact one's credit score, but only if someone quickly seeks multiple new lines of credit. The thought is that if I am applying for several car loans or credit cards, I am about to do something reckless, like purchase something I cannot afford. If, on the other hand, I bought a new house and got a couple of new credit cards offering 0 percent to furnish it, I might see a slight decline, but it'll bounce back when my spending becomes typical again.

Credit Limit Ratio—Again, if I have credit cushions, space between my balance and the amount of credit I could use—my credit limit—it shows the credit scoring entities that I am a reasonable risk because I seem to keep my balance to an amount I can afford. This same variable applies to each credit card or line of credit. The scoring process will lower my score when I push my balance toward the credit limit. The solution is to ask for a credit limit increase or use multiple cards.

A LESSON TO LEARN BY

"Anyone who stops learning is old, whether at twenty or eighty. Anyone who keeps learning stays young." —Henry Ford

I use my credit cards for everything. I can also get some perks and use their money for free for 30 days or more. We'll talk about that strategy in the next chapter. For now, I have a story about how my credit score was impacted by some of the variables the scoring entities consider.

My insurance education company occasionally offers destination classes. We'll get discounted group rates through a travel service, and our customers will buy them to join us in a tropical location. We teach class a few mornings, and the rest is vacation time.

Since I collect the fares for the destination travelers, I set the proceeds in a money market account until the contract payment comes due a few weeks before our travel date. When I pay, I use a credit card if they allow me. To get miles, points, or cash-back on tens of thousands of dollars is a big boon. Plus, I am getting the added incentive of having tens of thousands in a savings account, earning interest for at least an additional 30 days. It always pays to look for ways to make a few extra pennies.

There is a downside to this strategy, however. When I charge tens of thousands to a credit card, it will come very close to the card's limit, and my credit score will drop. The first time I did it, I was shocked at how far it fell and how long it took to recover. If I remember correctly, my 800 or so score fell to close to 600, like 200 points. It plummeted.

I thought it would jump back up when I paid it off about a month later. Nope—first, it took the credit-scoring entities to see that it was paid. They do not check account balances daily, and once they noted the payment, they seemed hesitant to give me the 200 points back.

The more I considered it, the more the process made sense. Just like the credit scoring entities do not know my income, job, or other variables that could impact my ability to pay, they also have no idea why I just charged almost $30,000. That purchase is unusual (at least for me) and could be a red flag for future financial concerns.

In the end, it didn't take too long to recover. Little by little, month after month, it would go up very steadily until it was back in the 800 range about four months later.

NOW, THE UGLY

"Some economists estimate that for every family that goes bankrupt, there are about 15 more who are in the same amount of financial trouble and would profit from bankruptcy but just haven't filed." —Elizabeth Warren

It isn't pretty, and it isn't fun, but sometimes bankruptcy or foreclosure is the best solution. Some might say that I hung onto our family home way too long, or I shouldn't have even purchased my ex-husband's share when I did, but I believe everything happened for the best. I learned a lot through that experience, and I had a lot of emotions to work through before I could let go.

You might be wondering, "What if things fall apart? How do things like foreclosure or bankruptcy affect one's score?" That depends, too, so let me give you the basics of what I know.

If someone is 30 days late on their obligation, their credit score can drop by 40 to 110 points. This is a broad range. How do they decide if someone gets a minor ding of 40 points, 110, or something in between?

If the person has a long-standing history of being a good borrower and this is the only debt unpaid, their score will be impacted on the low side of these values. Their score would drop in the 40-point range. However, if this person is not paying other debts and/or has a relatively new credit score, this unpaid debt will have a more severe consequence on their score.

If someone continues not to pay this debt and is delinquent for 90 days, this will cause their score to drop 70 to 135 points. It is important to note that the values would not be added to the amounts above, but these are cumulative. For example, the person who is 30 days late might see a 40-point drop in their score, and then when it gets to 90 days late, their score would drop an additional 30, bringing the total drop to 70 points. Of course, if the debt continues unpaid, the credit score continues to dip.

Foreclosure, short sale, or deed-in-lieu all have the same impact on someone's credit score: an additional 85 to 160 points. I won't define these here again. These were discussed in Chapter 4, "Debt is NOT Bad."

The point drops for bankruptcy are the highest on the list, ranging from 130 to 240, depending on the situation. Ultimately, most people suffering this hardship will see their credit score drop in the 200-300-point range. I have provided an overview of these values below.

The average points lost on a FICO score are as follows:

- 30 days late: 40 to 110 points
- 90 days late: 70 to 135 points
- Foreclosure, short sale, or deed-in-lieu: 85 to 160
- Bankruptcy: 130 to 240

A CREDIT CHECK

"If you don't take good care of your credit, then your credit won't take good care of you."—Tyler Gregory

There are several resources to check your credit today. Your bank or credit cards may reveal your score when you log in. You can install several applications on your phone to provide your credit score whenever you wish. Two that immediately come to mind are Credit Karma and Rocket Money. These tools can provide other measures of financial advice and assistance beyond just a credit score.

Some will say these types of resources are not entirely accurate. Provided it's close to your score, that is still an effective tool. We don't need the precision of a lunar landing to see if your score is headed in the right direction.

Your credit score is different than a credit report. A credit report will list all your sources of credit, balances, limits, start date, and more. Here you can verify that the information the scoring entities use is correct.

The U.S. Federal government mandated that every American consumer has the right to receive their credit report for free each year. You can access this free report via this website: AnnualCreditReport.com. It allows you to get your credit report from the three major credit bureaus: Equifax, Experian, and TransUnion. Each can contain different information reported by various lending institutions. Americans are entitled to a free credit report, not necessarily the score. The last time I used this site, I had to pay to get my credit score directly from the bureaus. The cost varied, but based on my research, it ranged from $5.95 to $9.95.

We have covered a lot of ground. We have some tools to manage our debt and make the most of every penny. We can reduce the cost of our debt while improving our credit score, and in the process, we hope we find lots of extra pennies to add to our coffers. We also have a few tools to help keep things on track. This book outlines six strategies to maximize debt usage to improve your financial future.

Below are the four strategies we have reviewed thus far:

- **RULE 1: MINIMUM PAYMENTS ONLY**
  - This gives us extra cash to save.
- **RULE 2: NEVER KEEP A BALANCE ON HIGH-INTEREST CREDIT CARDS**
  - Get a lower-interest line of credit instead.
- **RULE 3: OVERCOME OBSTACLES**
  - It pays to reassess and learn other money-saving techniques.
- **RULE 4: KEEP AN EXCELLENT CREDIT SCORE**
  - Pay our bills on time every month—it's that easy.

The next chapter discusses our final two rules for making money and building wealth from debt.

- **RULE 5: FINANCE WHAT WILL GROW**
- **RULE 6: USE CREDIT CARDS FOR EVERYTHING**

CHAPTER SEVEN

A MONEY MAKER

When & How to Use Debt

"There's a tremendous bias against taking risks. Everyone is trying to optimize their ass-covering." —Elon Musk

MANAGE MONEY LIKE THE BIG GUYS*

You might think, "Debt is a liability. It will cost me. Now, Renée, you're saying debt will make us money. You've lost it."

You are correct. Debt is a liability and can 'cost' us in more ways than one. It counts against net worth on a balance sheet. Any amount we owe is subtracted from our assets and reduces the value of what we ultimately own. The interest we pay is also an expense, and the payment reduces the money we have available for other items (opportunity cost). It can also be something we worry about, robbing us of peace of mind. Yes, there are several layers of cost associated with debt. Undoubtedly, borrowing money has variable costs associated with it. Still, this same debt can create wealth for our future selves if we apply our fifth rule to our decision-making process.

*My use of the phrase "BIG GUYS" is explained in Appendix II.

RULE: 5
FINANCE WHAT WILL GROW
DEBT CAN HELP US ACHIEVE OUR GOALS

"If we command our wealth, we shall be rich and free.
If our wealth commands us, we are poor indeed."
—Edmund Burke

To better understand debt as a wealth accumulator, I'd like you to consider a question: "When one of the BIG GUYS wants to expand his enterprise, do you think he cashes in his other investments and runs over with $100 million in cash to buy the next favored endeavor? Or do you think this multi-millionaire (or billionaire) will work with a few banks and lending institutions until he finds the most favorable terms and chooses to risk the lender's money instead? Or possibly find other creative means to pay for it, like asking a few rich buddies to pitch in or tapping into an investment capital firm for financing?" I'm using BIG GUYS here because, again, most of the wealth is held by men. (For more information, please check out Appendix II.)

Borrowing money and seeking other financing options can protect our wealth from risk. This is the same principle we discussed earlier, only on a grander scale. This is how those BIG GUYS get into that league. When we strategically use debt for other endeavors, we can keep money in savings for greater control, options, and future security.

To illustrate some of the fundamentals of this strategy, let's look at Elon Musk and his purchase of Twitter (now X). Musk could have come up with the $44 billion purchase price. He was worth well over $200 billion at the time—many billions over. He could have purchased Twitter outright with cash after liquidating some holdings.

But Musk didn't want to do that. At first, he tried to limit his cash contribution to the transaction to $15 billion. This was on top of Musk having already purchased almost 10 percent of Twitter's stock. He was into this deal, into multibillions anyway. Then, one of the financing options fell through. This required Musk to invest around $27 billion—well over half the purchase price. Why did Musk want to avoid putting so much cash in? One reason is:

Diversification—We typically hear this word associated with our investment portfolios, but the strategy can work in any financial transaction, or anywhere we want to reduce risk. Risk reduction is the entire purpose of diversification.

If we have all our eggs in one basket and that basket crashes, we will likely lose all our eggs. But if we diversify, put some eggs here, put some eggs there, and maybe have eggs everywhere, it is less likely that we will lose all our eggs.

The same logic applies to significant purchases. If we take all our savings and buy what we consider the best business venture, and then that venture fails, we can lose all the eggs in that basket. Or let's say we find our dream home and have the money to buy it outright. If we do that, and the insurance won't pay after a tornado tears it down, we may not have the cash to get new housing or to pay attorneys to fight the insurer's decision for us.

By diversifying the purchase through multiple sources, we can reduce our risk. This is one reason Musk wanted to limit his capital in the transaction. One of the reasons Musk was forced to add more cash to his Twitter purchase was due diligence. While we might see the due diligence process as limiting our options, the concept is designed to reduce risk, and, as a result, it can help protect our wealth, too.

Due Diligence—The $12 billion difference between the $27 billion Musk put into the purchase of Twitter and the $15 billion he originally intended was supposed to come from a loan secured by Tesla stock. At the outset, this sounds great. Musk must liquidate nothing. The stock is still his to continue increasing in value and could create dividends (if Tesla ever decides to issue them).

Musk would keep all the advantages of stock ownership and still get the proceeds necessary to buy Twitter. That sounds great if this were dollar for dollar—for every dollar the bank loans, that dollar is secured by one dollar of Tesla stock. However, according to Wikipedia, the lender wanted this $12 billion loan secured by $62 billion of stock. Risking the loss of five times the loan value if the whole thing goes defunct would not be considered a good deal by anyone.

There are many possible reasons for this, and as I read articles on it, one explanation emerged as the leading reason for this disparity—the risk the lender identified during their due diligence.

Due diligence (sometimes referred to as "underwriting") is collecting and analyzing information before deciding or conducting a transaction. By design, the due diligence process should identify weaknesses to help reduce loss and mitigate damages. At the time, there was much discussion that Musk's offer of $44 billion was twice Twitter's value. This disparity creates risk even if Musk can cover the loss or the purchase has significant growth potential. No one wants to get caught holding a bag that has no value.

Let's examine how the due diligence process might help us protect and secure our wealth. Banks, lending institutions, and other financing organizations will likely have more expertise in financial matters than we do. They've witnessed many times how a loan assisted someone in advancing their economic future in a positive direction; they've also seen the painful results of the reverse of this when the choice was costly.

These entities know what to look for to help keep our investment secure. We can consider them and their analysis as partners in this process. Granted, this partner wants to profit, so we must act wisely and review terms, but ultimately, their success is tied to our success, and vice versa. Suppose we are seeking financing on a new business venture, and the lender, through their due diligence, is concerned with this opportunity. They will not extend the funding we seek. In that case, we may want to reconsider the structure of our purchase. If this happens more than once with different lenders, maybe this due diligence will protect us, and the Flow will help us consider something different.

While we could see this as an obstacle, we could also see it as an opportunity to evaluate our choices. Due diligence will likely identify risks that make this cost prohibitive for the lender, which are generally the same risks for us. Another way lenders reduce their risk is by managing vested interests.

Vested Interest—If we want to finance a purchase with debt, the lending institution will want to see how serious we are about this opportunity. This is why we usually need enough cash to create a vested interest, like the down payment when we buy a home. It's as if we are in a partnership—the lender wants to ensure that we have enough at risk in this purchase that we will want to guarantee success.

Musk was required to invest a sizeable sum in Twitter—a $27 billion vested interest. This is akin to us putting a 60 percent down payment on a home. It doesn't sound very favorable when it's placed in those terms. One of the ways we can reduce our vested interest is to find others who might want to join us in this investment. Their contribution gives additional merit to our endeavor.

For Musk, this looked like $5.2 billion from investment groups and individual investors. In exchange for their capital, the contributors became Twitter shareholders. These dollars are like votes that say, "We think this is a good deal. We are with you." The more others are willing to put in, the stronger the vote of confidence.

This is no different than our parents or grandparents helping with college tuition, buying a house, or starting a business. These dollars, or votes, say, "We think this is a good idea and are willing to partner with you." A scholarship or money for a first-time homebuyer is the same thing. When we receive these benefits, the underlying message in this vested interest is, "We believe in you. We value your success and want to help." How much money others are willing to invest can help guide our decisions and determine if this is our best course of action.

It is important to note that everything we refer to is an investment in our financial future—a business, college education, real estate, etc. It is not a sound financial plan to use debt to ensure we can afford a daily latte, designer clothes, or a new car each year. Using debt to make money means we are borrowing to purchase or invest in something that will offer us security, income, or wealth—it's a money-maker.

FINDING THE MONEY MAKER

"Whoever said 'money can't buy happiness' really knew what they were talking about."
—Elon Musk, Posted on X in February 2026

I wasn't too involved in the headlines about the Musk Twitter buyout, but I know he wanted out of the deal for a while. Even if we were very engaged in tracking the news of this takeover, we can never be sure we are getting the whole story. Sometimes, the players involved don't see or can't admit the truth. Was Twitter not transparent regarding the value of the company? Was Musk in it for vanity and posturing? Maybe it's a combination of both or something else entirely.

In hindsight, however, it is clear this was not a money-maker for Musk. According to The Guardian, X (the new name for Twitter) was valued at $12.5 billion as of January 2024. Eek—that is close to a quarter of the purchase price. That's painful!

Musk has also experienced much volatility at Tesla since he began his purchase of Twitter (now X) in April 2022. In the two years since this highly publicized takeover, Tesla's stock suffered extreme volatility and dropped to less than $120 per share for a while. Some of this volatility might be related to Tesla's business, but all the news around Musk, Twitter, and X suggests that buying X was not a money maker.

Now that Musk has used this platform and spent a lot of money to get Donald Trump elected, maybe it was worth the investment. With Musk involved in the U.S. federal government, deciding which companies get government contracts, including his business interests, and eliminating Federal employees and departments overseeing his many business ventures, the few billion dollars lost pale compared to all the wealth he may amass with this alliance.

In fact, Elon Musk's purchase of Twitter (now X) occurred in October 2022, when his net worth was estimated at about $200 billion. By May 2026, it is estimated at over $800 billion—a more than fourfold increase, far surpassing others on the billionaires list. Some might argue that this purchase, along with his alliance with Donald Trump, played a role. By reflex, I might say, "Good for them." But you already know what I really think about that.

Here is the final critical nugget of strategy that Musk's story teaches us—we have no idea how it will turn out when we start into something. We might believe it's the best plan. We know this will be a money-maker, and then life throws us a curveball. We start college, planning for a certain degree, and our spouse gets sick, so we need to abandon that plan and go back to work instead. At that moment, on top of everything this curveball sent us, we now have college debt and no degree to back it up.

Life happens, and sometimes, even with the best planning, we find ourselves in a place we didn't expect or anticipate. Look at me with my dramatic income change and home loss. It was scary and turbulent, and I wish I had never had to go through it, but it gave me a new and valuable perspective on how to operate in times of stress and fear. From the most challenging experiences, I've also found that GOD has brought me new gifts I never knew I wanted, provided I keep myself aligned with the Flow, and do not allow fear to stop me.

My move to Mexico might never have happened if I were still in that costly and altogether too big home. As I type these words, I watch the sunset over the Pacific Ocean. Pink clouds are on the horizon, white caps are pounding the shore, and the sound of those waves mixed with the Spanish spoken around me whispers, "This is a blessing you never knew you wanted."

JOURNEY TO MEXICO—MY BATTLE WITH FEAR

"You're only poor if you give up. The most important thing is that you did something." —Robert T. Kiyosaki

As mentioned in earlier chapters, getting outside helps my creative writing juices, so I invested in an e-bike. After deciding to write my book, I knew I also needed to leave the dreary northern climate during the snowy season. The clouds may keep the temps warmer in the winter, but the lack of sun chills my mood.

I had traveled to Mazatlán several times to build houses in the city's impoverished areas. Because I was familiar with it, my insurance education business also selected this location for our destination classes. Many of the attendees loved the area so much that they kept coming back. One even started spending her winters here, so I asked her to help me find a rental for January to April 2023. She located an adorable furnished place a few blocks from the beach.

I didn't have the money for this—I didn't have a plan. Of course, I have my savings, but this is paramount and bears repeating—the continued growth of these pennies is imperative to a secure life, so I don't want to touch them. I only get those FREE pennies if I leave them there. We'll continue to develop this idea in the next chapter.

I also knew it wasn't likely that the income from my business would increase dramatically. Thankfully, it had stayed reasonably constant, but agents frequently told me they were retiring, and not as many new agents were taking their seats. Most state insurance licensing boards are seeing their numbers decline, too. It's not a dying industry, but it is certainly not thriving. Usually, I would not go on a vacation unless I had the money to pay for it. In this case, however, I considered this an investment.

Like starting a business, publishing a book is about generating revenue and, hopefully, income. However, book publishing is even more risky than most business start-ups to meet this objective. I was willing to take that risk at this career stage, in part because of my savings balances.

That's the practical side. On a Higher Plain, I felt a calling to get these ideas into the Universe and share them. I believed, and still do, that these choices were part of the Flow, so I went to Mexico to write and I wrote a lot.

Even though I had significant projects for my business, I still found considerable time to write, and the words seemed to Flow. I also began to think about the following winter. Even if I finished the book before the snow started flying, I knew publication would take several edits, marketing, and much research.

I could borrow money from savings the following winter, but that didn't seem sensible. My home would sit there empty for months, paying someone to shovel and check on it while still paying a heating bill, plus the expenses here in Mexico seemed a waste. I understand that others do it and are happy with that choice. However, I am just too frugal for all those wasted pennies! Even more importantly, I do not have that much cushion in my tight budget. One winter in Mexico, I could handle. But to spend my winters in Mexico routinely is not a lifestyle that is in the cards for me right now.

While still toying with options, uncertain what GOD might have me do, I discovered that a building in the area was starting to offer leases. I went over to check it out, and in 24 hours, I decided to sign an 18-month lease.

This change would require me to sort through various options, so I put them on the list and used the method discussed in Chapter 2 to "Find the Flow." Like a miracle, it all fell into place. I found a contractor to build a room in my basement to store my things, found renters to care for my home, and headed to Mexico. Once here, though, I found that all my plans didn't work as I hoped, and the fear crept in.

COMBATING FEAR WITH FAITH

"Happiness is not in the mere possession of money; it lies in the joy of achievement, in the thrill of creative effort." —Franklin D. Roosevelt

While packing and crossing things off my to-do list, I counted all the pennies I thought I would save moving here. The cost of living in Mexico has historically been less than in the U.S.. My transportation costs are lower, and so are my utilities by large measures.

I also thought I could rent out my house at a reasonable profit. Rent is so high right now, and I bought my home years ago when values were lower. This move meant I would not be teaching in-person classes throughout the state. I figured people who attend my in-person courses, which are expensive to host, would gladly meet in a cyber classroom instead.

It didn't turn out that way. In fact, not at all. I haven't found that my expenses are that much less. It might have been the transition costs. I had to buy things for my condo, which I hadn't expected. For example, it's fully furnished with sheets. Yay, but no towels or other items I needed, like cleaning supplies, blankets, a few small appliances, additional pillows, and various household items. The peso gained value against the dollar, so I had to pay more for my rent and other expenses in Mexico. I lowered the rental rate on my Minnesota home and took on many expenses to get the right tenant, someone I trusted to care for my property. After I rented out my Minnesota home on narrow profit margins, the water bill went up 70 percent, and sanitation costs increased by 50 percent.

The easy transition from in-person to virtual was, well, not as easy as I hoped. The winter months were okay, but it's spring now. Traditionally, I would start my in-person classes, and agents would register for those courses. Instead, things have dried up like the Sahara.

Although no one has said anything, I have the distinct impression that they were hoping I would come back and schedule in-person classes again. If I don't, they can always register for the webinars later. In the interim, it means low—very low—income for me. To top it off, the tenants I thought would care for my home damaged the landscaping, which forced me to pay for an attorney. I might have been able to navigate it without his assistance, but never having rented a property before, I preferred to get sound legal advice.

I am full of fear—scared every day. When I open my email, I don't see any orders when there are usually two or three, and a pit in my stomach grows. Then the hamster wheel gets rolling: "You were going to be able to save more money. What will my retirement look like now?"

Or this is a fun track, "How can I ever move back to the States on this income? I can't even afford to live in Mexico right now."

Here's another "oldie, but goodie" for the self-pity hamster express: "Everyone else has it better than me. They have (fill in the blank—a spouse to help them, stable income, rich parents, etc.)." You name it. The message, "My life sucks, and they have it great."

A new hamster wanted some time on the wheel. I think I like this one least of all: "Who are you to write a book? You're too old for this. No one will want to listen to you." When I was younger, everything seemed to turn to gold. Not so much now, or so it seems. I still connect wonderfully with my customers, but I've had a horrible time finding new customers, and it's zapped my self-esteem. Ageism is real. (Ageism is prejudice or discrimination based on a person's age.)

The words are slightly different, but these hamsters all say the same thing: "I could invest in this book and this method, and it would go nowhere. This could be another loss on your balance sheet of life."

As I wrote those words, I thought, "So what? I accomplished what I set out to do. I honored the story in my heart. I did it." If it goes nowhere, so what?

If this is a dud, something new will turn up, and chances are, it will be something good. I have been provided for all my years on this earth, and it has been okay. Earlier in these pages, I also said I didn't care about making millions of dollars—my primary goal is to help people. If I get a few sales that allow some people to get on track financially, that is what the Flow wanted for me.

That is me right now, this minute. That is not always me. Most of the time, I am a jumble of nerves, and I think the hamsters in my head mated and multiplied. Then I go back to the basics of where this all began, with the lists, the Energy, and the Flow. I prayerfully consider my options. What can I do? What should I do to steer my ship in the direction the Universe wants from me?

In those moments, I consider other options—get a job, reinventing my business, move home, etc.—things I might do, but in the end, the Flow brings me to this book. I sense this is the next step in my story, and although I have no idea where this might get me or what will come of it, GOD keeps putting enough road markers out there that let me know I am on the right path.

IT'S JUST THE DEAL

"You gain strength, courage, and confidence by every experience in which you really stop to look fear in the face." —Eleanor Roosevelt

Unless you have some miracle cure for fear or find a way to evict the hamsters in your head, you will likely encounter fear as you pursue your plan. But if you, like me, believe the path is right for you, and you've done your due diligence, we must persevere. If we don't, we will not know what destiny has in store for us. If we turn back or quit, I do not believe we are then living in the authenticity GOD intended.

Years ago, when I was about to start my business, I had a phone call with a friend. I was sitting on my front steps with the handset to my ear, and she asked, "Aren't you afraid it won't work out?" My response: "Of course—every day, but I must try. If I don't, I will always wonder what could have been. The regret will likely haunt me."

On the flip side, twice in my life, I did not pursue what I wanted. One was to move to the East Coast and enter the Wall Street world of finance; the other was to move across the country for a corporate promotion. I regret not seeing where either path might have led me.

I don't think we escape life without regret or thinking, "What if…?" We are not offered a do-over card, and there is no time machine to see how things turn out if we select the other option. Yet I know those two opportunities offered me something I cannot recover or recreate today. Those options have expired.

Today, I have a choice like the one I made then. Continue seeing where this book brings me, or cash it all in and try something else. The problem is that "something else" has no name and will likely cause the same fears. So, I persevere and look fear in the face. Here are a few things I have found that help me manage it:

1. **Have a Plan**—I figured I might have to borrow money before making this move. To ensure I had the best rate and lowest expenses, I got a Home Equity Line of Credit (HELOC). If things do not turn around with my business so that I can pay off what I have borrowed, I am considering moving some of the debt to zero-percent options. Here, of course, I will look at the entire cost of the debt with the strategies discussed in earlier chapters.
2. **Assess the Plan**—Like Musk's purchase of Twitter, I continue to do additional due diligence, contact others for advice, and seek new information or supplementary projects. I ask GOD what They would have me do, and I try to remain open to the Flow redirecting my journey. I always thought I would use social media to market my book, but I was going to finish the book first. Instead, I started a YouTube channel. It's taken time away from the finishing touches on the book, but I hope to have it monetized soon with a following of potential readers.
3. **Stick to the Plan**—Given that I applied fundamental financial principles to my plan, like the ones discussed in this book, I am committed to the course. Right now, I am continuing to put 20 percent into savings. I am borrowing money to cover expenses while continuing to fund my retirement and other savings. You might think that's nuts, but I think it fits right in with this strategy. The money in savings is there to pay off this debt if I need to go that route, but I'm hoping I don't because I want all those pretty pennies to make more pennies.
4. **Expect the Fear**—It's natural—and if I fight it, deny it, or shame myself because I have it, that only creates more stress. While it's hard to embrace it, I can honor it. Because fear is uncomfortable, it's a motivator. Each time I feel the fear rising, it allows me to reassess—to determine if I should add something new to the plan to help or if there are areas where I can reduce expenses. It also keeps me in front of this keyboard, pecking away. Fear is a communicator. Fear becomes a helpful tool if I expect it and use it to help me Flow through my plan.

When I sat on those steps back in 1999, chatting with my friend about my fears about starting a new business, I had no idea that business would sustain me and my family financially for decades. I would start a network of agents who felt like family and became lifelong friends. I would be honored to share ideas that benefited their finances and those of their clients, and I would have the opportunity to learn from them and expand my horizons.

For more than 25 years, I've been blessed to create a community focused on helping each other and building strong alliances. This book and social media are designed to bring all those same benefits from that classroom to your home. I aim to develop a new community with all the same beautiful ideals. When my mind wanders there, the fear disappears. Then I know I am in the Flow.

RULE 6:
USE CREDIT CARDS FOR EVERYTHING THE REWARDS SAVE OUR PENNIES

"I use a credit card for everything—and I choose one of the ones which gives me money back." —Frank Abagnale

While not as grand or impactful as buying a home, starting a business, or gaining an education, there is another way we can use debt to make a few bucks: "Credit Card Reward Programs."

It only makes sense to take advantage of all the free things credit card companies offer, provided we are responsible credit users. Whatever our passion is—cash back, frequent flyer miles, auto manufacturer bucks, retailer credits, and more—if we are making the purchase anyway and have the cash to pay it off, why not run it through a credit card first to buy ourselves some time and get something free in the process?

The rewards vary—some give 1 to 5 percent on different purchases. The card may or may not have an annual fee. We could be offered an attractive bonus up front. My jam is frequent-flyer miles. Because of this strategy, I receive about two free tickets for every ticket I buy. My credit card spending might be more than that of the typical person because of my business expenses.

One of the major U.S. airlines offered me 80,000 flyer miles (generally about two tickets or more) if I got their card and charged at least $3,000 in the first three months. As a bonus, if I charged half of that, $1,500, in the first month, they would apply a $200 credit to my account balance. This was all a no-brainer for me. Since the renewal for my company's server was that same month, I used this credit card for the entire invoice. I received all these perks for an expense I would have had anyway.

This worked so well that I jumped at it when I got another offer from another airline. This one was only 60,000 miles but had similar terms. After navigating their system and using the perks, I found that this airline was not as generous with redemptions as the first airline.

I cannot use miles to cover the entire fare. This flyer program requires about the exact miles as a zero-cost flight, 20,000 to 40,000, while asking me to still cover $100 to $250 of the ticket price. I have heard the same about hotel credit cards and other rewards programs. Some are more generous than others. My complaints disappear when I consider that I am getting these perks from my routine spending.

The value of the benefits varies based on ticket prices, demand, departure, destination airport, etc. The averages I mentioned are based on my experience over the years. There are always exceptions—during COVID, I used 8,000 miles to fly from Minneapolis to Raleigh. Four years later, when the crisis diminished, it was about three times that, or 24,000.

TOTAL COST —TOTAL RETURN

"For the best return on your money, pour your purse into your head."
—Benjamin Franklin

I've told you this before, and it's probably not the last time I'll mention it because it is so crucial, but we always must look at the total cost of any financial tool before deciding if it works for our goal. The most favorable of the two airline credit cards, the first one, charged an annual fee after 12 months. Unbeknownst to me, the card gave me the first year without this expense.

I don't typically keep credit cards with an annual fee. There are too many options without such fees that it hardly seems necessary to pay fees. The credit card company charges a percentage of each sale to the merchant, which is how they can afford to offer the perks, and as a result, they don't need the annual fee.

I wanted to keep the card, so I asked them to remove it. I have had much success getting fees removed. Annual fees, certainly, but even if my payment is late, the company will often waive any penalty or interest provided I have a good payment history, and these requests are not excessive. If my full payment is received one day late, which rarely happens, it becomes clear that this was a slight error, and the company will graciously waive the fee. It is always worth investing a little time if we can save some pennies.

In this instance, the credit card company was unwavering—they would not remove the fee. I didn't want to pay a fee to keep the card, so I asked if I could keep all the frequent flyer miles in my account if I canceled it. When they said, "Yes," I told them to cancel the card.

Two months later, when I flew on this airline and had to pay $50 to check my bag, I regretted this choice. That credit card gave me a free checked bag for each flight. Granted, I didn't know if I would be on this airline more than once a year, which would have fully covered that annual fee, but still, it was a nice perk.

When I booked another flight with this airline about six months later, an offer popped up on the screen: "Would I like to save $100 on today's flight by applying for a new credit card?" Of course, I clicked YES! Yes, I want to save $100, but I also want that free checked bag each time I fly.

Sadly, I was declined for the new card. I didn't get a reason, but I am confident it was the fact that I took all the perks the first go around. Then, I decided all those benefits were insufficient to overcome the fee. This company was unwilling to give me another shot to take more than I was willing to give.

IN IT TO WIN IT

"A budget tells us what we can't afford, but it doesn't keep us from buying it."
—William Feather

Working to get these extra benefits makes little sense if we don't pay off the balance every month. Even if we get a 5 percent bonus, it means nothing if I pay 18 percent or more interest. In that example, we have only reduced the initial interest to 13 percent. That is too big a price to pay.

It also makes no sense if we buy more than we can afford to get the perk. Had I not had the upcoming business expense for the airline card and instead purchased $3,000 worth of items I did not need, I would have been far better off buying two airline tickets to just about anywhere. The 80,000 frequent-flyer miles are not worth $3,000 UNLESS we would have bought those items anyway.

The typical adult receives frequent offers from companies offering credit perks. We certainly cannot take advantage of all of them. Sometimes, however, the opportunity could benefit us, so it makes sense to be prepared.

Even though some people in our classes occasionally disagree, I believe I came out as a winner in this personal story about taking advantage of the perks offered for credit use. Now that you are armed with the facts about the effects on your credit score from the last chapter, you can be the judge.

More than a few years ago, I was out for a leisurely day of lunch and shopping with a friend. I set about $200 worth of clothing items by the register. As the clerk began to process my purchase, she turned to me and said, "How would you like to save 10 percent today?"

What I heard her say was, "How would you like me to give you $20 to cover your lunch?" That's how quickly I did the math in my head. Since we had a little time, my immediate response to this simple question was, "Yes!"

So, she began to set me up with my new retail store credit card. As she was doing so, she said, "Did you know you can stop by our store anytime and make a payment?" My response, "I can?" She replied, "You can."

There was a little silence for a bit of pondering, and then I said, "Can I make that payment today?" Her response was: "You sure can!" Then another thought occurred: "Can I pay via credit card?" She responded, "I don't see why not!"

So, I laid down my travel Visa and got my $20 and 180 frequent flyer miles! Upon leaving the store, my friend turned to me and said, "I cannot believe you just did all of that!" I couldn't help but respond, "Well, why not? If we split a salad, I might have enough for an appetizer, too!"

Since then, having shared this story with countless other agents, they've told me plenty of reasons I should not have done that. Do you see any red flags when you hear my little saga of credit use? How is this behavior potentially harmful to my credit score?

They checked my credit, and as we talked about earlier, too much of that can hurt one's credit score, but I didn't do that in every store we went to that day. I've taken advantage of those opportunities whenever I wish and have had no adverse effects.

Some mention debt limit-to-income ratios, high levels of overall credit availability, a new account potentially subject to identity theft, and many other potential problems. As we reviewed in the last chapter, while those things can happen, none significantly affected my credit score, and shouldn't for you as well. It was a win, and the salad was tasty.

SAFETY ON PURCHASES

"I don't use a debit card. The safest thing is a credit card because I'm using the bank's money. If someone accesses our information, they are stealing the bank's money, not mine." —Frank Abagnale

U.S. Federal Law requires that consumers are not to be held liable for more than $50 of charges that result from lost or stolen card information. This means credit card holders are not responsible for unauthorized purchases because most companies cover the entire amount.

Your bank and debit card may offer the same protection, but it is optional. If the bank provides this protection, it can take weeks to resolve it, meaning we are without our cash during that time. If we use a credit card, they will credit our account for the fraudulent charges and issue a new card to stop the theft.

Another protection with credit cards is the ability to dispute charges. For those unfamiliar with this service, if we make a purchase and the vendor does not honor their commitment, the credit card company will credit the purchase price to our account while they 'dispute' it. This means they will follow up on our complaint and determine whether the seller is acting in good faith. Possible reasons to file a dispute are that we didn't receive the item, the product broke in the warranty period, they gave us the wrong product, we were promised a refund we did not receive, or a host of other problems a buyer could encounter. We can file a dispute if the seller is not handling these issues.

In my experience, credit card companies are not as favorable to cardholders regarding disputes as they once were. I loved this service and possibly overutilized it, but sometimes, what I received was unacceptable. The vendor would not make good on it. It was unfair that I had to pay for it; the credit card company would help me resolve it. Let me give you a recent example.

Canadian COVID-19—I went to Canada for my son's birthday in 2022. At this stage of the COVID-19 outbreak, the vaccine was readily available, and anyone who wanted to be vaccinated could do so multiple times. Treatments were also available to reduce the harmful effects of the virus.

However, I needed a negative COVID test to get on an airplane bound for the U.S. from another country. Anyone sick could fly any domestic flight without verifying they were COVID-free. Without the negative test results, one could drive into the U.S. from either border. I figure both these activities spread the virus around. Yet the rule about a negative COVID test was still in place for international flights into the United States.

Before I left to see my son, he told me he wasn't feeling well—no significant symptoms. Right now, I cannot recall if he even mentioned the possibility of

COVID-19, and honestly, it makes no difference. I couldn't see my kid for two Christmases because of this virus, and I had a trip booked to see him for his special day. I was going.

Sure enough, it was COVID. I caught it, I am sure, the moment I got in his car at the airport and he said, "Hello." Which set off a ten-second coughing spasm in the enclosed space. My symptoms weren't bad either, but that didn't matter when I failed my COVID test 24 hours before my flight. When I called the airline, they were great. "Sure, we understand. Just give us a call when you are ready to fly." In this discussion, I confirmed, "I will get a replacement ticket free of charge, correct?" The response was, "Yes."

The day before my doctor's exam to clear me to fly, I called the airline again to check flight availability in two days. There were openings. I asked if I should book now. The woman on the phone said to wait so we could ensure I was cleared to fly. There was plenty of room.

I immediately called the following day when I received my flight pass. I explained my situation to the gentleman and gave him my original trip confirmation number, and he said, "That doesn't matter. You will need to buy a new ticket."

I, of course, asked if he could see the earlier notes from the earlier calls. I explained that the call records should say I was eligible for a free replacement ticket. He denied there was any such thing in my account. I asked for a manager. He said he was one. I asked for the person above him. He said there was no one.

It's crazy—I know, but it's every bit true. I will add that I was upset, but not at first. My initial request was very calm. As much as I love my son, I was ready to go home. We made the best of his COVID-19 birthday celebration, but we were both ready for our space.

The anger hit me the first time the man on the phone said, "You'll have to buy a new ticket." The rest of his obstinacy could have been a reaction to me, but when he claimed he was the CEO taking customer service calls, I broke down in tears and hung up. After a few more sobs and a pep talk from my son, I called again. You aren't going to believe this, but the same horrible person answered. I thought I was in the Twilight Zone, or someone was about to say, "You're on candid camera!"

Or maybe John Quiñones was preparing to get on the line and say, "Thanks for being a part of the hit show; *'What Would You Do?'* Of course, you'll get your free replacement ticket, but can I talk to you about how corporate customer service, or the lack thereof, drives people crazy?"

None of that happened, so I hung up without a word. I never wanted to speak to him again. I've had enough narcissistic abuse to last a lifetime. I will not try to get something fair and reasonable from someone irrational. Had I been thinking, I should have had my son try, but instead, I decided to call in the morning to guarantee I would get someone new. I prayed it was the woman we spoke to earlier—so calm and confident that they would get me home without burden or cost.

I called at 6 a.m. the next day and was disappointed to hear a man on the other end of the line. It was not the same woman, but also not the man from the night before. I started again. Here's the issue, the number, and this man, too, says, "You'll have to pay for a ticket." Being better rested, I calmly said, "That is not what I was told earlier." Around we go.

Long story short, I put a new ticket for a flight that afternoon on my credit card. After another hour on the phone, there was no way around it. I called back twice, kept asking for a manager, and continued to tell them I was told more than once I would get a free replacement. Nothing worked, and I had to return home.

I also vowed I would dispute it. When it appeared on my card, I submitted a dispute and provided proof—the dates of calls, the COVID test, the travel release, the U.S. travel rules, and a letter outlining everything. I was concerned it might be too much, but I wanted them to know I had been forced to pay for a ticket and should not have been.

As is customary, temporary credit for the purchase price was applied to my balance. The credit card company contacted the merchant, who provided a copy of the policy stating that customers must pay for a new fare on cancellations. The credit card company denied my dispute. Again, Twilight Zone—they must have missed ALL the proof that I had COVID, which was an exception to that policy.

I filed it again, and it was denied again. Then I called. I was not going to let this go. I spoke with the review person and explained. Her response was, "You had COVID, were told they would get you home at no cost, and then did not? That's not good." Finally, someone was willing to hear me. We had a pleasant conversation about her experiences during COVID-19 and those of her family. She believed this was a time to help people, not take advantage of them. After this call, I got to keep my money. I also learned that when there are extra details, sometimes it's worth that phone call.

That brings us to the next section of our discussion—SAVINGS! How can we get more money to put away, where can we invest it, and how can we protect it? These are essential considerations if we intend to hit our financial goals and keep fear at bay. Here are six strategies to maximize debt use and improve your financial future.

- **RULE 1: MINIMUM PAYMENTS ONLY**
  - This gives us extra cash to save.
- **RULE 2: NEVER KEEP A BALANCE ON HIGH-INTEREST CREDIT CARDS**
  - Get a lower-interest line of credit instead.
- **RULE 3: OVERCOME OBSTACLES**
  - It pays to reassess and learn other money-saving techniques.
- **RULE 4: KEEP AN EXCELLENT CREDIT SCORE**
  - Pay our bills on time every month—it's that easy.
- **RULE 5: FINANCE WHAT WILL GROW**
  - WISELY use debt to further our financial goals.
- **RULE 6: USE CREDIT CARDS FOR EVERYTHING**
  - We get perks for this, but it only works IF we pay it off each month.

CHAPTER EIGHT

ALL THOSE PRETTY PENNIES

SEVEN SUCCESSFUL STRATEGIES FOR SAVINGS

"If you don't know where you are going, you'll end up someplace else."
—Yogi Berra

JUST GIVE ME THE PLAN, STAN

Now that we've reviewed the benefits of increasing our savings and found ways to maximize the value while decreasing the cost of our debt, it is time to dig into some savings goals. A standard suggestion in many financial circles is putting 10 percent of your annual income into savings. This standard works best for long-term savings goals if we've been doing this since our first career job, generally in our early 20s.

Conversely, starting later in this game will require us to contribute more money to catch up. Remember John Green, a tottering old man in his 30s. His savings account was $30,000 behind the teenager, who had put some cash in an IRA from their summer job. A 20-year-old can save less money each year than a 30-year-old to reach the same retirement goal due to compounding. A 30-year-old has a savings advantage over a person in their 40s. You can immediately see what a person in their 50s might need to do to catch up.

For example, a 25-year-old who contributes $3,000 per year to an IRA for ten years ($30,000 of contributions at 7 percent annually) and allows the account to compound until retirement age at 65 will have $338,000 in their retirement account.

Before moving on, I think it's essential to make this point: The 25-year-old above has $308,000 of FREE money. They didn't work for it, and nothing was sold to acquire it. This person allowed their $30,000 to sit there for forty years, and POOF! By the time they retire, their deposit has increased by more than ten times. It's so powerful, Albert Einstein said, "Compound interest is the eighth wonder of the world. Those who understand it earn it; those who don't, pay it."

Some of the exacting folks reading this may object to my use of the phrase, FREE MONEY. Typical reasons: "It's not FREE. They'll have to pay tax." Or maybe, "They had an opportunity cost." Opportunity cost means that while it was in the account, saved away, the person lost the "opportunity" to do something else with it, which has a "cost" associated with it. One could even stretch this objection to, "They probably had costs in the account, so it's not all FREE."

If someone who sees $300,000 wants to find something wrong with calling it FREE, okay. People pay taxes when they work hard for it, too. The taxes have nothing to do with how we acquired the money. My statement of FREE means it arrives over time through the power of compounding—PERIOD. We get more of it when we reduce fees. We'll talk about that later, and if ever we believe the opportunity cost is too much, we can withdraw it. Chances are, however, that $308,000 will be a better opportunity for our future selves.

What if our young person skips out on saving those first ten years and instead focuses on the car, the house, the kids, and paying off their debts? They begin saving $3,000 annually at the same 7 percent annual return at age 35. This time, they don't stop after ten years. They continue to contribute until age 65, $90,000 in contributions—three times as much as our 25-year-old, but their account is only valued at $303,000 at age 65—$213,000 of FREE money.

The earlier one starts saving, the better off they are financially.

Our analysis isn't done yet. The 35-year-old has $213,000 of FREE money. This isn't bad—it's terrific. It's still FREE money—additional gains only help our fearless future. Yet consider who you would rather be. The 25-year-old or the 35-year-old? It's silly even to ask.

Another thing to consider: What if our 25-year-old continued making contributions beyond the first ten years? It makes this comparison even more dramatic, but it is more realistic. What young saver stops after they see they are creating free money? If the 25-year-old kept going, saving $3,000 a year until age 65 like our 35-year-old, they would have their original $338,000 plus the $303,000 or $641,000.

To reach that same $640,000, a person starting to save at age 35 must contribute more than $6,000 per year for thirty years or $180,000 in contributions—our 25-year-old would have contributed $120,000 instead.

While starting earlier will have the most impact, whatever our age, it pays to save. There's FREE money to be made.

MAKING GOD LAUGH

"We plan, GOD laughs."—Yiddish Proverb

To help you plan, I want to give you some pat answers, like, "If you are in your 30s, contribute 15 percent instead. At 40, 20 percent...," and so on. But here is the problem with any of that: Regardless of what your age is today, you do not know what your future or your retirement might bring, and neither does anyone else. You can look up a retirement calculator online. It'll offer some insight. You can work with a financial advisor who can also share some ideas on contribution needs to meet your goals, but until you get there, you do not know what you will need or whether your goal was accurate.

I'll offer myself as an example again. I have been contributing to a retirement account since I was 21. I didn't plan it that way. I had a career job that I had been at for more than 12 months, so when profit-sharing came around, they put some money in for me. I thought that was incredible—FREE MONEY! Again, our skeptics may think, "Renée, that's not FREE. It's part of your compensation." Yes, and no. The company was not required to share the profits, and I didn't expect it. In fact, I had no idea at the young age of 21 that such bonuses existed. That puts this in the FREE column for me.

Then, I learned that if I made a 401(k) contribution, the company would match it. I thought that was even better. I saved money for my future, and my company gave me more FREE money. This was a no-brainer for a financially savvy 21-year-old. I started with the 6 percent match maximum and quickly went to the 10 percent recommended by advisors.

Other than a few years when I started my business, I continued to contribute each year. When we divorced, I had to give some to my ex. I also took some out for the down payment on my house in 2019. It's probably not hard to guess which was more painful. Even after "The Lost Decade," the recent series of bull market years has me poised for retirement. That does not mean I am counting chickens from my unhatched eggs. Anything can happen between now and then.

This book and my YouTube channel may take off, and my financial future will be greater than anticipated. Or, if that doesn't happen, and I'm saddled with the debt that has been rising lately, I might wonder if I should take out money to pay it off, get a job, reinvent a career, or find myself a husband quickly. (Is hunting for a husband considered a part-time job?) Other possibilities: I can't work because my health doesn't hold up. Or my kids or someone else I love needs help, and I put all this on hold to assist.

Even though I am down to the home stretch (about eight years, give or take), I have no idea where this will end up. Neither do you. Unless we are those lucky few with more than we need and nothing negative ever happens to us, most of us are always unsure where we'll end up due to financial transitions along the way. When we leap into retirement, even with the best of plans in place, nothing is guaranteed there either.

This is why we save as much as we can every day. Only through every penny making us more pennies will we have any sense of security. The more pennies, the greater the protection. The other thing that offers us security is perspective. Let's discuss pennies first and cover perspective later.

I KNEW YOU'D SAY THAT

"Think left and think right and think low and think high.
Oh, the thinks you can think up if only you try!"
—Dr. Seuss, "Oh, the Thinks You Can Think"

A few years ago, my daughter called me asking, "Mom, I was invited to participate in the 401(k) at work. Should I do it?" My daughter was only 21—like I was when I got the invitation, too. Unlike me, she was still in college, working part-time as a nursing assistant at the local hospital. It was a fantastic job for a student because she was responsible for staffing, and if all positions were filled, it allowed time to study.

It took me no time to respond to her 401(k) question, "Yes. You should participate." Of course, right? Her reply was, "I knew you'd say that." My kids grew up around my business and have been to my classes. They've learned these lessons firsthand. I almost jokingly replied, "Then why are you calling me?" She jumped in again before I could say anything, "I was calling to see how much I should contribute."

Ah, there we go, part of this puzzle I had not yet talked to my kids about, and this illustrates why there are no pat answers to these questions. Financial plans are not one-size-fits-all. So, I asked, "How much will they match?" She replied, "Six percent." Then I asked, "Can you afford that?"

She replied, "Mom, I work part-time for little money—six percent is not a lot." Of course, this still didn't answer my question. I couldn't offer my kids a free ride to college. I gave them a modest savings account for college, but it didn't cover the whole bill. When they left for college, I was single and challenged by my lower income.

My kids had to be responsible for themselves, and to a great degree, this offered valuable life lessons like this one. Since her response didn't give me the clarity I needed to provide a good answer, I again asked, "Even if the six percent isn't a lot, can you afford to give it up?" This time, she said, "Six percent is a couple of lattes. Yeah, I'll be okay."

To that, I said, "Then definitely do the six percent. If you can swing more, do that." I didn't explain the value of starting at 21—I hoped all the earlier discussions had sunk in. We chatted a bit about other miscellaneous things, and then we said our goodbyes. Maybe 10 minutes later, my phone rang with her name in the caller ID.

Although I was surprised to see her name again, I started with the standard, "Hello." Then my daughter said, "Mom, what's a beneficiary?" This simple question reminded me of how many levels of understanding come with these financial things—so many, indeed, that I might write a separate book on various nuances.

Since a beneficiary is a person or entity who will directly inherit the proceeds, my response to her was simple, "Just put my name on that line." I was kidding, of course. I explained a little more about her options and left her to choose. Who she decided to name and why she made that selection is not my concern as the parent of an adult child. Some might dispute that position, but it is indeed my belief. Although I still do not know, I believe she chose her boyfriend, whom she later married. He's a good choice in my book on both counts.

Here is the best part of this story—or really, the part of this story that speaks to the "get started early" point. When my daughter graduated from college about a year later and prepared to roll her 401(k) over to an individual IRA*, this nearly 22-year-old had $3,500 in the account by routinely skipping a few lattes and taking advantage of the employer match. (*A rollover or a transfer allows taxpayers to move their qualified retirement savings to another qualified account without paying taxes. The rules are in IRS Publication 590.)

If my daughter leaves it there and doesn't touch it, this $3,500 account can accumulate over $70,000 by retirement age. This assumes retirement at 65 and annual earnings of 7 percent on average. It's not a bad start for retirement savings for a college student.

1

The earlier we start saving, the more secure we are financially. Don't wait—save as much as you can today.

LET'S TALK ABOUT IT

"The only thing to do with good advice is to pass it on. It is never of any use to oneself." —Oscar Wilde

My other kid has a different story. My son, the older of the two, took a longer route to graduate. He's very good at managing money, and he's also all about enjoying life. In addition to his work/life balance, COVID-19 threw a significant wrench into his plans to wrap up his graduate degree. This nearly 24-month delay may not have been part of the original plan, but like any unplanned hardship, it must be calculated in the strategy.

In his late twenties, my son called with similar questions about his first retirement plan contributions. His employer offered the identical 6 percent match, but I didn't start there with him. I began with the 10 percent rule, as I did to kick off this chapter, and then I said, "But you are beyond the optimal early 20s target. It would be best if you could do 15 percent. Can you swing it?"

My son's response was a little like my daughter's perspective and resonates with anyone who scraped their way on a tiny budget through college, "Mom, I've been living on about 20 percent of what I now make. I could probably contribute 50 percent or more and be just fine, but…"

What do you think followed that "but"? Maybe something like, "I want ________." We could fill that blank with options such as a house, car, truck, snowmobile, motorcycle, vacation, furniture, and more. Right? When we find ourselves with a brighter financial future, there is always something we've been waiting to buy.

My son said, "Truck—I want to buy a new truck." That's no problem—we work hard to achieve, and we should enjoy some of it now because we never know what tomorrow might bring.

I asked, "How much is the truck you want?" My son gave me prices and payments that reminded me of the houses I considered buying in 1989. Times have changed, but some things remain the same—there are usually other options. I then asked, "Do you need that much truck?" He was considering a new large diesel, not that my son couldn't use it, but did he really "need" it?

We discussed his options a little longer, but he wasn't buying a truck tomorrow, so he committed to starting the 15 percent contribution with the understanding that he could always change it. Ultimately, my son didn't get a new truck for over a year. While not a miser, he is frugal. Since this company gave him a work vehicle, he ran around in his old beater until it died. By then, he had decided he didn't need that big new truck or the big payment that came with it. The used, more conservative model cost less than half the truck he first shared with me, which afforded him a little cushion for savings and other toys.

2

If we want our future to be as good as our present, we might need to reconsider what we "need" today and downsize our purchases.

MY MEXICAN DOWNSIZE

"You don't realize how much stuff you have until you try to put it in a box."
—Allison Vesterfelt

My recent move to Mexico was not my first downsize or relocation to cut expenses. The first was when my daughter and I moved from our family home to a nearby townhouse. That one was a slow move—it happened over a year or more. If you recall, we lost this home to foreclosure after many attempts to work with the bank on a favorable resolution. When that didn't work, I began selling and donating things.

Pictures of all the sale items still come up on my social media from that time. Too many of those items were never even used. So much money for so many unimportant things. Each item required a decision: Keep, donate, sell, or trash. Each week for at least six months, I had several items for each pile, but the smallest was always the "keep" pile.

After that experience, while living in the townhouse, before I would buy anything, I would think, "Do you want to move this?" Would this go into the "keep" pile, or would it just become part of one of those other piles the next time I moved? With my budget on a new, all-time tight level, I couldn't afford excess purchases. This was my way of asking myself, "Do you *need* this?"

That concept held until my move to the city. My finances were cushier, and I had this new, fun space to make homey. I have an eye for design and a temperament for comfort. Combined with a few bucks in my wallet, these attributes are dangerous when considering cute, crafty, or functional items. Thankfully, my passion for ecology and the environment was also growing. My desire to limit waste and reuse kept me from buying many new things.

Fast forward to the purchase of my existing home in 2019. Here, I needed lots of new things. I sold all the yard and lawn maintenance items when I transitioned to rental living. Investments had to be made in those things again. The big furniture I'd been carting around through all these moves would not fit in this new space, and a new sectional was ordered. There were lots of things, too numerous to list here. Thousands spent—much I still own, tucked safely in the little room in my basement.

One afternoon, as I packed boxes to the ceiling of that storage space, I thought, "If I can pack all of this up for more than a year, never touching it, how much do I need any of it?" And chances are, when I unpack this, wherever and whenever that may be, I likely won't remember half of it. If that's the case, how important is any of it?

I want to be a minimalist. I do, but the truth is, if I could pare down that far, I would. Regardless of the length of my travel, I can't stick to a carry-on. My purse is as big as a decent-sized backpack, and I'm afraid to downsize it. If I leave it behind, I might need something, so the big purse goes everywhere.

However, I feel better when I buy less. It's better for my finances, but it's also better for the world. One less package or item traveling around, and all these "things" are work. The more I have, the more I must clean, move, store, transport, fix, maintain, and possibly replace.

3

Always look for ways to reduce spending. If we don't spend it, we save it. If we save it, we gain FUTURE FREE PENNIES.

THE QUICK CALCULATION

"Money speaks only one language. If you save me today, I will save you tomorrow." —Genereux Philip

Everything is a trade-off, and every time we spend our money, we choose that item we bought over FREE future pennies. We don't always think of it that way, but it helps our financial future to put it into that perspective. Reviewing the items in any shopping cart, we can do a quick FUTURE FREE PENNY count before checking out to decide if it's worth the trade-off.

Suppose I'm 55 and thinking of buying a $20 item but decide to put it into savings at 7.2 percent instead. By age 65, it would double to $40 instead. A 45-year-old has the benefit of time to double twice before age 65, so their $20 would be $80. A 35-year-old, $160, and a 25-year-old could have that $20 double four times, so their $20 grows to $320. If a 15-year-old puts that same $20 away, leaving it stashed away for 50 years, it becomes $640.

$20 SAVED AT 7.2 percent UNTIL AGE 65

AGE 55 = $40

AGE 45=$80

AGE 35=$160

AGE 25=$320

AGE 15=$640

These simple calculations are brought to you by THE RULE OF 72—any value doubles in 10 years at 7.2 percent. We may have more or less on average. Jack Bogle explains, "You know the rule of 72, divide the number into 72, any number you want, and that's how long it will take your money to double." If we get a 2 percent rate, 72 divided by .02 is 36 years to double. If it's 10 percent, 72 divided by .1 is 7.2 years to double. I find 7.2 percent the easiest to work with because it comes out to be the nice round number of 10 years to double. If my return is higher, which is likely with historic long-term stock returns, I benefit from extra pennies from my conservative projection.

Since we are working with doubles, any round number works for this simple calculation. I used $20 as a starting point because of its simplicity, but you can begin with any trade-off value and apply this method. Let's say you are considering new furniture for $5,000 at age 35. That purchase today means $30,000 less at age 65. When you ponder those future pennies, you may postpone that purchase a little longer or skip it altogether.

Maybe you are thinking of a new car for $50,000 or a used one for $25,000. If you go with the used one and tuck away the other $25,000 at age 55, that's $50,000 at age 65. If our car buyer is age 45, that's $100,000; at age 35, $200,000; and at age 25, $400,000. Those are some pretty pennies!

This applies to any possible purchase—eating out, a fancy coffee or bubble tea, a premium oil change versus doing it ourselves, fuel cost versus taking my pedal bike, etc. Always remember that each is a trade-off because if we don't spend it, we save it, and if we save it, we gain FUTURE FREE PENNIES.

You might also be wondering (because I certainly did when I put together these calculations) why, in my mid-fifties, I am still committed to saving so much when my time horizon says it might only double by age 65. There are two BIG reasons:

FIRST: I have no idea what the future will bring, and as I have said too many times to count, it's safer to have money set aside. PERIOD. Even if it never doubles, it is there if I need it.

SECOND and equally important: Who says I will take it out at age 65? I am blessed with a business that creates income for minimal work hours. I may not use it until I am 75 or 85. Or if this book takes off, and my writing supports me in my retirement years, I never have to use it. That way, my heirs will inherit it when I die. If I reach my goal of becoming a happy and healthy centurion, this could allow 50 years of accumulation.

Any of these alternatives means I now get the multiple doubles that the young folks receive in our simple calculations. These two straightforward reasons, equally based on the uncertainty of the future, mean I will continue to work hard to put pennies into savings and explore other ways to pay for expenses to try to leave them there.

4

Before a purchase, quickly calculate to determine if it's worth losing FUTURE FREE PENNIES. Using the Rule of 72 and assuming a 7.2 percent rate, our value doubles every ten years.

KEEPING IT IN PERSPECTIVE

"The optimist sees the donut; the pessimist sees the hole." —Oscar Wilde

Let's take a moment and consider wealth accumulation and preservation from both ends of the spectrum. What if the 15-year-old does what I mentioned and doesn't touch their savings until they hit the age of 105? This is ninety years of accumulation. Their tiny $20 would provide a gain of over $10,000. That's not bad, but what if we stretch this envelope a bit? Let's say they started with $2,000 instead.

Math Hint: To calculate this, we add two zeros to each earlier number because $2,000 has two more zeros than $20. If you're a quick calculator, you know we end up with over a million dollars at age 105. See the list below.

$2,000 SAVED AT 7.2 percent

$2,000 at age 15
$4,000 at age 25
$8,000 at age 35
$16,000 at age 45
$32,000 at age 55
$64,000 at age 65
$128,000 at age 75
$256,000 at age 85
$512,000 at age 95
$1,024,000 at age 105

Before you start swooning too much over this final number, we need to rein this in a bit and put this into proper perspective. Below are some thoughts from the pessimistic hole in the donut.

- **Lack of Priority—**Most 15-year-olds can barely scrape together enough cash for a movie ticket, let alone $2,000. As we add a few years on and the possibility of a part-time job, scraping together this sort of money becomes a little more likely, but their 105-year-old self is not a priority compared to new jeans, shoes, phone, or car.
    - OTHER CONTRIBUTIONS: This is where people who love this kid come in—parents, grandparents, aunts, uncles, and older siblings could contribute on their behalf.
- **Too Many Expenses—**This teen is not very likely to resist touching that money for 90 years. Heck, it's unlikely I would leave it there until 105 myself, but at least I have several expenses in the rearview mirror that our young person is staring at in the windshield. Before this $2,000 even becomes $4,000 at age 25, it will likely go to a car, college, or household expenses.
    - SEEK ALTERNATIVES: While spending is highly likely, it pays to find other means to cover those expenses, like increasing our income or taking on wise, manageable debt.
- **Slow Going—**A reason many spend rather than save is because the initial growth is slow. Even at age 35—20 years in—the account is only valued at $8,000. It is hard to believe at that moment that it will grow to be anything worthwhile.
    - STAY STEADFAST AND INFORMED: This is why remaining steadfast is so very important. There were times through all these years that I kept thinking, "I will never get there." Now, in a day, my account value can change by thousands, just like the increases we see above.
- **Inflation—**We have yet to discuss the inflation factor. Ninety years from now, a million dollars will not buy what a million will today. To put this in perspective, what one could buy in 1934 (90 years ago from 2024) for $200 would cost $4,600 today.

    - EARN 7 PERCENT OR MORE: You might think inflation will eat up your earnings. However, annual average inflation for the last 100 years was around 3 percent. This means we are ahead if we earn on average each year in the 7 percent range or more. I'll offer more perspectives on inflation in later chapters.
- **Taxes—**While we don't know what tax rates will be when we withdraw our savings or if it will be taxed along the way, paying taxes is a near certainty in most accounts. There are exceptions, or partial exceptions, like Roth IRAs and municipal bonds, which we'll discuss in later chapters. Without these mitigating options, our gains will be taxed.
    - ALTERNATIVES: Compounding helps offset depletion caused by taxes. So can tax-deferred growth. This will also be discussed in another chapter as we seek ways to maximize your wealth.

5

It might take a while to see the value of saving, but if we stick with it, we will reap the rewards. Keep focused on the donut and not the hole.

MAKE A NEW PLAN, STAN

"Just slip out the back, Jack. Make a new plan, Stan. You don't need to be coy, Roy. Just get yourself free! Hop on the bus, Gus. You don't need to discuss much. Just drop off the key, Lee. And get yourself free!"
—Paul Simon, 50 Ways to Leave Your Lover

With these challenges facing us, how will we ever reach the goal? If you believe I am about to share a 'goal' with you, I lost you somewhere. Even if we have a goal in mind, we likely will exceed it or fall short, but to hit it is like winning the lottery. There are too many unknowns, and if anyone tells you anything different, they either lie or haven't thought about how life changes dramatically.

I have armed you with information on the value of saving. You know your age, how much you have saved, and your income versus your expenses. We discussed the savings rule of 10 percent and how ages above the mid-20s should contribute a higher percentage. With this, you can now determine what you should save. If you do not believe you can afford this amount, then it's time to consider areas in your budget you can reduce or eliminate, or methods to increase your income.

The simplicity of this may be a little frustrating. I envision readers thinking, "Renée, I knew that. I thought you were going to give me some real help." Let's think about that for a second. If you've been applying the debt ideas and reducing the cost of your payments, you've found some money there. Maybe you are now putting off a major purchase or downsizing the item's price. Perhaps you are following a dream and trying a new venture. Any or all of these will help you get closer to your goal.

There is no silver bullet here, no magical cure. Yes, some people win the lottery, become famous, or create the next multi-million (or billion) dollar invention or corporation. In reality, that will not be the case for most of us. For most of us, the only way we will find financial security is to consistently apply a three-step strategy:

- **Reduce Expenses and Purchase Wisely**
- **Consistently Manage Debt for Successful Outcomes**
- **Save as Much as Possible as Often as You Can**

In the coming chapters, I will equip you with fundamental investment and tax planning strategies to help you reach your financial goals. However, this is not a one-size-fits-all solution. That's why we spent time discussing wise decisions in earlier chapters. This framework is far more important than the pat answers on any financial planning website. A standard plan and pat answers will only get you so far in this messy business of securing your financial future.

A good financial plan is squishy. It's like crafting something with Play-Doh. You might set out to make a tea set, but you realize the handles won't stay on the cups (job loss), and your saucers continue to have cracks (health issues). So, you scrap the first project and build an adorable little house. It's not as elaborate but it is safe, sturdy, and something we all need.

This is how our financial plans must be. We must adapt, be willing to try something new, and keep working on it until we've built something secure. This is why tapping the Flow is crucial to our long-term success. GOD will likely illuminate ideas or plans we might not have considered. Of utmost importance as we Flow along is to set aside as much money as possible.

What is essential at this moment is to set your contribution target and stick to it. We return to where we began in the first chapter: "Pay Yourself First".

6

Since we do not know what the future will bring, we must go with the Flow and seek the best alternatives for a secure future.

STICK TO THE PLAN, FRAN

"Plans are nothing; planning is everything" —Dwight D. Eisenhower

Once you establish the percentage of your income or the dollar amount you should save, we circle back to an initial concept we discussed: "Pay Yourself First". This simple phrase is clear: Before we take care of any other obligation, we put money into savings. Each month or pay period, we set that dollar amount aside. 401(k) payroll deductions work great here, but we can also have automatic drafts from our checking account.

My monthly contribution allowance was established as part of my rationale for moving to Mexico. The cost of living there is less. I don't need to drive—skip those expenses. Healthcare and food are more affordable. Things were getting tight in the States (affording my home, other routine expenses, and savings allowance).

When I heard about the complex where I live, I was told the rent was 16,000 pesos. At that current exchange rate (May 2024), that was a little under $1,000 U.S. dollars per month. When I came to look at an apartment, I was told the only place available was the top floor at 20,000 pesos. If you do a little quick math, that is 25 percent higher, or around $1,250 monthly.

The place had great amenities. It overlooked the mountains. It would give me incredible sunrises, and the rooftop would give me beautiful sunsets. I loved it. It was perfect—all but that rent. I walked away at first and then talked to my son. He asked, "Mom, isn't the $1,200 rent still less than your living expenses in the U.S.?" I responded, "Yes."

Then he said, "It sounds like you loved it. Why would you give up something that brings you joy AND reduces your expenses?" I had no good answer to that question. It seems I taught him well, so I said, "I'd better let you go. I'm headed back over there to sign the lease."

I did, but I was clear with the property manager: "If something opens up on the lower levels, I want that instead." She agreed, and I signed the lease. Over the seven and a half months before my move-in date, I emailed her several times about a different apartment, including my confirmation of the December move-in date. She never told me of another option, so I moved into the upper-floor, more costly unit.

As I began to meet the other residents, I found that the lower units had been available because many rented them after I signed my lease. Even more frustrating, many told me their lease included two months of free rent. This meant my costs were nearly double those of the other residents. I was angry, but I knew approaching the building manager with that attitude wouldn't be helpful.

I scheduled a meeting and asked some questions. It became apparent that her English was not as good as I had assumed. This, combined with how all the residents kept her running around 24/7, was likely why I was never offered a different unit. I'm unsure if she understood my requests, had time to deal with them, or even wanted to move someone who seemed all set in their apartment.

However, saving 80,000 pesos yearly, or about $5,000 per year (depending on the exchange rate), was worth pushing the issue. The very amiable property manager was not very responsive, and it took much negotiation, but I finally received a lower rent. The problem is that by the time I knew anything about this, they were increasing the rent to 18,000 pesos, and because of my travel schedule, I could not get the two months' free rent. My $5,000 per year in savings on living expenses is now only $1,500.

Creating savings is worth the effort—I wish this had worked in my favor to a greater degree, but I am still very grateful to have lower rent no matter what. $1,500 per year is still quite a few pennies.

Reduced expenses provide a cushion—Right before I secured the lower rent, I began traveling around town to write. Initially, I thought the rooftop and other facilities would work great for tapping the Flow, but I had to get out into the community for the mental break I needed to write. The problem is that most Mexican parks do not have picnic tables, so I started going to coffee shops. It turns out my rental discount isn't going into savings but to the ever-growing coffee industry. Even if we can't put the savings into savings, it can help us to afford other things we might need. It pays to keep our eyes open and find pennies for our pockets.

7

Sometimes, finding the extra savings we need takes a little work, but it's worth the effort when we have more pennies to add to our savings or provide a financial cushion.

We've got a great list here of seven successful savings strategies:

1. **Start Early—**The earlier we start saving, the better off we are financially. Don't wait—save as much as you can today.
2. **Cut Expenses—**The story's moral is that if we want our future to be as good as our present, we might need to reconsider what we "need" today and downsize our purchases.
3. **Reduce Spending—**If we don't spend it, we save it. If we save it, we gain future FREE pennies.
4. **The Trade-Off—**Before a purchase, use "The Rule of 72" to illustrate the benefit of saving over the long term to quickly calculate if it's worth losing future FREE pennies.
5. **Keep it in Perspective—**It might take a while to see the value of saving, but if we stick with it, we will reap the rewards.
6. **Financial Plans are Squishy—**We must go with the Flow and seek the best alternatives for a secure future.
7. **Find the Money to Pay Yourself First—**Sometimes, finding the extra savings we need takes a little work, but it's worth the effort when we have more pennies to add to our savings or provide a financial cushion.

Now, let's maximize the value of setting aside all these "pretty pennies" by discussing "Plans for Your Pennies".

CHAPTER NINE

PLANS FOR YOUR PENNIES

FINANCIAL PLANNING CONSIDERATIONS

"If the plan doesn't work, change the plan but never the goal."
—Daniel Hurst

WHAT'S THE GOAL?

There are various ways to assess retirement income needs, each offering different levels of guarantees and security. Before discussing the pros and cons of these methods, it's essential to address a question from one of the proofreaders. As he went through the following few pages, he kept noting things like this in the margin, "What are their expenses? Isn't that important here?" By the third note, a couple of pages in, I could tell his growing frustration when he noted, "Shouldn't we know their expenses or the budget?"

Well, yes and no. The person planning their retirement should know their budget and typical expenses. But no, I don't need to note a sample budget on these pages. Since you, the reader, are seeking to fund your retirement, you can draft your own number, and I will provide you with planning tools that say,

"For every X amount of income dollars you need each month during retirement, you will need to save XYZ."

I don't know what X is for you, and as we just talked about in the last chapter, you don't know what X is either. You might have a rough idea: This is my current mortgage payment (and whether you'll have that paid off), so add your standard expenses. Those numbers can change even if you are as little as five years from retirement—heck, they could change next year. These ideas are provided solely to show what a healthy savings goal might look like.

$166,000 = $1,000/mo.—One method I share with our classes suggests that for every $1,000 of monthly income we'll need in retirement, we should have $166,000 in savings. This calculation assumes one will earn 6 percent annually on average, and we'll need the income for 20 years. We will be spending our principal and not solely withdrawing earnings. If our assumptions hold, the $166,000 will be depleted at the end of year 20, providing a secure income stream for the specified period.

To illustrate, if you believe you'll need $3,000 per month of income from savings, you will want to have $500,000 in your account when you retire (3 x $166,000 = $498,000). The $1,000 monthly income is in addition to other sources of income, like a pension or Social Security. Your projected monthly budget may be $5,500, but you may also expect $2,500 monthly income from Social Security. Then, you only need $3,000 per month from savings. I'll show you how to determine your future Social Security benefits later in the book.

If either of the two variables is off—the 6 percent and 20-year assumption—so is our baseline assumption. Say we earn 7 percent on average; our money lasts longer. If, on the other hand, we live longer than 20 years and only earn 6 percent a year, we run the risk of outliving our money (frankly, for those of us in the average earnings category, we almost always run that risk). If we wish for greater security in retirement, we will want to have more than that saved.

One problem with this calculation is that it does not assume inflation. We'll talk more about the impact of inflation on our plans in the coming chapters, but what you can buy with $3,000 today will likely cost twice that in 20 years, so any solid plan should have an automatic increase in withdrawal amounts in the calculation method. This method assumes one will withdraw $3,000 monthly from year 1 to year 20. That is simply unrealistic.

The 4 percent Rule—A well-known, easy calculation option incorporating inflation is the 4 percent rule. If you believe you'll need the same $3,000 per month in income (or $36,000 for the year), you will want $900,000 in savings when you retire because $36,000 is 4 percent of $900,000. This strategy assumes 60 percent of the portfolio is in equities (stock), and the other 40 percent is in fixed income, typically bonds.

Please note how the $500,000 we needed in the last example almost doubled with the 4 percent rule. If our needed income withdrawal will likely double at the end of the term due to inflation, we would expect a significant increase in the required savings to accommodate this higher income.

In this calculation method, we adjust our withdrawal amount for inflation. So, if there is 3 percent inflation that year, we would add $1,080 (3 percent of $36,000) to the $36,000 and withdraw $37,080 the following year. We would apply this inflation calculation method to each of the subsequent years.

Based on historical market and inflation trends, the typical portfolio using the 4 percent rule would last 30 to 35 years. This offers better long-term protection, but this strategy is not without drawbacks. It's a very conservative liquidation method and, therefore, requires a savings goal that is more difficult for the typical saver to achieve.

DYNAMIC PENNIES

"Good fortune is what happens when opportunity meets with planning."
—Thomas Edison

While these guidelines give us some perspective around savings goals, no strategy is perfect. The Play-Doh of financial planning is too squishy to apply a stagnant withdrawal structure. The best plans reevaluate, reconsider, and remain ever dynamic. Here are a few things to consider:

Flexible Withdrawals—As life experience has taught us and we've discussed, our financial needs can change. Planning for specific withdrawal amounts each year can be difficult because we do not know what the future may bring. Granted, in retirement, we can still use the debt strategies outlined in the earlier chapters, but as discussed, sometimes it makes better sense to withdraw from savings to cover the cost. A successful strategy affords various options.

Income Needs Decrease—Although we will have to contend with inflation, the people who help retirees navigate their income needs say the withdrawal requirements generally go down instead of up. It is logical that we are young and healthy when we first retire, so we will do most of our vacations, projects, and hobbies. As we age, these activities (and expenses) begin to dwindle. Many also downsize their homes or consider renting instead, which can reduce housing expenses.

Life Changes—Medical bills are generally the exception to reduced income needs as we age. If, as we age, our health begins to fail, our expenses and income needs are likely to go up. Other life changes, like the sale or purchase of a home, inheritance, and the death of or acquisition of a life partner, can also create dramatic shifts in one's retirement income needs. Any plan must be adaptive to these variables.

This list could go on and on. Suppose you were to research this on the internet. You'd find blogs about concerns with the continued viability of Social Security (SS) or possible tax law changes impacting Roth IRA or other retirement accounts. Any tax change can affect our retirement savings' longevity and income possibilities.

I will address these matters in the next chapter because they are vital to consider, but first, I want to put your mind at ease. The likelihood of the bottom falling out of the U.S. economy, or the defunding of Social Security, is slim to none. I would go so far as to say you have a better chance of winning the lottery tomorrow (even if there is NO drawing) than for either of these two pillars of economic stability to collapse. In the following sections, I'll explain why I believe this in numerous ways.

Here is one big reason: More people are working for the betterment of the American people than not, and those working against the average Joe or Jane still want us to have some money to spend and buy stuff. Middle America drives the economy with its purchases, and even if you constrict Social Security slightly or the typical household income by small margins, it has dramatic ripple effects throughout the economy. This is the stuff recessions are made of.

They—whoever "they" are and irrespective of their intentions—do not want to force too many of us to go broke. A significant number need us to have enough money to feel comfortable spending it if "they" will have any success, and yes, this also means our elected officials, which means we must vote wisely. To do that, we must be armed with the truth—more about that in the next chapter.

To give you the tools you need to build your pile of pennies, we will enter the land of MONEY—places where dreams are made or squashed. The rules here are as dynamic as your squishy financial plan. Too many folks in MONEY LAND want to take yours before you get theirs, believing it is legitimate to cheat to win. Through awareness, we hope to recognize and thwart them.

GOLDEN RULE WORLD

"When I was teaching children, I began every day writing this on the blackboard: 'Do to others what you would like them to do to you,' telling them how much better the world would be if everybody lived by this rule." —Common Sense, Thomas Paine

Ah, yes, "The Golden Rule"—if only we could come close to this ideal. We've repeatedly discussed this concept in the ethics classes I instruct. Time and again, we are all challenged by how easy it is to break this rule. Frankly, if we could all find a way to adhere to this straightforward concept, there would be no need for any ethics classes or possibly this book.

In the "World of Golden Rule," everything is based on equity. People are paid well, things are reasonably priced, and fees cover only the actual costs. No one would want to take too much from another to benefit themselves because they wouldn't want that same treatment. We would all then live in a land of abundance—and I mean ALL. Even those in the poorest regions would be met with a surplus because we would be able to see the needy through the lens of empathy, and we would share. In the "World of Golden Rule," there is no need to discuss protecting your "pretty pennies" because everyone else cares about your pennies, too.

I realize that is very Pollyanna-ish. It is not something we can likely achieve. Considering it, though, gives us a new perspective. When Mr. Paine says, "if everybody," he implies some folks must follow this rule. Many of us think we do, but I'd like to challenge your thinking to say we all break the rule. Oh yes, yes, we do. Let me give you a straightforward example.

A friend invites you to a party. This friend is spending a lot of time and effort planning and setting up. They told you how excited they were to see you there. On the day of the party, you don't feel like going. You're not sick and have no conflict in your calendar—it's just that a party is not what you want to do.

If we are practicing "The Golden Rule," we will likely go. We've hosted parties before and realized the work that goes into it. We also know that when someone attends, it shows they care. This friend told you they were excited to spend time with you. When people don't show up, and there's no genuine conflict, the underlying message says they don't care. This is why many people lie and say they are sick, or something came up, because they know it is hurtful if they say, "I just don't feel like going."

When we 'hurt' other people, we break "The Golden Rule." We all break it because none of us is exempt from having hurt another. Empathy and compassion can almost universally better guide our choices and actions. This truth likely holds in every capacity of our lives, including the financial realm.

THE FINANCIAL SERVICES INDUSTRY

"The financial industry is a service industry. It should serve others before it serves itself." —Christine Lagarde, Inside Job (Documentary)

Christine Lagarde served as France's finance minister in 2008 when the financial crisis occurred. My first exposure to Ms. Lagarde was while watching the documentary *Inside Job*. It's about the systemic corruption and changes in policy that created the financial meltdown—greed, plain and simple. It's excellent. I encourage you to watch it.

When Ms. Lagarde said the statement above, "The financial industry is a service industry. It should serve others before it serves itself." I thought, "Heck yeah, that is exactly what this industry is missing!" The point isn't to make as much money as possible, because that means I might be taking more than I need or deserve, but to help others achieve their financial goals. Sadly, too much of the industry has lost that perspective—if it ever had it.

The financial services industry is not alone in this perspective about the Almighty Buck—how I get mine before you get yours. Healthcare should "care" about people and their lives, yet too many can't afford it because of the profit built into the system. We could add to this list the oil and gas industry, killing our planet to keep us dependent on fuel, and other environmental concerns like pollution and waste in food production, plastics filling the oceans and landfills to remain there long after we're gone, on and on. The world is suffering. The living things on this planet are in jeopardy, and we keep doing more of the same.

In the same documentary, Christine Lagarde also said about the pending financial crisis: "And I clearly remember telling Hank (Paulson): 'We are watching this tsunami coming, and you're just proposing that we ask which swimming costume we're going to put on.'"

That is precisely how ridiculous so many things are today. People are robbing us of our pennies—billions in tax cuts to the rich and subsidies to their companies. Yet the rich and powerful point at the immigrant, the mom on welfare, or the millennial trying to pay off their student loans and tell us, "Don't let them take that from you." Or, worse yet, flat-out create and repeat lies about the status of the programs or government spending. Then, the masses turn against those we could, or maybe even should, help instead of considering the BIGGEST problem of all—greed and corruption. This subterfuge is used by the wealthy and other influential groups with an agenda, like the NRA (National Rifle Association), to motivate people to vote against their very own best interests.

Don't get me wrong, these are complex issues. There are no simple fixes for any of them. If we take a moment and consider this through the lens of compassion, a viable solution becomes clear. When our focus is on the people and not the profit, we are in the Flow. Holding that lens at the correct angle is difficult when we discuss money. I've been challenged by my perspective even as I write these chapters.

I'm not sure about you, but tapping into the Flow and feeling connected to Purpose and Power requires less effort when I am a part of creation. Looking at the stars, putting my feet in the sand, holding a newborn baby, and watching hummingbirds flitter at a feeder all fill me with awe and wonder when I remember to align myself with Everything. Natural creation helps me connect and be grateful for the moment.

Humans created money. It's a made-up thing—like Kings and Queens or any title or position of authority. Buildings, cars, malls, dams, airplanes, roads, weapons (another list that doesn't end), they're all made up. They are not part of the Natural Universe. Instead of being a pathway to the Creator, these things make it even harder to break through. They distract us from what is of Greatest Value. Too much focus on the created instead of Creation can zap the Flow.

This is a tricky balancing act, between the natural universe and our daily lives, and I'm not always good at it—sometimes I forget to try. The best I can do most days is remind myself often that GOD is with me and for me while I try to accomplish tasks in the world. It's easy to fail in the balancing act of these two worlds. However, as I'll remind you repeatedly (which also serves as a reminder to me), the more I let GOD in, focusing on the Flow as a guiding force, the more readily answers come to me, accompanied by more peace in the process. Let me tell you a shocking story about the perspective of whom we 'serve' in the financial industry.

JUST A LITTLE HELP FROM A FRIEND

"It is not the creation of wealth that is wrong, but the love of money for its own sake."
—Margaret Thatcher

When I left corporate America and started my own company, I moved my 401(k) to a self-directed IRA. (Individual Retirement Arrangement—I know we typically use Accounts for the "A," but IRS Publication 590 for IRAs uses Arrangements.) Given my background, I felt confident I could adequately select investments and balance my portfolio.

Even without the same access to information via the internet we have today, managing my portfolio in 1999 wasn't difficult. A functional portfolio is easy unless one puts all one's eggs in a risky basket. There are so many tools out there today. We'll talk more about things to look for later in this chapter.

I kept my IRA in the same spot until about 2012 or 2013. While volunteering in the children's ministry at church, I met a young man starting his career in financial planning. We became fast friends. The whole crew of volunteers would attend the church service together and do other social activities.

He never pushed transferring my investment business, but I know how this industry works. Most people who are entering financial planning or insurance first try to get sales from their family and friends. From that, they hope to get referrals, and things will grow if they do a good job. Since I respected him and saw his promising future, I suggested I transfer my IRA to his firm.

It is also important to note a few things—the firm he started with was a company I didn't respect much. I would have never chosen to do business with this firm, and in hindsight, I wish I had done a little more research at the time. My thought was that little could go wrong—and little did. I was relieved when he elected to leave that company about four years later. Without saying anything, I assumed he found out what I already knew to be true of this company: profits, not clients, were their top priority.

He put some of my money into a few funds that I had similar profit-focused concerns about in my asset allocation mix, but since they made up little of my portfolio, I went with them. I realized he was new. He still had a lot to learn. Part of the problem, however, is that financial planners get most of their education from firms and companies pushing their own investment vehicles. This means the story financial planners hear will likely keep them from seeing some underlying problems.

For those unfamiliar with the phrase "Asset Allocation Mix", it's a diversification strategy that helps minimize your portfolio's volatility. One would mix in differing assets (investments) that typically react differently in various markets. In theory, when one investment goes down, another goes up. We will talk more about this in the chapter "More FREE Pennies."

Last note: I did this to help him. Sure, I hoped that maybe he would offer me something I was unaware of—as I think back, I can't recall anything. It was nice to email him if I needed something. He or someone on the staff did it quickly, which was terrific. It was one less thing I had to take care of, but truth be told, I could do anything he could do, and I had more experience.

I was still happy to do it. He was a young man starting a new career. He met his wife through our friendship group. They have three or four—or maybe it's five children now. I lost count. He continued to mentor the boys he started with in that children's ministry through high school. He was making a positive difference in the lives of many people. I was glad that I could, in some small part, help him help them.

Fast-forward to writing this book. One item I wanted to offer my readers was recommendations about financial planners. I contacted my financial planner (and friend) to ask where I could find my fees. This was deducted from my monthly account for their services. Like always, he promptly got back to me. I checked with a friend who is a partner in her financial planning firm, and she told me that those fees were excellent. They were akin to the fees they offered their best clients. This was welcome news.

I couldn't shake the fees, though—the percentage, but more specifically, what that percentage meant in dollars I was paying in fees. It kept popping into my head. This was a monthly expense, just like interest on a loan, and my thought was, "Do I need to be paying this?" The quick math in my head wasn't helpful either. Every time I thought of my portfolio doubling, I realized this fee would double, too. The fee also makes it more challenging to double my portfolio. All of this didn't seem right or fair.

I was the one who worked hard to get money there, and managing $100,000, $500,000, or $1,000,000 is the same work. Why should someone make ten times the money for basically the same job? One could argue that a financial planner's incentive is to help you grow your portfolio—sure, but that incentive is there regardless. People will leave if they don't manage the money well.

He also collected this fee when the market and my portfolio performed poorly. I get it—he still needs an income and is still there to help me, but my losses are more significant, and these fees ensure it takes me longer to recover. This wasn't adding up right for me, and I did not like it.

This caused me to go to my financial planner friend and discuss this with him. He proceeded to tell me things of value he offered me. None of them equated to the dollar amount I saw on my sheet. One point he brought up was that he could be helpful in the liquidation phase when I needed the money for retirement. That could be true, but that doesn't mean I must stay here, paying hundreds of dollars a month until then.

The dollar amount was considerably more than any of my routine bills. It was more than I paid monthly for food or electricity, and more than I spent a year on clothing by a large margin. Combined for the year, it was more than I paid for most vacations and was growing. If I had met my goals, this number would have continued to increase, and it didn't seem worth it. I'm trying to cut all these expenses, yet this cash flows out of this door.

At one point in the discussion, I said, "If I hit my savings goal, these fees will be more than half my annual contribution." What I didn't say, but was thinking, "And I would NEVER cut a check and just give you that amount of money—EVER."

His response was, "You aren't paying our fees. It comes out of your account balance." Oh my, we are back to word games to act like this isn't a substantial expense. I felt like I was zapped back in time and was again talking to the guy at the mortgage company when I asked about closing costs.

I immediately retorted, "But that is still my money. Even if I don't give you a check for $500 directly, but you take that from my account balance, it is still an actual cost to me." It means I have fewer pennies working for FREE pennies—this is a big deal. He is an intelligent man. He knows how this works and the concrete cost. He also works in a world where he always hears that line, "You aren't paying the fees…"

I didn't want to give up on our working relationship. None of this changed my initial motivation to help and work with him. Plus, I needed the research. I suggested to him that I split my account. I manage half; he manages half. We'll see which side did better. I thought this was an intriguing solution. I was interested to see how this might turn out. If he was correct and offered value that I could not find anywhere else, the side he managed would have a higher value. If not, my side would do better, and I would at least cut the fees in half.

He took about a day to reply. I got an email that read (paraphrased), "We are no longer interested in working with you. You are not required to move your funds to another holding company, but if you choose to move them, we will not assist you with the process."

Are you as flabbergasted as I was? Never had I ever thought that would be the response. My friend didn't even call me. When I replied to his email with (paraphrased), "Are you serious, {insert name}? This is how you treat a friend and a long-time client?" I received no response. I haven't heard from him since.

I wrote to him an additional time on the first anniversary of my rollover. I moved my IRA to another firm specializing in lower-fee self-directed IRAs.

My email thanked him for pushing me along. I shared my new account balance with him. While I knew the market had done exceptionally well from 2023 to 2024, I would not have seen the 30 percent gain in those 12 months had I stayed with the firm. I wished him well and told him how this experience was exactly what I needed as research for my book. I ended the note with a promise to mail him a signed copy upon publication. I also told him I still care about him and his family. He didn't respond to that message either.

WEALTH OF SPIRITUAL FIBER

"The spirit of man is more important than mere physical strength, and the spiritual fiber of a nation than its wealth." —Dwight D. Eisenhower

I do not believe my financial planner friend intended to hurt me, yet he had to know that cutting ties in that way would have that effect. I still cannot believe it. Not only is it rude on a personal level, but it is also unprofessional. Two things are at the center of my beliefs about this situation:

1. He put money before our friendship. Knowing he is a man I met through church, admired, and wanted to help makes that even worse. Even if he wanted to move away from a working relationship with me, he could have done it tactfully and gracefully. This is why my next book is equally important to this one. In it, we discuss how conflict avoidance does not help maintain successful personal and professional relationships and various other methods to navigate life choices.
2. My account would have won if we had proceeded with the suggested split. He didn't want to consider it because he knew my NO FEES account would win. Part of me thinks that since we are friends, he could have even told me that, but then there is the matter of all the fees I already paid him and the

cognitive dissonance of resuming his work after admission. It's easier to avoid it.

I'm not even mad about paying him fees for those ten years. If I were to add it up and then calculate missing returns, I could get pretty worked up about it. There seems to be no point in that. I was motivated to help him. I believe that was a GOD thing. The Flow brought me to that choice, and I gave it to the Universe as a gift. It isn't 'mine' anyway. What comes around goes around.

I think my desire to start with the fees for the research was a GOD thing. My initial thoughts for this chapter were pointers and advice on how to find an advisor. I wasn't planning to write a chapter starting with the downside of financial services. I also believe the fact that I couldn't get the concept (of all those fees compounding) out of my head was a GOD thing. That was something the Flow wanted to illuminate.

Deciding to put these concerns into a book that I plan to market to the agents who attend my classes causes me grave concern. I don't want to offend them, and I don't want to lose their business. It could be a killer to my day job to publish a book that illuminates the downside of the financial services industry.

When faced with a professional dilemma, I did what I typically do: I brought it to them. This scenario became a point of discussion in one of our ethics courses. The attendees, many working in financial services and planners themselves, resoundingly agreed: A planner should be able to account for the value of the fee, or it shouldn't be charged.

Many have further shared that the type of questions and concerns I expressed are part of the job. Whatever the discussion, it should always be treated with the client in mind first. In the majority opinion, a curt email canceling the relationship and preemptively refusing any offer of assistance does not reflect the client's first mindset.

Nearly all financial professionals have canceled a client or two. Everyone in any industry has had to decide to separate from a business relationship. Most said it was due to abusive or temperamental behavior from the clients. Even then, it was handled with more tact and grace than this email. In an instance like this, many described how they have seen clients leave after drawing a boundary, such as, "We can only work with you if the entire account is here." That, to me, is a legitimate request. I could then decide how I wanted to proceed.

After my research, what is now my recommendation regarding a financial advisor? Here are a few suggestions based on a variety of preferences and comfort levels.

CHAUFFEUR, ANYONE?

"Money is only a tool. It will take you wherever you wish, but it will not replace you as the driver."—Ayn Rand

Okay, maybe "chauffeur" is a little extreme compared to a financial advisor. In the end, however, if you have a financial advisor, you are paying someone else to do things you could do for yourself.

I believe the industry should adopt a flat fee like a CPA for a tax return or an hourly amount like an attorney. This percentage of the portfolio is not fair. I wanted to add, "...to the middle-income person," but it is also unfair to the rich. Having fees set as a percentage of the portfolio is costly and potentially unnecessary. It also means advisors will likely go after big-buck clients instead of helping everyone equally.

If the industry begins to reexamine its fee structures, it has a long way to go. When my financial advisor fired me, I went to my friend, who owns a financial planning firm, and asked her, "If I were to hire your firm as consultants, how much would your advisors charge?" I thought I would have them review my asset allocation mix every year or so and make any recommendations based on trends and new information.

Guess how much they wanted to charge me for this service? I still can't believe what they said--$500 per hour with a two-hour minimum. They figured it would take four hours to review everything and to meet—$2,000. It was the

$500 per hour that killed me. That is more than the typical attorney who had to pass the bar. There is no such measure for a financial advisor. It's more per hour than a typical physician who can save lives, went through eight years of education, and had to pass multiple boards.

To become a financial advisor, one needs only a securities license and an insurance license. Each takes about 40 hours of training plus an exam. Many continue with training beyond that, but that is all the education required to put out a sign offering financial advice. If you commit to researching and educating yourself, you can do the same.

Below, I've listed some possible options for varying degrees of self-involvement and contracting out the plan. The beauty is that you can start with any of them and change to another option at any time. It's your money—your plan, and do not let anyone scare or bully you into keeping your money anywhere. None of this is rocket science.

To prove that, put this book down for a moment and open YouTube. Type JOHN (or sometimes called JACK) BOGLE in their search engine. He's the founder of Vanguard. Watch anything he's in. It's all good and will build your investment confidence. As you take in different messages from Mr. Bogle, watch his videos titled "John Bogle: How much do investors lose in charges and management fees?" and "John Bogle: All you need to know about investing in three words." While you are at it, watch "Jack Bogle: My Essential Advice for Any Investor."

Do-it-yourself: This is not complex, as illustrated by the three recommended videos featuring Jack Bogle. There are many tools just like that out there. By doing this yourself, you have nothing to lose. CORRECTION: You lose the penny-eating fees. If you don't like it or believe you need more help, no problem. Get yourself an advisor. Just because you begin with one plan or strategy does not mean you need to stay there.

The Early Bird: An economical way to do this is to get yourself an advisor early on when your portfolio isn't extensive, learn as much as you can, and then, when you feel you are ready to fly, move your portfolio. This requires getting the right advisor—one willing to educate you. It also means you will commit time and effort to these visits and study other resources to expand your knowledge.

Eggs in a Couple of Baskets: Although the person I was working with opposed allowing me to separate my portfolio, it is common for people (especially those with more considerable sums) to work with several people on their accounts. This way, we get multiple levels of diversification because money is in different investments and managed by various people. Most advisors have requirements for minimum portfolio sizes, so you may face challenges with this alternative.

Virtual Advisor: Many investment firms offer a web-based artificial intelligence (AI) advisor alternative. When I moved my IRA to Vanguard, I considered this route and still might try it. You will get up-to-date advice, an automatic rebalancing of your portfolio, and an advisor who can meet with you whenever it's convenient for you at less than half the cost.

A Given Scenario: Another option is to visit an advisor when your life circumstances change, such as an inheritance or acquisition of a new business, or when you need a specific product, like life insurance, after the birth of a child, or are considering an annuity for retirement income. We will discuss some of these products and life needs, but it is always a good idea to check things out with people you trust in the field.

A Jockey for Your Prize Pennies: You might decide to pay the fees and get an advisor for the long haul. It is an option, and you would not be alone. Many get an advisor. Primarily out of naively thinking that they need to do this, but it's also possible that doing this self-study in the world of money is not your thing. You would rather pay someone else to do it.

Should you adopt any plan with an advisor involved, please keep Jack Bogle's words from the video "How much do investors lose in charges and management fees?" in your mind before proceeding—

"We put up 100 percent of the capital, take 100 percent of the risk, and get about 30 percent of the market's long-term return."

While I have not verified Jack's claim that we receive only 30 percent of the long-term return, I figure the 2 percent fee is more than 25 percent of the 8 percent return because it comes off the top, grows in dollar amount over time, and is paid regardless of the return. This is a considerable expense to overcome, so whoever we work with must be worth it. The final section of this chapter is a few suggestions on what to look for in an advisor if you go that route.

PICKING YOUR PONY

"If money is your hope for independence, you will never have it"
—Henry T. Ford

The number one determining factor in ruling an advisor in or out is whether they operate under a "fiduciary" or a "suitability" standard. A fiduciary must legally act in the client's best interests before anyone else, including their own. You will want the advisor's commitment to a fiduciary standard in writing. Even then, there are so many grey areas that it is also best to rely on your instincts regarding the person's adherence to these principles.

To illustrate, my advisor friend is a fiduciary. Do you think he acted in my best interests when he fired me because I was concerned about the fees? Was he thinking of me when he told me the firm would not assist me in a transfer? After all my account paid him over the years, he couldn't even take the time to call me to discuss why a separation might be best. Maybe that is part of the inherent problem with this relationship: Many clients like me are best served by not paying advisor fees, yet the fiduciary has a conflict of interest because of the loss of fees that is not addressed.

To that end, you can negotiate fees, so do not be afraid to do so. Every little quarter percent you save adds up to many more pennies in your pocket. If you decide lower fees are essential to you, and this possible advisor won't entertain your negotiations, you have your answer on whether they are a good fit.

You will want someone whose philosophy of money aligns with yours. Suppose you now believe the principles in this book that responsible, manageable debt is okay, especially if it allows you to save additional pennies. In that case, you do not want a financial advisor who believes debt is rooted in all kinds of evil, someone who wants to put you in high commission or high fee products, or maybe doesn't believe some of your investment goals are necessary.

For example, toward the end of our working relationship, I asked my financial advisor/friend about "Green Investments" —companies and funds that are environmentally friendly. His response was, "We don't do that. There is no way to tell if the company does what they say they will do." I responded, "That may be true, but it is important to me and might be to your other clients, too." He politely dismissed me with, "We haven't had anyone ask about it."

Your investment ideas, concerns, and objectives are probably different from mine, but you deserve someone who will take them seriously, research them, and explain the pros and cons so you can decide. This is your portfolio, and you are spending many pennies for this person to help you. The right person will honor you and the dollars you pay for the service by taking the time to help you, including your unique interests.

In hindsight, my advisor dismissed my idea because he had a set formula for his asset allocation mixes. This is a one-size-fits-all solution; you do not need to pay an advisor for that strategy. You could put your money into specific mutual funds that provide an asset allocation mix. We'll discuss this and other product-specific ideas in the coming chapters.

Part of what you want from this relationship is education. Your advisor's ability to help enlighten you depends on how much time they spend educating themselves and on their educational source. These variables are not always equal. Be sure to prepare specific questions for your first meeting to determine if this person's thoughts align with yours and if you believe they are well-versed in several financial areas.

Important to note, this does not mean the person must have years in the business or several letters after their name indicating professional designations. A youthful advisor with enthusiasm and perspective who stays up on current trends can be just as good as a more mature person. While a professional designation for some indicates a commitment to learn more and develop their trade, it can also be shielding incompetence or rigidity. Neither is a good quality for the person you'll partner with for your financial future, so look first at the person and their reactions to you.

Let your conscience (the Flow) be your guide—pick someone you enjoy being around, who talks to you as an equal, and who is kind and considerate. If the person says, "That's a good question; I don't know, but I'll find out for you." and then he or she does get back to you with the answers or does some research while you are there, this is a positive sign, not a negative. It illustrates follow-through, honesty, and integrity.

Most importantly, remember that this is not a lifetime commitment. You can always change to a new advisor or none. Your financial plan is squishy Play-Doh. What works and feels good today will likely change tomorrow —Flow with it.

Before I give you a basic understanding of diversification strategies and an overview of various investment classes, it is essential to understand how the government fits into your financial strategy. Social security, taxes, inflation, interest rates, and more will directly impact your pennies and planning. As Yvon Chouinard said, "The more you know, the less you need."

CHAPTER TEN

THE GOVERNMENT & YOUR PENNIES

THE MORE YOU KNOW, THE BETTER YOUR PLANS

"Democracy cannot succeed unless those who express their choice are prepared to choose wisely. The real safeguard of democracy, therefore, is education."
—Franklin D. Roosevelt

VOTE WITH YOUR PENNIES (AND COMMON SENSE)

In the State of the Union Address (SUA) on February 7, 2023, some Republicans in attendance began to heckle and boo when President Joe Biden told Americans that a handful of those Republican lawmakers had their eyes on reducing or eliminating Social Security (SS). The jeers were calling Biden a liar for such remarks, so he went about offering proof. I won't list the sources he provided here. If you're interested, type "Transcript of the 2023 State of the Union." For a more dramatic flair, I encourage you to go to YouTube and search for a clip of Republicans and Social Security at the 2023 State of the Union Address.

As Biden continued with various points to confirm that a minority of Republicans had an interest in defunding SS, the boos, heckles, and jeers continued; Biden went off script and gained agreement with these words: "So folks, as we all apparently agree, Social Security and Medicare (are) off the books now, right? They're not going to be struck? {APPLAUSE} All right. We got unanimity. Social Security and Medicare are a lifeline for millions of seniors. Americans have been paying into them with every single paycheck since they started working. So tonight, let's all agree —and we apparently are —let's stand up for seniors. Stand up and show them we will not cut Social Security. We will not cut Medicare. Those benefits belong to the American people. They earned them."

I used to say, and still mostly agree today, "No elected official would vote away Social Security because they would never be reelected." It would be political suicide. No one who works for a living or counts on someone else who does should ever vote for someone who didn't support Social Security—EVER. But today, I wonder how many voters would believe it. Would yet another alternate reality be created?

I can hardly speak of it. I never know what to say because there is a camp of people living in a place where truth is elastic, and they are creating beliefs from lies. When gathering information, I try to go directly to the original event—the State of the Union Address, the hearing, the trial—and if there is no live stream, I am reading the transcript. I get my news from popular media, but I can determine trustworthy sources if the information aligns with what I witnessed firsthand. Although it's a time commitment, it is worth it, and to the best of your ability, I encourage you to do the same.

There is a great deal of misinformation, and without making an effort to stay informed, it's easy to get caught in it. I'll be honest—before September 11th, I was largely disconnected. I paid little attention to the news or to what was happening on Capitol Hill. After that, I followed events closely for a time, but eventually drifted away again until the election of Donald Trump.

I didn't vote for him. Although I'm an independent, I had typically voted Republican, but I could not support him as the nominee. My concerns about his leadership style dated back to watching The Apprentice, where I found his approach off-putting.

Even so, when he was first elected, I gave him the benefit of the doubt. I hoped he would surround himself with capable people, listen to them, and serve the country well. Over time, however, it became clear to me that he was unwilling—or unable—to take in new information and adapt his approach.

During that same time, the research in my classes and the discussions it sparked revealed some interesting patterns. Despite frequent claims that Republicans perform better on the economy, the data did not consistently support that view. Across several key indicators—national debt, inflation, unemployment, and wages—we often observed stronger outcomes during Democratic administrations and weaker trends during Republican ones.

My purpose in sharing that information is not to tell you who to vote for, but to let you know that over the years of teaching financial matters, I have come to understand which government policies help drive the economy and benefit the mostpeople. We can all agree, as an example, that "Trickle-down economics" doesn't work. Since it was instituted under the Reagan administration, the wealth gap in the United States has widened, placing an undue financial burden on most Americans. At the same time, the rich have gotten so rich it's mind-numbing.

We are told a story about what will benefit us as voters and Americans. Too frequently, those with the money and resources to push their agenda build that story, and that story helps them. It does not help me, it does not help you, and it most certainly does not help those in greatest need. I should offer a correction: Some of it has helped us. That is true, but more and more, the people of the world are buying into BIG LIES. This makes it incredibly important to hone our ability to see the truth.

I will arm you with truth and facts in these pages. As we explore some common misconceptions and disinformation campaigns, I hope it helps you navigate all the various resources in the future to separate the truth from lies and opinions from facts. The more informed and better educated we are about all sorts of things, the more impactful we can be in our finances, families, communities, nation, and the world. The more we know, the less we fear. Education can set us on a beneficial path; the good news is we have complete and utter control over it.

THE SECURITY OF SOCIAL SECURITY

"Elections belong to the people. It's their decision. If they decide to turn their back on the fire and burn their behinds, then they will just have to sit on their blisters." —
Abraham Lincoln

It's surreal that the quote above is almost 200 years old, and we still haven't learned that lesson. As I type these words, Donald Trump is in office for his second term with a laundry list of craziness. I could provide a list of today's lawless, corrupt, and cruel policies from the highest office in the land, but it will likely change again in the coming days and make the freak storm of today a memory for the new horror unfolding tomorrow. This is what you get when 77.3 million people believed Trump's lies and ignored the evidence that he is a convicted felon, an adjudicated sex offender, and fomented an insurrection after lying about an election. The other 168 million voting adults (90 million that didn't vote, plus the 75 million that voted for Harris and the 2.8 million that voted independently), the children in the U.S., and the rest of the world must live with this reckless choice. Hopefully, we are spared the future unraveling of decency and democracy by removing him before 2029.

One would think people would know better than to put a corrupt man in power. Apparently not. I've said all my career, and even in earlier pages, "It's political suicide to eliminate Social Security." With Trump and Project 2025, they seem not to care, because part of the agenda is to take over and force us into their system without future elections. With American independence baked in, I cannot see this ever happening. From what I can tell, they are giving it the old college try anyway.

Everything Project 2025 and DOGE are doing is utterly self-defeating. Robbing the American people of their safety nets and protections is so ludicrous for prosperity that I wonder if the administration ever considered the economic impact of these grand controlling ideas. Government programs that help put wealth, safety, and security in the hands of the people also help to make the rich wealthier and the government more stable. It is a prosperous cycle. In the most basic sense, autonomous citizens are productive people. In a hopeful turn of events, it seems that some of Trump's attempts have fallen flat, and with the people speaking out, some Republicans have begun breaking from the fold.

There has been a long-running campaign to sway Americans to question Social Security's viability. To illustrate, I want to use a video we use in our classes to discuss these essential points. I've shared stories like this with my customers for years, hoping they would avoid sitting on some blisters, as Abe would say. I hope you might benefit from the same.

Attempting this in a written format will be challenging, but we can manage it if you switch between this written word and a means to watch the video. First, search YouTube for the video "Social Security Trust Fund planforamerica." You've found the right one if you see a 3-minute and 20-second (3:20) video with little stick cartoon characters. The description line should read, "'Trust' should be a four-letter word when referring to the SS Trust Fund." (Source: https://youtu.be/moG31hGZl14)

Before you watch it, I'd like you to find a pen and something you can write on. It might even be the margin of this book. You won't need much room. Once you've got that, I'd like you to draw out a small box—1 x 1 inch will do, or something larger, if you prefer. This is for your notes, so it does not need to be perfect.

Once you have the small box, draw a line down the center so you have a box with two columns, just like the one below. Then, put the word TRUE at the top of the column to the left, and yup—you got it—FALSE at the top of the right column, like the image below.

As you watch the video, add a mark to the TRUE column whenever you hear something you believe is correct. When you think it's FALSE, put a mark to the right. Use X's, slashes, checks—whatever works for you to identify an incident of truth or not. This way, when the video is over, you can quickly determine if you believe there was more FACT or FICTION in this video.

TRUE	FALSE
xxx	or ||||

Now, watch the video, make your marks in the columns, and come back to read the next section.

AND THE WINNER IS...

"Anti-intellectualism has been a constant thread winding its way through our political and cultural life, nurtured by the false notion that democracy means that 'my ignorance is just as good as your knowledge.'"—Isaac Asimov

Your research is done. You've watched the video and made your marks. The only thing left is to see if your beliefs about Social Security align with the facts. In live classes, I ask the audience to text their results—more TRUE than false, or more FALSE than true.

Most people get it wrong. Maybe 30 percent of folks answer correctly. This disparity is not because they're dumb, uneducated, or naive. It's because they've been lied to and not from one source. This video is riddled with misconceptions that float around and come at us from various broadcasts. If you have more check marks under the TRUE column than the FALSE, you have also fallen victim to these falsehoods.

I want you to roll the video back to the beginning (0:00) and watch it around 0:22, where she says, "…lots more money coming in than going out, so…" That is 100 percent true. The trend of more workers than seniors probably continued into the 1970s. The Carter administration (1977-1980) started to work on the problem, but it was in the 1980s that it became clear that something must be done. Longer life spans and demographic shifts like the Baby Boomers entering retirement age required some BIG changes to Social Security.

Go back and roll the video. Just let it run only about four seconds to 0:26, and I want you to imagine an enormous buzzer going off when she says, "…it was put into a trust fund for future Social Security retirees." BZZZZZT—WRONG!

There was a trust fund back then, but it was created to cover annual shortfalls like any prudent reserve. If, in any given year, they collected more than they needed, it was placed in reserves for a year when contributions were less than expenditure. But the actual SS Trust Fund that she proceeds to discuss, where Republicans and Democrats come with their big ol' trucks to steal all the money, was created with intentionality in the early 1980s.

Social Security was already beginning to feel the financial effects of the demographic shifts at that point. Early in the 1980s, Reagan called upon Congress to act, allowing Social Security to borrow money from other entities to cover a current shortfall and seek out long-term solutions for solvency. This led to several changes, like phasing in an increase to the full benefit age from 65 to 67 and beginning to impose a federal income tax on Social Security income.

Yes, that's right. Before 1984, retirees received their Social Security benefits income tax-free, and get this—the base income levels when these taxes are imposed have not been indexed for inflation. This means that, 40+ years later, as seniors require a greater income to maintain the same lifestyle, an increasing proportion of their Social Security checks are taxed.

This is also the stage of the game where the U.S. government became intentional about setting aside money into the trust fund to cover the trillions of projected shortfalls. What she is describing in this video was planned. This is not a conspiracy. This was and is an attempt by the government forces to shore up and secure this critical income stream for the American people.

To talk further about that—and the other things in the video like the trucks hauling away money or the deadbeat roommate, I want you to scroll the video to 1:44 and watch until about 2:30. I am sure as you watch this, you are now able to see other FALSE statements like, "…expanding and increasing the benefits by politicians since 1935." We just talked about some of the reductions in benefits.

In fact, Social Security went through what would be called the expansion phase (1935 to 1972) where the program expanded by adding benefits and covering more people. Costs increased in this period, but again, the demographics of the day allowed for it. However, around 1973, we entered a period of retrenchment, which reversed the expansion by reducing benefits and increasing taxes. This has certainly not been a spending frenzy, and it was our lower-middle-income citizens who felt the most dramatic effects of these rollbacks.

When we are armed with historical accuracy and facts, misleading statements become apparent. Having the facts also helps to reduce fear. These conspiracies that float around make us feel like we can't trust our elected officials or other people in government. I am not about to tell you that they are all wonderful people thinking about you every moment. That is evidently not the case, but I will tell you that I firmly believe there are more who care than there are who do not.

To discuss this further, I want you to focus on the section where she says, "SHOW US THE MONEY!"

JERRY MAGUIRE'S MONEY

"SHOW! ME! THE! MONEY! A-ha-ha!
Jerry, doesn't it make you feel good just to say that?"
—Rod Tidwell (Cuba Gooding, Jr.) 1996 movie "Jerry Macquire"

Perhaps some of you haven't seen this movie, but for my generation, it was a cult classic. In the film, as the agent, Jerry (played by Tom Cruise) was supposed to get a football team to show Rod, the athlete, THE MONEY—the most significant contract possible. But did Rod expect Jerry to come over with a pile of cash as he's jumping all over the screen shouting, "SHOW ME THE MONEY"?

Of course not, right? The woman in this video, around the two-minute mark (2:00), challenges us to say to our elected officials SHOW US THE MONEY in the Social Security trust fund, and then goes on to say, "They can't show us anything, because the trust funds are empty." What? Whoa. Let's consider this.

Do you have money? I assume you do. You bought this book because you're an adult interested in financial matters. If you are going to invest time and effort (and a few bucks) into this book, you probably have some money you'd like to manage.

If I turn to you and say, "Show me the money"—how will you do that? Are you going to pull out a pile of cash and say, "Here you go, Renée. Here's my money." I doubt it. Most of us don't have our cash tucked in our freezer. It would not be wise or prudent to do that.

You would likely show me your bank and investment account statements. The same holds for the Social Security trust fund. They publish an overview of the balance sheet (search "social security trust fund balance"). All historical information regarding Social Security can also be found at ssa.gov.

When I showed this resource to people in class, some said, "Why don't they tell us that?"

I can't answer that question. I wish our elected officials would do a better job of educating us, but typically, when participants ask that question, I have a question for them: "Would you be attending this class if it weren't required for your license to do so?" Many answer, "No." Therein lies part of the problem—we prefer sound bites of information instead of learning the whole story.

Let's go back to keeping cash in the freezer because, believe it or not, it's a critical point. You can't show your money to people who ask to see it because you do not keep all your money in your house.

Why is that? Besides the risk of theft, why don't you keep money in your freezer? Because you want "FREE pennies," right? We know what will happen if we have cash sitting around. It will deflate. We invest somewhere, so the value increases. Remember all that doubling every ten years? If we have it sitting around in our freezer instead, we miss out on the growth opportunity and do not have a hedge for inflation. As the cost of goods and services increases, the money in our freezer buys less and less—it loses value.

The same holds for the money in the trust fund. If they just let it sit there, it will deflate. Plus, we might like to see its value double in ten years, right? The same principles that apply to us regarding why we save and invest are also applicable to why the U.S. government would want the money in the trust fund to grow. It is smart, wise, and prudent to invest in it.

Imagine that the United States turns to the global investment marketplace and says, "We are going to have $2 trillion in this Social Security Trust Fund. Which investment firms want it?" How many of you reading this feel a sense of panic and dread when you think of that? This is a scary vetting process—so much risk for corruption. Consider this further: $2 trillion is market-moving money. If the government were to invest this in the standard markets, the value of the selected assets would increase (for now), and other investments would suffer. Not only is this a daunting proposition, but it is also unfair to the global markets.

Instead, they chose to invest it in U.S. government bonds. This isn't some conspiracy—it is part of the plan. Granted, it isn't a perfect solution—investment strategies are never ideal—but it is the better option compared to these other alternatives.

The 2015 shortfall date she mentions in the video has now passed. I wrote this book in 2024, and nothing had fallen apart. If you looked up the "Social Security trust fund balance," as suggested earlier, you could see that the fund's proceeds are being used to pay income recipients as planned for these shortfall years. Nothing has fallen apart, it didn't break. She is right—in 2035, the reserves will be gone, and if we don't take corrective measures before then, seniors will receive a percentage of their original benefits.

However, we can fix that as well. Just like they took corrective measures in the early 1980s to plan for this trust fund, we can also resolve the shortfall in the future. This is why it matters that we have informed voters. I do not want the next generation to go through another benefit cut. There is no need for that. We can address the funding deficiencies by adjusting the taxes slightly.

IT IS POSSIBLE

"Sometimes, it takes a while to recognize that someone has a special ability to make us believe in ourselves, tie that belief to our highest ideals, and imagine that together, we can do great things." —Caroline Kennedy

In the presidential debate of June 2024, Biden said, "The rich pay on average 8 percent tax. If we get them paying closer to 20 percent, we can balance the budget, pay down the debt, and secure social security." He also said, "The lowest wage earners pay the most Social Security. Those at the top don't pay the tax on all wages. That's not fair. If we correct that, we no longer have a funding problem."

Both quotes are paraphrased—he also discussed reducing the national debt, funding childcare, improving education, and more by increasing the tax rate for the wealthy. In the next section, we'll talk about historic tax rates on the rich, and the information will likely surprise you. In 2024, during a heated election, not everyone believes that Joe Biden did a good job; however, in my opinion, he will go down in history as one of the best American presidents. He had many good ideas for the American people, and he was able to get much of that legislation passed.

I know that Joe's ideas would have benefited millions of Americans. There was still more work to be done, but we would have benefited from those changes for years to come. Now that Trump was elected, it appears Republicans are working to roll all of that back and do real damage to Americans' security.

Joe Biden is very much like Franklin D. Roosevelt (FDR), a beloved president elected four times who is touted as having saved the country from the Great Depression and put it on a trajectory for the most prosperous times for the middle class in U.S. history.

You might wonder, "If Biden is like FDR, why don't people see the good things Joe has done?" I believe the problem is two-fold and intertwined:

1. Most people do not take the time to know what is happening in government, the economy, and the world. FDR had fireside chats, and everyone tuned in around their radio.
2. Today, people listen to sound bites. We are not always getting information from the source, and the content is easy to manipulate. Too much of it is misinformation, and some of it is outright lies.

In his book, *"Beyond the Big Lie,"* Bill Adair tells us what we need right on the cover: "The epidemic of political lying, why Republicans do it more, and how it could burn down our democracy." Adair claims that he noticed an uptick in Republican lies early in the 2000s, but it hit untold proportions when Trump entered the scene.

The New York Times had an article that fact-checked Trump and Harris's campaign speeches on the same random day in the fall of 2024. Here's the breakdown:

More than one falsehood every minute—In an hour and 3-minute speech, Mr. Trump made 64 statements that were either false, inaccurate, or lacking context.

One-tenth the lies—In her 23-minute speech, Ms. Harris made six statements that were false, inaccurate, or lacking context.

While both sides lie and posture, there is a fundamental difference in where you will find more truth. There are people in the Republican party who are of moral integrity, and the more truthful crew might be deemed classic Republicans versus the MAGA (Make America Great Again) Trump-following variety. Many of these classic Republicans endorsed Harris for the 2024 election because they saw Donald Trump and the MAGA tribe as a risk to our democracy, especially in view of the events of January 6th and the agenda in Project 2025.

Remember, I saw and can still see value in a conservative approach to government. Not exclusively—many policies on the left will enrich the lives of Americans. We cannot wear binary glasses here—no political side is ALL GOOD or ALL BAD. Depending on personal preferences, each side of the ticket and each candidate will have good and bad qualities. I am not trying to tell you that all Republicans and their ideas are horrible, while everything Democratic is excellent. Or that every utterance from MAGA proponents is a lie, and the Democrats are always truthful. The world is not exclusively dualistic, and that is not my perspective.

Like everything else in this book, I am offering you facts and perspectives so you can make better decisions that will improve your life and the lives of your family, friends, community, business, employer, and, honestly, everyone in the world. These choices matter. Everyone and everything is affected by our political decisions. Your vote has paramount consequences.

Just as a fair financial exchange requires truth and full disclosure, a fair voting system depends on an informed electorate. When people are misled, they cast votes based on promises they believe are real but often are not. That is not a fair exchange—it is deception.

I considered listing examples, but the pattern is well established: Donald Trump has repeatedly made claims that are false or misleading, and those claims have shaped how millions of people understand reality. This is not occasional—it is persistent. It is tempting to assume that once he is gone, things will improve. I am not convinced. Others are watching, learning what works, and refining it. The next version may be more disciplined, more polished, and far harder to recognize.

If you are getting your news primarily from right-leaning outlets, you may need to step outside that ecosystem and compare sources to fully understand the story. Take the 2020 election as an example: Donald Trump repeatedly claimed he won, despite a lack of evidence to support that conclusion. That claim became widely known as the "Big Lie," a term popularized by Bill Adair.

Some media outlets amplified those claims. In the case of Fox News, internal communications later revealed that certain hosts and executives privately questioned the accuracy of what was being broadcast. Lawsuits brought by companies such as Dominion Voting Systems and Smartmatic led to major legal and financial consequences, including a substantial settlement.

The broader issue is this: when misinformation is repeated often enough, it shapes perception. That is why it is critical for all of us to examine multiple sources, question what we hear, and verify claims before accepting them as fact. Without that effort, it becomes far too easy for false narratives to take hold—even on major issues like elections or an administration's performance.

POLITICS OF COMPASSION

"The focus of a politics of compassion is the alleviation of suffering caused by social structures." —Marcus J. Borg, The GOD We Never Knew

Compassion and empathy are part of the solution to finding truth. Let's look back to the Social Security video. Around 2:56, she says, "They don't really care about any of us." "They" in this statement are our elected officials.

Do you think that is true? Do you believe none of the elected officials care about us?

I hope not, because there is no hope if no one cares. I think there are people in government who do care about us. I tell the group in our classes, "It's clear some of them care. Look at Bernie Sanders. You might not agree with him or think he's a little nutty, but he cares. It is evident in every impassioned speech he makes." No one has yet disagreed. He also isn't on a 'team'—he doesn't vote with the crowd, and will vote against them if he believes a "yes" vote will not benefit hardworking American people.

Bernie knows what side he's on and will take risks to protect his ideals. That's integrity. Do you know who else has done that? Liz Cheney, Adam Kinzinger, Mitt Romney, Mike Pence, and a whole list of Republicans who risked their political careers and lives to stand up for their principles and the good of the American people. Rand Paul, Kentucky Senator, as another example, has some convictions I personally disagree with, but he believes he is doing good by his constituents, and will not be swayed by the Trump fever. He is boldly speaking out against the lawlessness. His risk-taking and decision to stand by his convictions indicate to me that he cares. Some are more consistently committed than others, but the United States and the world would be very different without the valor of those who care about people, the rule of law, and morality in times of consequence.

In 2020, when it was decided that Joe Biden would be the Democrats' nominee for president, I was disappointed. Among all the potential contenders, he was close to my least favorite, but even then, I remember thinking, "At least he seems like he genuinely cares." Joe continued to prove that to me. The night before the inauguration, I was brought to tears when our newly elected president and vice president stood at the Lincoln Memorial Reflecting Pool with 400 candles representing the 400,000 Americans who died of COVID-19. Finally, we had a president who could honor the pain and fear that our nation felt, and I knew we were in good hands. The legislation he passed and the vision for his presidency was an outcropping of his care and compassion for the American people and the world. We need to elect more people like that—lots more of them.

SSA.GOV

"People like Bernie Sanders and Alexandria Ocasio-Cortez have been very busy educating America about just how much socialism we have, from Social Security to Medicare to public schools to public universities, and how much we love that. The truth is that there is no pure socialist or capitalist economy on earth."

—Lawrence O'Donnell

Before moving on from Social Security to other government and macroeconomic topics, it's worth highlighting a valuable retirement planning resource: "My Social Security" at Social Security Administration (ssa.gov). You can use this tool to verify the accuracy of your income history and determine your future benefits.

It has been a while since I created my account, but I remember it required unique validations to establish your sign-in, like answering credit questions only you should be able to answer. For example, you got a mortgage in 2022—which of the following is your lender? You are then provided with multiple choices. You will likely have to correctly answer a few questions like this before you are granted access to your account.

Once logged in, you can verify that your earnings have been correctly reported and what your projected retirement benefits will be. It will show you an income amount if you start collecting at age 62, full benefit age (age 67 for most of us), and the benefit if we wait until age 70. The projection assumes we will earn the same amount until retirement, but the calculator allows us to change any variables.

To illustrate, you can see your benefit if you started collecting at age 65 instead of 62 or 67, or if you partially retired and worked part-time. A couple of things to note: Your benefit amount is based on your 35 highest earning years, which are indexed for inflation. This is important because if you have 50 reported years of earnings (age 16 to 66), the 15 lower-earning ones (for instance, through high school and college) do not impact your benefit. This also means that if you would like to explore a lower-paying job for a season of your life, this, too, would have little impact.

The benefits listed in the calculator will increase over time for two primary reasons. One is that income typically increases over earning years. Of course, this is not universal; some may see declines, but most see increased earnings through many pay periods. The second reason is COLA—Cost of Living Adjustments. I will better define COLA later in this chapter, but your Social Security benefits will receive annual inflation increases. This happens most years when we collect our benefits, but these inflation allotments are also applied to our projected benefits. This is why checking this resource routinely as you plan your retirement strategy is valuable.

One must work forty quarters (or ten years) to qualify. This dispels another myth that immigrants collect Social Security. First, they must work for at least ten years to qualify, and it's not prorated. If I work 38 quarters, I'm not collecting.

To qualify for any government benefits, one must have proper documentation. Because of the forty-quarter and documentation rules, it is far more likely that non-citizens will pay into the system and never collect benefits.

TAXES = THE DONUT ≠ THE HOLE

"We don't pay taxes. Only the little people pay taxes." —Leona Helmsley

We could address a significant portion of the wealth disparity and budget constraints in programs like Social Security through better equity in the tax system. The U.S. tax system is disproportionately unfair to middle-income earners and too favorable to those at the top. Don't get nervous. When I say "top," I mean those making an annual income of $24 million or more. I don't mean to be presumptive, but if you are reading this book, chances are you are not quite in that category (yet).

Did you know?

- The U.S. income tax system has only existed for a little more than 100 years. The 16th Amendment, ratified in 1913, allowed the U.S. government to tax the people.
- In 1913, the highest personal marginal income tax rate was 7 percent. Today, it's 37 percent (2026). However, it was at 70 percent or above for nearly 50 years of the last century (approximately 1935 through 1981).
- During the most prosperous time for middle America, the 1950s, the highest federal tax rate was over 90 percent. Yes, you read that right—**90 percent.**
- The extra taxes that were collected were invested back into America through education, housing, business loans, healthcare, and infrastructure. This investment propelled the U.S. strength for decades.

- There were two periods when we dramatically reduced the tax burden on the rich—the 1920s and the 1980s. During these eras, the wealth gap between the poor, middle America, and the rich grew wider.

Have you ever heard, "If you tax the rich, it will slow the economy?" Or the reverse of that, "If you reduce the tax burden on the rich, they'll invest, and it will trickle down." Our economic history tells us that those theories are not true. What seems to work better is redistributing wealth by taxing the rich and investing in what most Americans need—roads, bridges, internet, renewable energy, education, healthcare, childcare, etc. This is precisely what FDR did to pull us out of the Great Depression. The Infrastructure Act under Biden, which had bipartisan support, incorporated the same idea.

It is the American worker who keeps this economy healthy and thriving—people like you and me, and millions of others, including immigrants, both documented and undocumented. From a purely economic standpoint, offering a path to citizenship for those working without a criminal record would likely strengthen the system and reduce inefficiencies. Yet much of what has occurred over the past several decades has not been driven by what best supports the economy or the prosperity of the average American.

It's the "US" in the U.S.—it's the people who are working hard, trying to do the right thing, taking care of our families, and having to figure out ways to spend less so we can save. It's all the spending we do that keeps the economy humming. Without us and our pretty little pennies, the people at the top will cease to generate wealth.

The people at the top have the opposite problem. Their wealth is growing so fast that they cannot find a way to spend it all. So, it sits there. They aren't making jobs for us. They didn't decide to share more with us by offering higher wages, employee tuition programs, lifetime pensions, or universal healthcare. Nope, most just kept taking more of it, and now that Trump is reelected, they are continuing with massive tax cuts to the rich and cutting more benefits from the middle class.

I shared some of these ideas in a class lately—about imposing higher tax rates on the rich—and one person said, "Then they'll leave." This means the rich would leave the United States to escape the tax. I haven't thoroughly thought that through, but at first, my reaction was, "Oh no, that wouldn't be good." Today, as I type, my feeling is "Good riddance, and don't let the door hit you on the way out."

If a person in the elite class fails to recognize that the policies, infrastructure, resources, and people of the U.S. have contributed to their wealth and refuses to share, do we need them here? Right now, I think not. The wealthy are using their power to create policies that benefit them, to the detriment of most Americans. It certainly isn't a true democracy, or a representative republic, if all our voices aren't equal.

With today's political climate, I wonder where they'd go. Living in Mexico, I see firsthand how things are different in other countries. I'm not sure if other places will offer them the same benefits they've received in the U.S. Some areas of the world already have lower tax rates than the U.S., yet I don't see a mass exodus of wealthy Americans to those areas.

Please bear in mind that the rich, just like any group of people, are not monolithic. Some people with great wealth are doing amazing things to help people, like MacKenzie Scott, Jeff Bezos's ex-wife and co-founder of Amazon.

When they divorced, she pledged to give most of her wealth away. Her giving to date exceeds the multi-billions, and the motto of her philanthropic website, Yield Giving, is: "Yield is named after a belief in adding value by giving up control." That, indeed, is letting the Flow take care of it. Some wealthy individuals advocate for higher taxes because they have firsthand experience that the current system could be improved. They realize we are all in this together, and when we benefit the masses, we all benefit. I think we can use more of that kind of thinking.

PROUD TAXPAYER

"I'm proud to pay taxes; the only thing is, I could be just as proud for half the money." —Arthur Godfrey

If you are paying taxes, that's not a bad thing. I know that's an unpopular sentiment, but paying taxes means you are making money. That's good. If we reduce our tax burden, we keep more pennies, and thankfully, there are some tax benefits in the realm of savings. If used strategically, we gain advantages when we put our pennies into tax-qualified accounts. Below, you'll find a short list of standard tax benefits and some of the typical account types that offer them.

Tax Adjustments—In this category, you'll find Health Savings Accounts (HSA) (if we contribute outside of an employer-sponsored plan) and Individual Retirement Arrangements (IRAs). Most people would refer to these two accounts as "Tax Deductible," but technically, these are reported on Part II of Schedule 1 on one's 1040 tax return. That might be too many details, but what it means is it further reduces one's AGI—Adjusted Gross Income—and if you ever noticed, it's this number that usually gets us in or out of certain benefits. An "Adjustment" acts like a tax deduction; it's just better.

Tax Credits—A deduction or adjustment is good, but a credit is better. Tax deductions and adjustments reduce taxable income and save us taxes based on our bracket, but a tax credit is a dollar-for-dollar reduction of our tax liability. It comes right off our tax bill. Typically, a tax credit is not associated with a specific kind of savings account but is offered to particular investments; this will be covered in the next chapter.

Tax Deferred—This means we pay no immediate tax on our earnings—taxes are "deferred" for a later date. Because of this feature, the value compounds faster. Many tax-qualified accounts offer deferral; it's impossible to name them all, but below is a basic list.

All IRAs and HSAs are tax-deferred, as are other common retirement savings accounts, including 401(k), 403b, Simplified Employee Pension (SEP), and Savings Incentive Match Plan for Employees (SIMPLE). Accounts designed to save for education expenses, such as a Section 529 or an Educational Savings Account (ESA), also qualify for tax-deferred growth. We also find the cash value in a life insurance contract and annuities in this category. We'll discuss these further in the insurance section, "Protecting Your Pennies."

Tax Free—This one is rare. If we're making money, we pay taxes, but some "qualified" exceptions exist. I call out "qualified" because there are special rules or other benefits we give up to "qualify."

One is a Roth IRA. With a Roth IRA, one sacrifices the tax adjustment on contributions to the account—the contribution is taxable. However, the earnings accumulate on an income tax-deferred basis, and when we take them out for retirement (provided we have had the account for five years), they come out tax-free. Disability, death, and first-time homebuyers are also qualifiers for tax-free distributions.

When I say tax-free, I mean it. IRS Publication 590 for IRAs defines these qualified Roth distributions as "You don't include in gross income..." This means it does not even go on one's tax return. Because of the Secure Act of 2022, any of the retirement accounts listed above--401(k), 403b, SEP, SIMPLE—can have a Roth component added. Since these accounts allow for more significant contribution limits, this means more money for tax-free distributions later.

Another example I can think of is distributions from an HSA for Qualified Medical expenses. These are defined in IRS Publication 502 and are the same as an FSA (Flexible Spending Account—discussed below). With an HSA, we pay no tax on contributions due to the adjustment or salary reduction. It accumulates tax-deferred, and if we take it out for medical expenses, it is tax-free.

Salary Reduction—An employee's salary reduction means that money is automatically deducted from an employee's paycheck. It's considered a voluntary reduction, and since it does not go through standard payroll, the employee pays no tax. If any accounts listed above are offered through an employer-sponsored program, they qualify under salary reduction and are usually not adjusted for on one's tax return.

This is where the FSA comes in. It is also known as Section 125 because that's where it's found in the IRS code. Employers offer these to employees for childcare and medical expenses. These accounts do not provide the other tax benefits discussed above. FSAs do not earn interest, and the participant can use the proceeds for the qualified expenses or lose them.

Other rules can impact all these qualified accounts, including contribution limits, early withdrawal penalties, and qualified expenses. Since those rules can change over time, I will leave it to you to research them.

IMPORTANT NOTE: This list refers to income taxes. There are different laws for capital gain and estate taxes. Taxes in your state will vary, too. For this book, we won't dive into that right now. Those topics work better once you've accumulated many much-needed pennies. Before we wrap up this section on government policies and programs, it is important to discuss two economic factors that have an impact on your pennies: Inflation and Interest Rates.

INFLATION & INTEREST RATES

"It is a way to take people's wealth from them without having to openly raise taxes. Inflation is the most universal tax of all." —Thomas Sowell

Some people believe that the U.S. Federal government controls interest rates and inflation. If we look at this in a roundabout way, I guess you could say that, but it isn't accurate.

No one and no entity controls inflation. If that were possible, we might do away with it, but we can't. It's like consumer confidence--it's always there in varying degrees, but no one can control how confident people are about their economic future. When I wrote this section in the fall of 2024, the U.S. had record-low unemployment, wages were rising, the stock market was breaking record highs, and our inflation trends were lower than most other nations—we were the envy of the post-pandemic world, according to "The Economist" in their October 2024 article.

Yet, Americans still said they were worried about the economy.

There are levers we can pull, buttons we can push, and facts we can share, but in the end, no one controls any of it, especially with an economy as large as the U.S.. It takes some mighty big buttons and levers to move it in any direction.

The Federal Reserve controls some of those buttons and levers—namely, interest rates and the money supply—to stave off inflation and recessions. They aim to keep the economy humming so we are all happy campers. However, the Federal Reserve is not an agency of the U.S. government like the IRS or the Social Security Administration.

The Federal Reserve System, or "the Fed," is not owned by anyone nor is it a private, profit-making institution. Instead, it's an independent entity within the U.S. government, deriving its authority from Congress. The Fed comprises a central governing board, the Board of Governors, and 12 Reserve Banks operating in different geographic areas.

The president appoints the Fed Chair for a four-year term with congressional approval. You've probably noticed that sometimes the Fed Chair is around for more than four years and serves under different presidents. Like the Supreme Court, the position is not supposed to be impacted by elections or popularity.

HISTORICAL CONFIDENCE

"The best argument against democracy is a five-minute conversation with the average voter." —Winston S. Churchill

To offer a bit of perspective, I will start this at the beginning of the Federal Reserve. I think it's the best way to understand what the Fed does, its value to the economy, and how economic trends come and go—and illustrate how many of these trends have been far worse than the U.S. economy's performance during and post-COVID. Pennies and perspective are fundamental to a fearless financial plan.

At the turn of the last century, from 1890 to about 1910, there was much volatility in the markets—and I do mean 'markets.' There was a railroad bubble that burst in the 1890s. Banking was crazy—there was no centralized monetary system. Money transfers between people and entities were cumbersome and took many days. We were becoming industrialized, but our systems did not support this growing economy. This problem had been going on throughout the 1800s, but it accelerated because of voluminous economic growth.

In 1907, another panic caused a run on the banks—there had been many over the years. At this time, there was no FDIC (Federal Deposit Insurance Corporation) to protect certain deposit limits. Excessive speculative investment, driven by loose monetary policy, wreaked havoc again. Wealthy tycoons of the day, like J.P. Morgan and John D. Rockefeller, came in to shore up the banks. Yes, this meant these wealthy men made a personal investment to bail out the banks. This sparked a discussion about the need for a central bank.

In November of 1910, six men —Nelson Aldrich, A. Piatt Andrew, Henry Davison, Arthur Shelton, Frank Vanderlip, and Paul Warburg—met at the Jekyll Island Club off the coast of Georgia. They wrote a plan to reform the nation's banking system. The meeting and its purpose were closely guarded secrets, and participants did not admit that the meeting occurred until the 1930s. However, the plan written on Jekyll Island laid a foundation for what would eventually be the Federal Reserve System, which was established in 1913.

This meeting was secret, not because it was nefarious, but because people then, like today, were afraid of change and of things they didn't understand. I felt the same about the Affordable Care Act (ACA)—granted, it is not a perfect piece of legislation. It has needed some tweaking to improve coverage and healthcare access in the U.S., but I was concerned when it first came out. It was costly to implement, but now, I see the benefit and wish they would expand it. Some people today still see something wrong with the ACA, and they want it to be repealed. In Trump's One Big Beautiful Bill Act (acronyms OB3; OBBBA; OBBB; BBB), Republicans voted to reduce the tax subsidies, essentially defunding the ACA in hopes of eliminating it. Many of those same people do not like the Federal Reserve either. This stems from the same place as the misleading information about Social Security—people are not getting the facts to make informed decisions. Instead, they are being told and believing stories that hype fear and stir the pot of discontent.

For the vast majority of situations, the Fed has taken numerous steps to help the economy using monetary policy. Is the system perfect? No. Like ACA and Social Security, there are things we can improve and others we should change, but thankfully, their maneuvers have helped the economy in many instances. Let's examine two key lessons learned by the Fed.

STRIVING FOR GREATNESS

"In preparing for battle, I have always found that plans are useless, but planning is indispensable." —Dwight D. Eisenhower

The Great Depression: Many looked to the stock market crash in 1929 as the beginning of the Great Depression, but it actually started much earlier or later, depending on one's perspective. The Fed's monetary policy of the day had much to do with the stock market crash. Not intentionally—they were new at this and a little giddy when they first started up, so they put lending rates low. This meant a ton of cash flowed into all parts of the marketplace.

Have you heard the phrase "roaring 20s"? Much of this prosperity was generated by this flow of money. In the early days of the Fed, investment oversight was also minimal, allowing for high leverage or margining of stock accounts. To explain a margin account, let's say you had $100 to invest. The firm would lend you the other $900. You have $1,000 invested for your $100. This works out great if the stock goes up and you can pay it back, but it's not so good if the value goes down. You still owe $900 plus interest, regardless of stock performance.

The Fed realized there was too much unbacked money in circulation, so it pulled back the money supply. In the 1930s, the Fed let the banking system collapse. There was tremendous deflation, which contributed to the economy's contraction. The newly formed Fed refused to intervene. Their theory was that the market and the economy would correct themselves. This theory was wrong. They learned that their role is to assist, and this is why when the 2008 crisis started to happen, the Fed poured over a trillion dollars into the money supply to fight off this same problem.

The Banking Acts of 1933 and 1935 changed the balance of power within the Federal Reserve System in favor of the Board of Governors, especially concerning monetary policy. The Acts made clear the Board's power to set the discount rate and gave the Board a majority of votes on the Federal Open Market Committee, including the chairmanship of the Committee. The legislation also gave the Board new authority to set reserve requirements for banks and margin requirements on loans to purchase securities. Similar forms of legislation for the newly created Securities and Exchange Commission (SEC) were made during this same era.

The Great Inflation: In 1964, inflation measured slightly more than 1 percent yearly and had been in this vicinity for six years. Inflation began ratcheting upward steadily in the mid-1960s and, by 1980, reached more than 14 percent. The 1970s were known as The Great Inflation, which had a significant impact on Carter's presidency. Unlike most recent inflation, the Fed didn't want to step in and raise interest rates at the time. Rising interest rates are not popular, but neither is inflation.

Since the existing Fed chair was in place from Ford, in 1979, Carter nominated Paul Volcker for the Fed Chair position. After congressional approval, Volcker wanted to increase interest rates, but the board would not agree. These hikes are not popular, so Volcker took the brave (and roundabout) method to curb inflation by reducing the money supply. This naturally increased interest rates without an official board vote to accomplish it.

Although people didn't like it, higher interest rates were necessary to curb the inflation trend. Volcker's policy was working, and interest rates were in the 20 percent range by 1981. It had to go this high because the Fed took too long to react. Inflation was at record highs; only record-breaking interest rates would fix it. As you'd imagine, all of this caused a long-lasting recession in the early part of the 1980s.

This wasn't fun, and it wasn't pretty, but it was heroic. If Volcker had not taken these dramatic steps, the U.S. economy could have exploded like others that blew up when inflation ran rampant and people in power did nothing. After all, it's the lower tiers of the economy that are most dramatically impacted by inflation.

Volcker served two terms as Fed Chair until 1987, and once inflation was under control, Reagan accepted his resignation. At least, that was the public story. Volcker knew he would not be reappointed. He did the hard job, and it was time to move on to a new era with Alan Greenspan. Volcker was not popular at the time. However, economic historians today appreciate his willingness to put people and future prosperity before popularity.

YOUR HAPPY PLACE

"Someone is sitting in the shade today because someone planted a tree a long time ago." —Warren Buffett

I tend to be an optimist—or at least I try to focus on what helps me move forward. I still have moments where I wallow, but I don't find it useful to stay there. What helps me regain perspective is context. So let's put the inflation concerns of the 2024 election into historical perspective.

COLA (Cost of Living Adjustment)—We might not have liked the recent COVID-19 inflation, but from the perspective of the 1970s, it was a tiny blip. The SS website COLA adjustment chart is an easy-to-understand guide that I use frequently in our classes. It provides the annual values dating back to 1975, when automatic yearly adjustments were implemented. Before that, it required an act of Congress for SS recipients to get an increase. This chart (and others like it from official websites and vetted sources) provides historical evidence to keep economic trends in proper context.

Social Security Cost-Of-Living Adjustments

Year	COLA	Year	COLA	Year	COLA
1975	8.0	1995	2.6	2015	0.0
1976	6.4	1996	2.9	2016	0.3
1977	5.9	1997	2.1	2017	2.0
1978	6.5	1998	1.3	2018	2.8
1979	9.9	1999 [a]	2.5	2019	1.6
1980	14.3	2000	3.5	2020	1.3
1981	11.2	2001	2.6	2021	5.9
1982	7.4	2002	1.4	2022	8.7
1983	3.5	2003	2.1	2023	3.2
1984	3.5	2004	2.7	2024	2.5
1985	3.1	2005	4.1	2025	2.8
1986	1.3	2006	3.3		
1987	4.2	2007	2.3		
1988	4.0	2008	5.8		
1989	4.7	2009	0.0		
1990	5.4	2010	0.0		
1991	3.7	2011	3.6		
1992	3.0	2012	1.7		
1993	2.6	2013	1.5		
1994	2.8	2014	1.7		

[a] The COLA for December 1999 was originally determined as 2.4 percent based on CPIs published by the Bureau of Labor Statistics. Pursuant to Public Law 106-554, however, this COLA is effectively now 2.5 percent.

(Source: https://www.ssa.gov/OACT/COLA/colaseries.html)

- The highest annual COLA adjustment in recent years was 8.7 percent applied for 2022.
- The next highest value is 5.9 percent which was applied for 2021 inflation.
- 2023 put us on a more reasonable trajectory of 3.2 percent.
- As I edited this section in October 2024, Social Security just updated the new COLA for 2024 at 2.5 percent.

It seems that the Biden administration (and really, the Fed chair, Jerome Powell) brought inflation to reasonable levels in just two years without a recession. I know of no other time in modern history that this feat has been accomplished.

Compare that to the late 1970s and early 1980s. The highest COLA adjustment during those years was 14.3 percent in 1980, but that is not the only double-digit increase—1981 represented an 11.2 percent increase, and 1979 was close to 10 percent, at 9.9 percent, with a deep recession to follow.

It is also important to note that the values are compounded, as in your savings account. If eggs increase by 14 percent in 1980 and then rise by 11 percent the following year, the total increase exceeds 25 percent because 11 percent is applied to the inflation increase from the prior year.

Please also look at the COLA values since the 1990s. Many of these values are in the 2 percent range or less. There are also three zeros in the chart—for 2010, 2011, and 2016—years with no inflation or possibly deflation. Focusing on the last 10 or 15 years, you'll see an even lower average overall. This trend is due to the Fed's focus on keeping inflation in the 2 percent range, rather than the 3 to 4 percent range we had historically.

I don't know about you, but the COLA adjustments don't seem so big when I consider the recent inflation hiccups of 2021 and 2022 in the context of these historical values of the last decade or more. I am also grateful that the Fed reacted when they realized that it was not just a temporary supply chain problem that was driving inflation. As we'll see below, today's interest rates are in the normal range, and, as a result, inflation has been in line with average trends.

Interest Rates—Although the Fed has many levers it can adjust to change interest rates, it does not set the prime interest rate. The prime rate is defined by The Wall Street Journal (WSJ) as "The base rate on corporate loans posted by at least 70 percent of the ten largest U.S. banks." It is not the 'best' rate offered by banks. Any bank can declare its prime rate. Some smaller banks will use a larger bank's prime as a reference for pricing loans, but most use the Wall Street Journal version.

The highest prime rate was 21.5 percent on December 19, 1980. The lowest prime rate since 1975 was 3.25 percent. This occurred on two occasions: December 16, 2008, and March 16, 2020. The historical long-term average of prime rates is 6.84 percent.

Mortgage interest rates are usually a lower percentage and do not always change at the same time as the prime lending rate. In October 1981, mortgage rates reached 18.63 percent. The average 30-year fixed rate reached a record low of 2.65 percent in January 2021. Average rates were then increased to 7.79 percent in October 2023. This is close to the median 30-year mortgage rate of 7.41 percent (1971 to 2024, according to Freddie Mac).

WHY CAN'T THEY SEE IT?

"The only thing worse than being blind is having sight but no vision."
—Helen Keller

If all these points are factual, and they are, why couldn't American voters see that in the 2024 election? I believe the answer to that is complex, but it relates to many of the things we've already talked about. Trump and pundits lied—but we know that. I think his voters even know that. So, why didn't those who lived through the '70s and '80s do or say something to educate people in their circle?

I have no idea. I would be teaching classes, and until I brought it up, it was as if most people had no recall of these events. There's an advantage in dealing with these numbers and this information all the time—I can't ignore it. But I think the problem is much deeper than forgetting the past.

We can easily get trapped in the negative. Clickbait is the headline that shocks the most, and "Inflation is Back to Normal" is not going to be viral anytime soon. A feeding frenzy can begin, wanting to gobble up the negative, so the shock stories flow.

This is where being willing to learn, consider, research, and take the time to find balance is so critical. Clickbait is often fear-driven, so it's vital to step back and assess. I do not know how we can recreate that with more people, but maybe that puts greater responsibility on those of us who do have some perspective to be willing to share the vision.

HOPEFUL PERSPECTIVE

"Life is about perspective and how you look at something... ultimately, you have to zoom out." —*Whitney Wolfe Herd*

That's a lot of numbers and stuff. I could give you more, and I thought about doing it. I considered adding information about median income for each decade compared to average home prices, and then I thought, "The interest rate matters when calculating the payment." That is the real affordability test. I should calculate that. Then, I thought of taxes and insurance. I could have built you some complex charts and graphs. Sounds fun, doesn't it? (Insert tongue in cheek.)

If I did, the real point would be lost in the numbers. The whole reason we went through any of this was to gain perspective. My intent was for you to find hope and possibility in that perspective. To feel empowered for your financial future. Instead of more numbers, I'll share a personal story of a young man who found some hope in this historical perspective.

My son was researching to prepare to buy his first home. Like many Millennials, he was discouraged by current interest rates and home prices. While discussing it, I asked, "What are interest rates right now?" This was sometime in 2023, and I knew rates were rising, but I had not been following them.

He told me some rate—I can't recall, but I remember my thought and response, "Oh, that's pretty normal." His response equaled my same level of surprise, "What? These interest rates are normal?"

At that moment, I realized all the stuff we old folks know that is valuable to young people; financial education about what to do with today's pennies is equally essential to understanding it from a historical perspective. My reply to him was, "Yes, there was a time I thought a 7 percent mortgage rate was like gold."

I told him everything we've discussed on various pages in the book, including that my first mortgage was 10 percent, which I thought was reasonable considering what happened in the 1980s. I also told him how often I refinanced for lower rates, closing costs, and other things we discussed in earlier chapters about debt management.

I remember saying, "Those 2 percent interest rates are not the norm. I don't know if we'll ever see them again." I don't know if we want to see those near-zero rates on the macroeconomic level. On a personal level, that's wonderful, but low interest rates are offered to get money moving in the economy. This happened because things slowed down to a near standstill during the pandemic. Ultimately, we don't want that again. The outcome could have been far worse than what we experienced.

His expectations fit his experience, which was in a low-interest-rate environment. When our expectations meet the historical perspective of the boom and bust and an ever-changing market that is sometimes up and sometimes down, forces are working to correct it and offer an improvement, and we start to see hope. Hope is one of the most impactful things in any economy. That is consumer confidence, and our choices based on that confidence are the ultimate driving force.

This isn't to say that there aren't many challenges facing young people today, because there are—and I do not intend to minimize those challenges with the following statement,

"Every generation has had its financial challenges. They've all had their BUST!"

I wanted to put the current economic situation into perspective by illustrating past bust markets in the graphs and charts I considered creating. However, that's like putting together a chart of historical weather patterns to say, "It's okay if it rains today. We'll get through it." All we need to know is that we will get through it.

Part of the Hope for future financial blue skies comes from who is at the helm and from the crew's temperament. Consumer confidence might be the engine, but this ship will not ultimately reach its destination if we do not have a captain and a crew with the experience, knowledge, and fortitude to get us there, who make it their priority to help the people instead of to help themselves. This is why we need to add another point to the list of actions for financial success: "Vote Wisely and Always Vote."

Keep doing these basic things, and as time goes on, you'll achieve financial success:

- **Reduce Expenses and Purchase Wisely**
- **Consistently Manage Debt for Successful Outcomes**
- **Save as Much as Possible as Often as You Can**
- **Continue to Expand Your Education and Rely on Facts**
- **Vote Wisely and Always Vote**

CHAPTER ELEVEN

MORE FREE PENNIES

ASSETS AND ALLOCATION

"An investment in knowledge pays the best interest."
—Benjamin Franklin

THE PERFECT INVESTMENT

What if you could create the PERFECT INVESTMENT? No limits—this imaginary investment can offer **absolutely EVERYTHING** you'd want, all in one package. It's "perfect."

Most folks start with HIGH RETURNS. Absolutely—we want "high returns"—a fabulous place to start. We love these "high returns"—so much, we always want to have them. Let's make them GUARANTEED. So, we've got "guaranteed high returns," which also means our principal, the initial contribution, is also "guaranteed" because we have NO LOSSES. **PERFECT!**

This looks good, but we are not done yet. Nope—what good is all of this if we cannot access our money whenever we wish to without penalty? We need LIQUIDITY—penalty-free withdrawals anytime —and tax benefits on these withdrawals. How about we get a tax deduction, tax-deferred growth, and tax-free withdrawals? This makes our PERFECT INVESTMENT, with no tax at any level. It's **PERFECT**!

Sounds great. If this product existed, there would be no need to even continue with this chapter. We'd all put all our money into it, and away we would go. As much as we'd like this investment to exist, it does not. We all know that. We encounter risk-reward balances as we try to achieve this perfection, but the concept of a **PERFECT INVESTMENT** drives Asset Allocation. We create an investment portfolio comprising products and investments that offer components of these individual benefits. When these individual investment products come together, the sum comes close to the Perfect Investment.

THE EFFICIENT MARKET THEORY

"Don't look for the needle in the haystack. Just buy the haystack!"
—John Bogle

Some investment strategies are actively managed. In an actively managed investment, one routinely seeks opportunities to buy low and sell high. In this strategy, assets are traded more frequently in an attempt to capitalize on potential growth when it exists. This process isn't perfect, and there are costs associated with this type of trading.

Some have found success with this strategy. Berkshire Hathaway Inc. (Berkshire) is a publicly traded holding company and conglomerate based in Omaha, Nebraska. It's known for acquiring and managing businesses across multiple industries, including insurance, rail transportation, energy, manufacturing, and retailing. Berkshire Hathaway has historically outperformed the broader market by about eight percentage points annually. Since Warren Buffett took over in 1965, Berkshire Hathaway's annual compound return has been 19.8 percent, compared to 10.2 percent for the S&P 500.

This sort of outcome is rare. Although the goal is to buy low and sell high, it isn't easy. For most of us, our instinct is the opposite: To sell low out of fear that the value will continue to fall and then buy high after the time to capitalize has passed. Even seasoned money managers cannot get this right consistently because most managed funds do not beat the S&P 500. If this sort of timing were easy, it stands to reason many more of us would be multi-millionaires.

Many economists explain this difficulty using the "Efficient Market Theory." A simple way to consider it is:

> The stock market is an open market, meaning both buyers and sellers are willing to trade at the same price. Both entities involved in this transaction have equal access to the same information, and communication systems in each marketplace have very few secrets. Secrets and unknown information create actual opportunities for gains or losses. As a result, it's nearly impossible to buy low/sell high consistently. Investing in the market as a whole and holding might make more sense. This strategy should generate long-term gains because, historically, the market has increased over time.

This is also why John Bogle says, "Just buy the haystack." Instead of trying to pick stocks (finding the needle), buy a bunch of stocks instead. Hence, Jack Bogle is a fan of buying index funds. In addition to having lower fees, we are purchasing a bundle of predetermined stocks that meet specific criteria.

Although we've discussed the S&P 500, there are also several other well-known (and not-so-well-known) U.S. indices, as well as those that comprise foreign stocks. Don't get too overwhelmed—even as we consider index funds, there are many options. If you go the index-investing route, start with the S&P 500 and branch out from there. As time passes, the Flow will help you add the investments that suit you best. The two resources below offer additional information:

https://www.fool.com/investing/stock-market/indexes/
https://www.investing.com/indices/major-indices

THE INVESTMENT CHA-CHA

"Wide diversification is only required when investors do not understand what they are doing." —Warren Buffett

I am reluctant even to discuss some of these additional investment concepts. You will make money if you consistently save, put it in the S&P 500, and don't touch it. Maybe not the first day, month, or year, but your portfolio will grow if you do those three things and don't stop. It's that simple.

There is no need to discuss some of the complexities of portfolio building. Please do study it if you are passionate about learning more and want to dive deeper. A gentleman I met here in Mexico, who spent his career in mechanical engineering but is now retired, wakes early to start day trading as soon as the markets open. He consumes a great deal of literature on financial matters and surrounds himself with like-minded people to share ideas. I am grateful to be one of the people with whom he exchanges information.

It won't surprise you that he retired early. He's so passionate about these financial matters that he learns and trades daily, as if it were his job. If you are like that, fabulous. You will likely build an enormous portfolio. Maybe you'll also help a great many people build wealth. It is a blessing if that is your passion, but it is not a requirement for a secure financial future. Having spent my career in money matters, I am not interested in learning the nuances of individual stocks, options, and other means to take advantage of market trends. I am more of a generalist and lean into bigger-picture ideas around finance.

You can have a very successful financial future without perfecting your asset allocation mix or even considering this section on correlation. I offer this only to introduce the concept or, if you are already familiar with the theory, reinforce it so you can determine whether you want to incorporate assets with various *correlation coefficients* into your portfolio. A correlation coefficient is a numerical measure of linear correlation —the statistical relationship between two variables —and is not nearly as complex as it sounds.

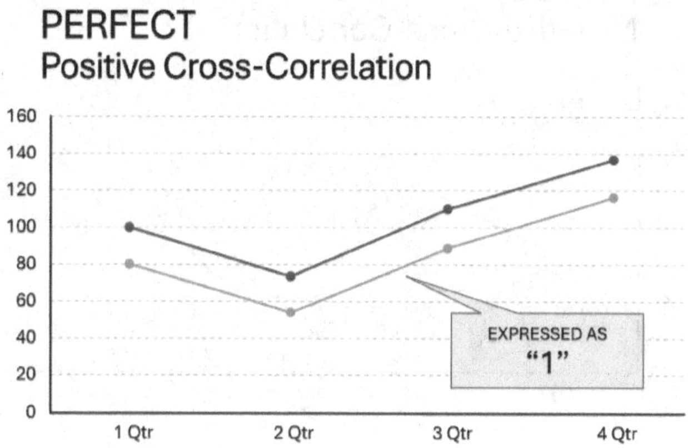

When comparing two investments, some assets offer a "Positive Correlation." The graph above shows a 100 percent positive correlation, and no two investments showa 100 percent positive correlation. Some investments have more positive cross-correlations than others. If you look at the graph, the investment represented by the black line (the top line) decreases as the grey line decreases. As the investment represented by the grey line (the bottom line) increases, the black investment increases as well. This graph reflects a "Positive Cross-Correlation."

Only the same asset would ever be represented by "1" in a correlation test, which reflects a 100 percent positive correlation—the graph above represents a "1." Both lines increase and decrease by the same measure, but we see a positive correlation in the market. For example, when the stock market reopened after September 11th, two sectors were hardest hit by losses: Airlines and Insurance Companies. All airline stock values did not drop by the same margin or percentage—that would be a 100 percent positive correlation—but all of them did fall. That is a positive correlation. On the same day in the stock market, other stocks performed well—for example, Security and Cell Phone Companies—which brings us to our next concept: Negative Correlation.

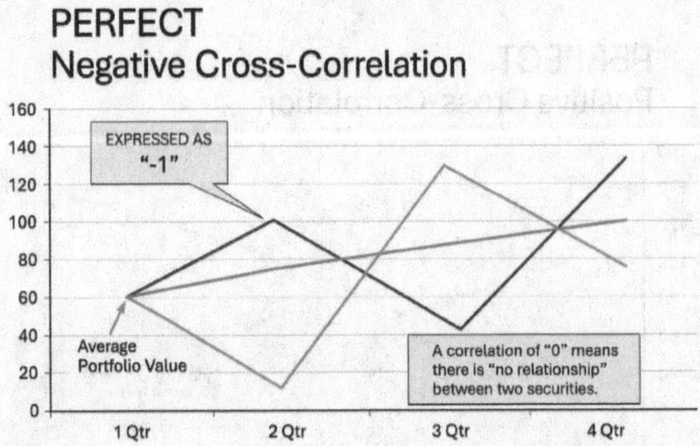

This graph for Negative Correlation is the opposite of the last. Here, as the grey line investment goes down, the black line increases. Then, as the black line investment decreases, the grey line increases. This is a Negative Correlation, and if we were to average returns at any point in the graph, we would see a portfolio value that increases steadily over time (represented by a grey, diagonal line in the center). This is the Negative Correlation benefit and the main objective of Asset Allocation. It is challenging to achieve a perfect 100 percent negative correlation, represented by -1.

Assets that show very little correlation are equally important. In a correlation test, these assets are represented by a value close to "0". With these concepts in mind, the following section includes various correlation charts.

SEEKING THE NEGATIVE

"The intelligent investor is likely to need considerable willpower to keep from following the crowd." —Benjamin Graham

Index Correlation Test

The Diversification Delusion, Tradecraft

Ticker	MDY	NAESX	S&P500	Dow	Nasdaq
MidCap SPDR	1.00	.68	.83	.70	.81
Vanguard Sm Cap Index Fund	.68	1.00	.61	.49	.67
S&P 500	.83	.61	1.00	.91	.84
Dow Jones	.70	.49	.91	1.00	.60
Nasdaq	.81	.67	.84	.61	1.00

This chart is from the article "The Diversification Delusion." It contains a correlation test on five stock-based assets: Mid-Cap SPDR, Vanguard Small Cap Index Fund, Standard & Poor's 500, The Dow Jones Industrial Average, and the NASDAQ. The assets in each line of the chart are the same as those in each column; however, the columns contain the trading symbol. For example, the Mid-Cap SPDR is also MDY, so the first box includes a "1" because they are the same asset. That is also why "1" runs diagonally throughout the chart.

If "1" is a 100 percent positive correlation, "0" is no correlation, and numbers with a negative sign represent a negative correlation, what does this chart tell us about the correlation of these stock assets? First, there are no negative signs; therefore, no negative correlation. None of the numbers are close to zero. Most of the numbers are closer to one than to zero. As a result, we see a strong positive correlation in this chart. Based on this assessment, we would expect these assets to move in tandem, and we are still seeking an investment that provides the expected buffer against negative correlation.

Let's try to find assets that may show a negative correlation. First, we'll look at bonds.

Bond Correlation Test

The Diversification Delusion, Tradecraft

Ticker	VWEHX	VFICX	VBMFX	S&P500	Dow	NASDAQ
Vanguard High Yield Corp Bond fund	1.00	.51	.52	.03	.02	.03
Vanguard Interim-Term Corp Bond fund	.51	1.00	.93	-.07	-.09	-.13
Vanguard Total Bond Market Index fund	.52	.93	1.00	-.05	-.08	-.11
S&P 500	.03	-.07	-.05	1.00	.91	.84
Dow Jones	.02	-.09	-.08	.91	1.00	.61
NASDAQ	.03	-.13	-.11	.84	.61	1.00

Again, this is another correlation test from "The Diversification Delusion" and contains three stock assets: Standard & Poor's 500, the Dow Jones Industrial Average, and the NASDAQ. However, this chart includes three Vanguard bond assets: High-Yield Corporate Bond Fund, Intermediate Term Bond Fund, and Total Bond Market Index Fund. The chart is constructed in the same way as the prior chart: the assets represented in each line are the same as those in each column; however, the columns contain the trading symbols.

Here, we see some negative signs representing a negative correlation. Also, some numbers are very close to zero, representing little correlation. As a result, we hope the bonds represented here do not follow the same valuation curve as the stock assets and, therefore, provide additional diversification.

Correlation Test: Gold, Bricks & Euros
Source: FinPortfolio.com

Ticker	VGPMX	ICPGX	QRAAX	S&P500	Dow	NASDAQ
Vanguard Gold & Precious Metals	1.00	.28	.18	.09	.13	.05
Franklin Templeton Global Currency	.28	1.00	.21	-.08	-.07	-.09
Oppenheimer Real Asset Fund	.18	.21	1.00	.01	.01	.04
S&P 500	.09	-.08	.01	1.00	.91	.84
Dow Jones	.13	-.07	.01	.91	1.00	.61
NASDAQ	.05	-.09	.04	.84	.61	1.00

I've included one final example of correlation. This chart contains three stock assets: Standard & Poor's 500, the Dow Jones Industrial Average, and the NASDAQ. It also includes three other asset types: Vanguard Gold & Precious Metals, Franklin Templeton Global Currency, and Oppenheimer Real Asset Fund. The chart is constructed in the same way as the prior two: the assets represented in each line are the same as those in each column; however, the columns contain the trading symbol.

As in the bond comparison, we see some negative signs indicating a negative correlation; however, it is not as pronounced here. More of these numbers are very close to zero, representing little correlation. If appropriately applied, little correlation can also work well in an asset allocation strategy. Let's take some time to look at these different investments. It's essential to understand how they work and their pros and cons before deciding whether to include them in our portfolio.

TWO PRIMARY ASSET CLASSES

"Know what you own, and know why you own it." —Peter Lynch

Although theories differ, in my mind, two primary asset classes exist: "Own It" and "Lend It."

Own It: Our most popular investments fit in this category. Here, we put stocks. Corporate stocks are sometimes referred to as equities because they represent ownership in a corporation. Real estate falls under our "Own It" category. We generally hold these assets for two possible primary goals—growth and income. We hope the value will increase so we can capitalize on a gain when we sell, and there will be a possibility of consistent income while we hold it. Stocks can produce dividends, which are corporate income distributed to the investors. For real estate, we can rent the asset.

Some "Own It" assets depreciate, meaning the value of the investment is expected to decline over time. Here, we can find items such as equipment leasing. This can be anything from cars and planes to cargo containers, which are big boxes that can be loaded onto boats, trains, and trucks. Investors provide capital to buy the equipment and then lease it to a company that uses it. The income is higher because the underlying asset depreciates, and no investment gain is expected.

Anything people need or use can be bundled into an investment to help create profit and returns. For example, you can buy shares in catfish farms. Investors pool their money, and the proceeds are used to purchase the equipment necessary to raise catfish, such as large pools, water filters, food, etc. They run a little hatchery there and place tiny baby catfish in the pools. The farm feeds and cares for the fish until they are big enough to harvest and sell to the market. If we do this right, it's fully sustainable, and our investors make money when we sell the fish.

Just as we can buy individual stocks, we can also purchase these investments in bundles like we would with a mutual fund or ETF (Exchange Traded Fund). Like a mutual fund, an ETF is a bundle of securities (stocks, bonds, and other investments), and each share represents ownership of the underlying asset. ETF share prices fluctuate all day as the ETF is bought and sold; this differs from mutual funds, which only trade once a day after the market closes. ETFs offer low expense ratios and fewer broker commissions than buying the stocks individually and most mutual funds.

Another way to bundle assets is in an REIT—Real Estate Investment Trust. There are REIT ETFs with many of the characteristics listed above. When we explore tangible assets as investments, liquidity (the ability to trade the assets for cash) can be of greater concern. It will be something to consider when adding it to your portfolio.

I invested about $7,000 in a medical REIT about 15 years ago. The investors' proceeds were used to purchase buildings and rent them to the medical facility. This worked great for several years. I was getting about a 7 percent income stream while interest rates in the market were much lower. The REIT management team has been liquidating some of the assets and returning some capital to the investors, but I have about $3,600 left in the investment.

When I moved my IRA, the new company could not take my REIT asset, and I could not liquidate it because there was no open market to sell this investment. I now have this one small account sitting there with the other firm. I also don't know when I will ever be able to liquidate it fully. The managing company wants to hold the assets as long as possible. While not of enormous consequence, I would like it invested elsewhere now, as the returns are lower because they've reduced the holdings. This is the sort of liquidity concern you should consider before investing in these assets.

Another form of "Own It" investment that can be illiquid is a Limited Partnership (LP). LPs own a bundle of tangible assets—real estate, equipment, farms—and place them in the partnership. LPs issue units, whereas mutual funds or ETFs issue shares. Each unit in an LP represents all underlying assets. Another difference with an LP is taxation. With a partnership, the depreciation of the assets passes through to the investors to offset the income. Unlike mutual funds, REITs, and ETFs, LP investors have no voting rights. The Managing General Partner is responsible for all decisions within an LP. This option is the most illiquid of the alternatives discussed thus far.

Some LPs offer tax credits—a dollar-for-dollar reduction of our tax bill. One form of LP tax credit is for low-income housing. Instead of the government building these residences, Congress authorizes investment firms to raise capital from investors. Since investors know that low-income housing will not yield significant gains or consistent income, the government entices them with tax credits to offset other earnings. These also create passive losses that can offset the earnings from another LP, which produces passive income.

Lend It: There are several debt instruments (debentures), the most common of which are bonds. Instead of owning anything directly, investors lend their money to others to purchase things. These are typically interest-bearing investments, but bond values can also fluctuate.

Let's make this easy by saying we invest $10,000 in a bond paying 10 percent, and interest rates rise to 12 percent. We'll continue to get our 10 percent earnings each year ($1,000), and that's good. If we want to sell our bond, it is not attractive to other investors who can get 12 percent. We would need to offer the bond at a discount, bringing the price to around $8,300. The lower purchase price would ensure that $1,000 in interest (10 percent on our original $10,000 investment), is closer to a 12 percent return to the new investor.

The inverse is also true. In a declining interest rate market, our 10 percent bond becomes more attractive, and buyers are willing to pay a premium of more than $10,000 in bond value. These changes in value only matter if we want to sell the bond. Like with our home, or with stock appreciation or decline, the value is only consequential if we liquidate our holdings. Since mutual funds and ETFs can hold bonds, valuation changes can affect their prices and the value in your portfolio.

One of the risks anytime one lends money is default—if the person or entity does not make payments, there are no earnings to collect, and investors may also suffer the loss of investment capital.

Even in the safest debentures, like U.S. government bonds, which have not defaulted, we still face risk (opportunity cost) due to inflation. The interest rate, or earnings, on a debt instrument is tied to the risk of default. If the risk of default is high, investors are enticed into the purchase with higher interest rates. The reverse is also true—if default risk is low, the interest rates will be low, too. Since U.S. government bonds have little default risk, interest earnings are typically lower. This, combined with taxation and rising prices, means we may not earn enough to keep up with inflation, which is a real risk to our portfolio.

There are several types of government-issued bonds: from U.S. and foreign governments, as well as state and municipal bonds. Special offerings can be made for projects like building a school, a government building, or a stadium. An array of corporate bonds are issued for numerous reasons. Specific bonds are also issued for items like mortgages, used to cover or raise money given to borrowers, and war (yes, war) bonds, issued by governments to cover the cost of conflict.

Bonds are generally rated, which indicates their credit quality. Independent rating services such as Standard & Poor's and Moody's evaluate a bond issuer's financial strength or ability to pay a bond's principal and interest promptly. At least, that's what they tell us. Before the 2008 financial crash, many mortgage-backed securities that subsequently failed had received a triple-A rating, the highest you can get. Many claim the problems in these mortgages were evident enough that these rating agencies should have known. There were investigations, but nothing came of them.

All things being equal, these ratings are like our credit score. It does not illustrate every nuance of one's creditworthiness. Any rating system is likely to have flaws and potential avenues for corruption.

It's like three students getting an A in the same class. One student worked hard for it—studying day and night. Another student cheated. Although entirely undeserving, they have the A nonetheless. The third student is taking the class for the second time. They knew much of the material from the first go-around but were there to raise their GPA.

Other debentures—a bank Certificate of Deposit (CD). All bank deposits can be lent out, so they're all debentures, including those in essential savings or checking accounts. Same with a Money Market—usually, these offer higher interest rates than standard bank savings accounts because short-term government securities back them.

OUTSIDE THE BOX

"If everyone has to think outside the box, maybe it is the box that needs fixing."
—Malcolm Gladwell

Before we wrap up this overview of investment options and move to the insurance section, I want to discuss two other ways people have made (or lost) money: Crypto and Options.

Cryptocurrency: It seems that cryptocurrency became all the rage when people began taking advice from social media. Elon Musk, Kim Kardashian, and anyone with media influence posted their buys, and followers were buying in. Some people made money, but too many did not. I know the SEC was looking into charges against some of these influencers. I am sure nothing will come of it. Let me tell you what I know about this investment class and what I believe happened when the bottom fell out.

Crypto is currency. Unlike the U.S. and Canadian dollar, the yen, the euro, the peso, or any other currency backed by a government, crypto has no backing. It has no value other than the value assigned by people who choose to buy it; the price increases as sales volume increases. Yet, crypto operates similarly to any other form of currency.

Many government currencies, such as the U.S. dollar, are no longer backed by gold and are considered fiat. Fiat is a Latin word meaning "by decree"—fiat currency only has value because it is decreed. In the crypto world, these decrees are far more meaningless, and the managers are too often more corrupt.

Regarding crypto, many influencers state as fact the benefits of crypto without offering any downsides or other perspectives. Here's my understanding of a few things I've heard.

Blockchain Accounting—With the cryptocurrency hype came many questions about blockchain accounting, which was positioned as a unique benefit of crypto. That is not the case. Blockchain is a centralized accounting method. As the internet evolved, so did accounting practices. Crypto adopted blockchain, and unless prohibited by law, so can other investments and companies. There are certainly benefits to blockchain accounting, but it is evident that this accounting method did not save this particular investment class from a severe downturn.

No SEC Regulations—The SEC stands for the Securities and Exchange Commission. It is a government agency established in 1934, following the 1929 crash that triggered the Great Depression. Its job is to oversee and regulate the investment marketplace. Before the crypto crash, I frequently heard, "Crypto is not regulated by the SEC." Or sometimes these words would be added, "…won't ever be…" implying that this investment class will always be outside the scope of regulation.

I am not sure why being unregulated would benefit investors. Time and again, we have seen that only the rich benefit from a lack of regulation. Regulations are designed to protect us. They can be cumbersome, and some are less effective than others. However, the regulations enacted after 1929 protected investors, and the deregulation before the 2008 crash illustrates that regulations are not your enemy.

Beyond that, who says the SEC won't ever regulate crypto? This is nonsense. If money is being made or lost and there is a possibility of defrauding investors, you better believe the SEC will step in. At least they should—it is their job to protect investors. I just searched "Has the SEC started regulating crypto?" One of the top links was to a page listing all the SEC cases and charges brought against crypto companies.

Currency Valuation—Crypto isn't that unique. It might be relatively new, 2009 —about 15 years before this book was written—but in the end, it operates like any other investment. If I buy gold today, do they mail me some big old bars? If I buy stock, will I get several certificates showing how many shares I own? Same with bonds? Or how about if I put money in a currency fund, do they mail me some pesos, yen, euros, baht, and whatever else the fund holds? Of course not—it is all electronically held, just like crypto.

Living in Mexico, I've noticed some trends about the peso versus the dollar. Point one—since the Mexican economy is doing well, the peso is strong against the dollar. When the 2024 eclipse happened, the peso was even more robust. People bought many things in Mexico—airline tickets, hotels, food, etc. Mazatlán was ground zero for the event—everyone was coming here to see the eclipse. Okay, maybe not everyone, but we were the first land mass to see the total eclipse, and the weather here is typically stellar. Rarely a cloud in the sky. So, the world's banks saw lots of their currencies being converted, and the peso got even stronger until it was over. I told my friends we'd be able to get more pesos with our dollars in mid-April, and sure enough, the price changed.

When the tourism season is hot in Mexico, in the winter months, the peso is stronger than in the summer when there is less travel to the southern regions. It's June here now, and pesos are a bit of a bargain compared to earlier in the spring. The recent presidential election in Mexico shook things up a bit. I took this as an opportunity to buy up some pesos. I feel like a squirrel saving for those lean winter months.

This is no different from crypto. The value went up when Elon, Kim, and other influencers shared their little tips and raved about how everyone should get into cryptocurrency. This increased demand raised the conversion price, and it is no different from converting to other currencies or from the way stock prices rise. Increased demand when supply is limited means increased cost/value.

The crypto market was all driven by the influencers. The more they could get everyone else to buy, the more money they made. Why did the price fall? The rich folks bailed, leaving everyone else with losses. I know there were other reasons, like some possible criminals involved in the offering. What happened in crypto was a shame. It was also a sham, and it's why I want everyone reading my books to consider how our financial choices impact others. Are we really winning when other people are losing?

If you haven't heard of the movie "Dumb Money" about the GameStop stock purchase, look it up and watch the trailer. This movie is about one of the few times this buying frenzy has worked for the little people. The rich lost money on this because they were 'shorting' GameStop—and this brings us to our next out-of-the-box investment.

Options: Those "shorting" GameStop were using options to do so, which is also why they were in an unlimited loss position. If you ever hear words like "hedging" or "straddling" associated with investments, they are talking about options. Options can be purchased or sold on any asset one believes will change in value—stock, commodities, precious metals, currencies—anything; options are sometimes referred to as "futures."

It can be very much like gambling. One person says, "I think it will increase in value." Another says, "Nope, you're wrong. It's going down." Then one of them says, "You want to bet?" And they do. They put their money in on the gamble. For this to work, someone must take the other side of the bet.

There are various positions. Some are more protected than others, and, as in the GameStop example, sometimes the risk is unlimited.

Regarding these two out-of-the-box investments (Crypto Currency and Options), I own a small amount of crypto. I wish I had bought Bitcoin when I first started discussing it in class, when it was about $300 each, but sadly, I was skeptical of its future value then. That same $300 bitcoin is trading at $110,000 today (November 2025). It's also possible that some of my other investments have purchased options on my behalf, but I have never entered that marketplace directly.

Admittedly, I am a good card player but a horrible gambler. I have won a few Hold'em bar tournaments, where the buy-in is dinner and a few drinks, but I don't put my money on the table at the casino. That is probably reflected in my investment strategies as well. I have a head for this stuff. My timing and decision-making are pretty good, but I like safer bets. Over the years, I've added a few sectors to my portfolio that worked well for me. We'll discuss that in the next section, so let's wrap up this chapter with some variables in the equities market that can help build a diverse portfolio.

A DOUBLE STEP

"I don't look to jump over seven-foot bars; I look around for one-foot bars that I can step over." —*Warren Buffett*

Under the umbrella of equity funds, there are several different types. An equity fund can fall into one or more categories based on the kind of stocks it invests in or its overall investment objective. Some of the basics are:

- U.S. equity funds: Only companies listed on U.S. stock exchanges.
- Foreign equity funds: Only companies listed on foreign stock exchanges.
- Global funds: A global fund invests in stocks from anywhere in the world.
- Large cap: Companies with $10 billion or more in market capitalization, which is the total value of the company's shares.
- Mid-cap: Companies with a market capitalization of $2 billion to $10 billion.
- Small cap: Companies with $300 million to $2 billion in market capitalization.
- Sector: Concentrate on a specific industry or market (e.g. energy, information technology, medical, etc.)
- Growth: Companies that invest heavily in expanding their business and have the potential for significant growth in the near term.
- Value: Companies whose stocks are undervalued based on market analysis.
- Income: Companies that offer high dividend yields on their stocks. Typically, blue-chip stocks are issued by large, well-established companies that have dependable earnings.

It is important to note that these categories can be combined. One could invest in a Global Index Fund, whose portfolio could include holdings from several index funds worldwide. Or a Foreign Value Fund, where the investment team might seek undervalued companies in other countries. The list of combinations in the equity funds arena is endless.

The S&P 500 index fund falls into three categories: U.S., Large Cap, and Index, as it includes the top 500 U.S. corporations by market capitalization. We could add "blue-chip" because those at the top of this list would also qualify under that term.

I've had a lot of fun and success adding sector funds to my portfolio, and this is where keeping up on political trends can help your portfolio. It gives us two benefits from our factual research. I added an energy fund to my IRA years ago. It paid off as businesses and governments continued seeking renewable energy solutions. Plus, I can feel good about investing my money there.

Medical care was another sector I added. Like energy, healthcare is pretty recession-proof—the demand is relatively constant. This sector also has a lot of new research and development. New technology creates opportunities for growth. Moreover, governments are willing to make investments in these areas.

This is precisely why I asked my financial advisor friend about green investments. Under the bipartisan Infrastructure Investment and Jobs Act (IIJA), more than a trillion dollars would go into the economy, mainly through businesses. The Biden administration had focused this plan on going greener. Because of this, I wanted to find funds that knew this and were working to capitalize on this money flow. It is a shame I was working with someone who was unwilling to help me research this opportunity. I am confident his other clients would have benefited from this, too.

When looking at unique sector funds, we can support causes and groups that matter to us. Some funds invest in companies owned by or managed by women, people of color, LGBTQ+, and any combination of those groups. As with GameStop, the values will naturally increase as more investors recognize the value of stepping out of the greed mentality and begin putting their money into areas that benefit society.

I don't know what you think, but I'm impressed we got through all that in just this chapter! Congratulations—you absorbed a pretty good overview of basic diversification strategies and various investment options. We turn our attention now to insurance to "Protect Your Pennies." You'll find out shortly that there are several unique ways some insurance company products can also give us FREE pennies. It all fits in with a comprehensive plan.

CHAPTER TWELVE

PROTECT YOUR PENNIES

INSURING THE PLAN

"The most contrarian thing of all is not to oppose the crowd but to think for yourself."
—Peter Thiel

THE AGE-OLD QUESTION

Maybe it's not AGE OLD—you might not even be familiar, but for those of us in the insurance industry, this question began, it seems, the first time someone decided to buy a life insurance policy:

"Buy term and invest the difference **OR** buy cash-value life?"

You might be thinking, "Really? With all today's issues, it doesn't seem like it should be a dilemma." Do you want to know something? I agree 1000 percent. This question is not an issue. It's only made into an issue because some in the first camp, the "buy term" team, see no value in the cash value life side. They have taken this position by explaining the benefits of each and presenting an "either-or" proposition, where one can *only* do one thing and *never* the other.

This is precisely why, chapters ago, I suggested that binary choices are rarely helpful choices. The honest answer to this question of term vs. cash-value life, just like most questions of its kind, is both. Your selection will depend on your needs and preferences. Let's talk about what each of these options offers. That way, should you need life insurance, you can decide which is better for you, or you may choose a little of both as your solution.

Term Life—the name implies we purchase the insurance for a specific term—a period of time. The contract is normally renewed annually. As each year passes and one gets older, the risk of dying increases, so the premium usually increases with each renewal. We can get a guaranteed premium for a set number of years—5, 10, 15, 20, or possibly more. If we go this route, the initial premium will be higher than a policy without this guarantee.

It depends on the policy whether one can renew at the end of the guaranteed term. Typically, a policy that renews automatically without needing health history underwriting will cost more after automatic renewal. If they are healthy enough to qualify, most people will apply for a new policy at a much lower premium. People who exercise auto-renewal typically make this selection because their health has declined, and they no longer medically qualify for the lower premiums.

Because of the inherent renewal risk with a term life insurance policy, the premium rates here are typically lower than those of the cash value life alternative. This is where the "invest the difference" concept comes in—the premium savings can be diverted to another investment. An ETF (Exchange Traded Fund) with a diverse stock mix would be the typical recommendation.

Cash-Value Life (CVL)—also called whole life because these policies are designed to cover someone during their 'whole life.' We might also hear "permanent insurance" or Universal Life (UL) for that reason. Sometimes, you might also hear IUL—the "I" stands for Indexed. We'll discuss this after the annuity section, since it is an option in both contracts—annuities and life insurance.

A CVL insurance policy has a savings component in addition to life insurance. The savings in the policy are the cash value (CV). Premiums are paid using after-tax dollars; the earnings accumulate tax-deferred. The cash value can be withdrawn via a low-interest loan. This allows the policyholder to pay the proceeds back into the policy by repaying the loan. Or the policy owner can create a distribution. In the case of a distribution, the withdrawal is not taxable because it is considered a prepayment of the Death Benefit (DB) and will reduce the life insurance by an amount equal to the distribution.

Imagine you have a CVL insurance contract with a $100,000 death benefit and $20,000 in cash value, and create a withdrawal of $10,000. After that, the new CV is $10,000 (the $20,000 original CV minus the $10,000 distribution), and the new DB (the life insurance amount or "death benefit") is $90,000. The withdrawal may not be taxable, but it reduces both the DB balance and the CV.

Unlike a term insurance contract, the CVL policy is renewable for the insured's life, and the CV can be used to pay the premium. However, earnings in the account can vary, which could prompt a client to contribute additional funds to cover the policy's cost. These policies also have guaranteed rates, so the CV consistently earns something.

Other Considerations—As mentioned above, but essential to clarify, the DB for a life insurance contract passes to the beneficiaries income tax-free. It is important to note, but it will not be discussed here because it impacts so few of us, the DB could be subject to estate taxes.

Lots of folks make a big deal about the tax-free nature of the DB. It is an enormous benefit to our heirs to receive this money and not lose a significant share to taxes. However, nearly every insurance benefit we receive is income tax-free. We pay no tax when we have a major surgery, and an insurance company pays $100,000 in medical bills. Thank GOD. A new roof or damage to our car that is covered by insurance is not taxable either. While receiving insurance benefits income tax-free is quite impactful, it is not unique to life insurance.

Many employers offer very affordable life insurance options. It's typically best to take advantage of these because the group policy usually offers lower rates, or employers help pay for them. In most contracts, we can also add coverage riders. (A rider is a smaller, supplemental coverage added to the policy.) It's like having a mini-policy in the main policy. Riders can offer life insurance coverage for children, or prepayment of the death benefit for disability or long-term care for assisted living.

PUTTING TOGETHER THE PLAN

"If a child, a spouse, a life partner, or a parent depends on you and your income, you need life insurance." —Suze Orman

That was a lot of rules and information, huh? Let's make this a little more interesting by illustrating these insurance principles with a story about my life insurance choices at various stages of my life.

When I got my first full-time job, my employer offered a basic term life insurance policy at no cost. In the 1980s, this was about $25,000. It was enough to cover final expenses (casket or urn, burial space or cremation, memorial service, etc.) but not much else. I wasn't married and had no kids or a mortgage, but the cost to buy more was so cheap that I added on and had a $250,000 DB policy.

Working for an insurance company at the time, I learned about CVL insurance early on. With high interest rates in the 1980s, buying a policy paying 11 percent was a no-brainer. I didn't buy a HUGE death benefit—$85,000. In those days, though, $85,000 covered most mortgages. Because I was so young, the premium was meager. I bought one for my soon-to-be husband, too. The benefit of purchasing this policy when young is that the premium stays low as we age. Another bonus: the guaranteed rate was 5.5 percent. Even when the Fed's lending rate hit zero, I still got 5.5 percent.

A Baby: Fast-forward to my first child in 1992. I still had $335,000 in life insurance, and now my retirement savings had grown to about $40,000. Nothing huge at this point, but since my mortgage was in the $120,000 range, my husband could work, and I would leave them with about $375,000, I was okay with that.

Others might say, "Get more for the kid's college fund, too." Or they might say, "The single-parent dad will need more childcare options." Or not. My mother would gladly help care for the kids. Each case is different, and, as with everything else we've discussed, there are no hard-and-fast rules.

These death benefit amounts worked for me, but, of course, I didn't die either. The "what if" never happened, and I am grateful it did not. My children's emotional health would have been vastly different. But even if I focused on the financial side, my ex wasn't as good with these economic principles. He blew through much of the money I gave him in the divorce. I am confident this $400,000 would not have lasted much longer.

This is an important consideration. One should consider the temperament of the person who will carry out your final wishes and arrange as much as possible in a will, a business continuation plan, or a trust. These items will not be addressed here, but they are worth discussing with an attorney or researching on your own. Many legal forms are available online to handle these matters.

Another Baby and A Job Change: 1998 brought baby number two, but I still held firm with the current life insurance plan—$250,000 term, $85,000 CVL, and now about $75,000 in retirement savings. Then, in 1999, I accepted my employer's severance package and started my education business. This also meant the cheap $250,000 term policy went away.

I was relatively young—in my early 30s. I was healthy and could readily buy another policy, but I did not. My retirement savings were doing well—the 90s stock market was kind. I think the value was inching closer to $100,000. At this stage, too, my kids had some college savings. I've been working on the plan, and I keep the $85,000 CVL.

My family was financially exposed with this lower life insurance amount. I know it. If I had died in these years, they would not have had enough, especially since I had a greater earning potential than my husband. I also know our budget and the odds. Things were tight then, and as cheap as a term life insurance policy might have been, I also knew it was unlikely that anything would happen to me. Was it possible—yes, it is always possible. Looking back today, given that I am sitting here, I would have likely paid about $200 per year for maybe 20 years, so, $4,000. It's not a lot of money, but it wasn't a priority compared to the other things I could do with my pennies.

This was my other thought, and it will likely be yours as well. If I am packing away the pennies, there is a point at which the savings cover the loss—I no longer need life insurance because I have the cash to self-insure. Here's the other consideration: as time goes by and the savings grow, our children's (or others') dependence on us is dwindling. Each year means fewer years to be responsible for their needs. Now, 25 years later, my kids are launched. If I die, everything I leave them is a bonus. Considering that, the gap period with too little life insurance was far fewer than 20 years.

IMPORTANT NOTE: Although I was underinsured, I was never uninsured. I don't believe we should ever leave other people holding the bag for our responsibilities—and as an adult, one of your responsibilities is your final expense. To practice "Morality of Money," we should ensure we have life insurance or enough savings to cover final expenses. We should also consider a cushion above that. Dealing with someone's estate at death is a lot of work. The person who is doing this is grieving your loss. While money is no replacement, it can provide a cushion for the person responsible for this work. If you have children or other responsibilities, do all you can to ensure enough to provide for them, too.

ALSO IMPORTANT: The responsibility noted above will likely be challenging to achieve for people with disabilities if their health status prohibits them from getting life insurance or earning enough to save a lot. That is entirely understandable, and there is no shame in recognizing any possible limitation. Collaborate with the people who love you. They will likely have no problem stepping in to help fill any gaps. In this instance, the responsibility lies in beginning these difficult discussions with the people who love you.

Back to regular programming—Renée's life insurance saga.

Child Rider: Fast-forward to 2017, when my son was turning 25. Years earlier, when my children were born, I added a child rider to my CVL insurance policy. A child rider offers a small life insurance benefit for our children. It's typically a few extra dollars a month, and I think this one was for a $25,000 DB. This is only a little more than the final expenses, so sometimes parents buy their children a CVL policy independently, since this could also increase their savings for college and other expenses.

I opted to cover my children with the rider and open other savings accounts for them. My son's coverage was about to expire because this rider's coverage ends at age 25. These riders usually include a conversion option that allows the policy owner to convert it to an independent policy for the child. The option offers security, but it's typically expensive. As before, people use this option only if their health history does not qualify them for preferred rates.

I thought about letting it expire. He'd been living independently for years, but he didn't have a partner at this stage. If something happened to him, I would be responsible. I had the money. That wasn't the issue. The concern was whether I could move on from my son's death and go back to everything. Could I resume work and other life responsibilities as I had before? The answer to this crucial question was "No." Parents who lose children are NEVER the same again. I would need time to piece myself back together again.

Since he was working on his graduate studies, he had not built up much savings, so I bought a term policy on his life. I paid for that policy until he got his first job, which offered life insurance, and he then picked up that responsibility. Since then, he has accumulated other savings, so this was a short-term need that I am still grateful I did. Taking these steps also proved to be a good opportunity to discuss the uses of life insurance with my son.

As I wrote this section, I realized my daughter turned 25, and the rider expired without the same concern. I didn't even think of it. Like her brother, she is still in graduate school with little savings. The difference is that she has a partner. I am unsure what they have done for life insurance; maybe I should ask. I know I would be equally devastated if something happened to my daughter, but I am also in a very different place. My savings have grown in the last six years, and I am even closer to retirement. She's also the last of my "littles." I don't have any other children to care for. I'm not in the same place I was when my son turned 25.

CVL Withdrawal: In 2019, two years after my son "aged out" of the child rider, I decided to buy a new home. It wasn't something I had time to plan. My landlord sprung an unfavorable lease change on me within the 60-day notice period—move to the lower-level unit and pay $250 more monthly rent or move out of the building in two months. I decided on option two. Since I didn't ever want to be at the whim of a landlord again, I decided to buy.

This is precisely why it is crucial to put away pennies. If I didn't have savings, I would have limited options. If that happened to someone with no savings, they could become homeless. Without significant cash reserves or a means to get it, responsible renters can find themselves without options.

I decided to take some money from my CVL for this new home purchase. The 5.5 percent I received in this account is good, but the other investments were better. I would have to sell some of that for the house, but I could limit the damage by using some of the cash value. Since my kids were grown and my retirement savings would make a sufficient gift, the CVL death benefit was no longer necessary.

The life insurance policy had about $20,000 in cash value. I didn't want to drain it entirely because I wanted to keep the insurance in force, so I took half, or $10,000. I paid no tax, and my death benefit became $75,000 instead of $85,000.

OTHER PEOPLE'S BUSINESS

"I'd rather be honest than impressive." —Unknown

A TikTok Sale: A friend kept seeing a video on social media about a life insurance policy that worked as a savings account, and the earnings were tied to the stock market. My friend asked me if I knew anything about the featured Index Universal Life policies (IUL). I told her I'd never sold one but was familiar with them. I answered a few questions, and since she was interested in learning more and possibly buying one, I put her in touch with someone I love and respect in this business. Thankfully, I know many such caring professionals.

They were able to talk by phone soon after I made the introduction. My friend explained her situation, and as a thorough professional, the respected advisor I'd referred had a few questions.

When those were answered, she (the advisor) said, "I wouldn't bother with the life insurance. Your kids are past 18 and doing fine. Just continue to fund your retirement account as much as you can. Since you seem to want to make sure your kids don't have to worry about your final expenses, it might be worthwhile to visit a funeral home and prepay those expenses."

How is that for reputable? She could have made an easy sale, but put the client first. Sadly, that isn't always the case. Let me tell you a case I fear falls into that category before discussing final expense policies.

The Mother of ALL MECs (Modified Endowment Contracts): I recently met a woman who said her retirement was funded through CVL insurance. I do not know many specifics other than what she told me. She knows it's unusual, but she retired a few years ago, and everything is going okay. She also told me she had worked for years with the gentleman who had recommended this strategy. She did ask me if I knew of this strategy, and I told her, "Yes, but normally, life insurance is not used exclusively for retirement planning."

That was all she asked me, so I didn't share my other concerns. One must buy too much life insurance to fully fund one's retirement with cash value in a life insurance policy. This is because the CV can only be a small percentage of the DB to qualify for the tax-free distribution rules. I'll offer a more in-depth discussion shortly—for now, know that life insurance has an inherent cost, and, as with any other expense, we should only buy what we need. It would be like needing a car on vacation, but you purchase a brand-new one instead of renting one. That is the kind of price difference we are talking about.

The reason to buy life insurance is that you need the insurance benefit. If there is no need for life insurance, other savings vehicles can offer many of the inherent advantages of a CVL contract. There may be exceptions to this rule, but at this moment, I cannot think of one.

The woman in my story may have set all of this up before June 21, 1988. That was the effective date of the Modified Endowment Contract (MEC) rules. Before that date, the cash value could nearly match the death benefit, and the contract owner would still get all the same tax benefits. After that date, if there isn't a nice roomy cushion between the cash value and the death benefit, the contract is deemed a MEC, and the tax benefits on loans and withdrawals go away.

This woman would have been in her 30s in 1988, so she may have taken advantage of the rules before the MEC changes. I still don't understand why; however, in 1998, when the Roth IRA came on the scene, this advisor didn't suggest that as an alternative to the MEC. It certainly would have cost less than any life insurance policy and would still pass to heirs income tax-free. This is why I am concerned that this advisor was seeking a higher commission on life insurance. I have considered asking more questions and sharing my concerns, but her plan is in place. I fear stirring this up might sow discontent where all is well.

A BIG BOW

"A person without money is like a bow without arrows" —Indian Proverb

Let's wrap up this section with some miscellaneous concepts related to life insurance. These items will also serve as a platform for transitioning to our next insurance topic, annuities.

Final Expense Policies: This life insurance policy is designed to cover mortuary and memorial expenses. Often, these are MEC (Modified Endowment Contracts), so no health history review is necessary. As the cash value increases, so does the benefit amount; hopefully, it continues to cover the burial or crematory expenses that increase over time. These contracts are usually irrevocably assigned. This means the person cannot withdraw the cash value, but it also means these dollars are no longer part of their estate and are therefore not subject to Medicaid spend-down. We'll discuss Medicaid in the next chapter, "The Penny Thief," which highlights healthcare in America.

Credit Life (and Disability): These forms of insurance can be added to a loan. If you die or become disabled, the insurance component will either pay off the balance or make the payments on your behalf. These policies have limited underwriting, so they don't fully assess one's health risk. When an insurance company cannot determine risk, premiums cost more. For those who qualify, it is far better to have other insurance that covers the risk of death or disability than to buy a credit life or credit disability policy. Disability insurance is also discussed later. These remaining points transition us to annuities and can apply to both contracts.

Surrender Charges: CVL and annuity contracts usually have a surrender charge in the policy's early years. A surrender charge is a percentage of the CV that the policy owner is charged if they decide to cancel. It is put in place so the insurance company can recover the policy's initial expenses.

Imagine you put $10,000 in an annuity contract, and that company pays the writing agent a 5 percent commission ($500). They also must pay their employees to process and issue the contract. There are probably other internal expenses, so we'll assume the company's cost is 3 percent or $300. The surrender charge would likely be 8 percent (the 5 percent commission plus the 3 percent internal expenses) the first year, declining by 1 percent each year thereafter until zero in the 9th year.

You might wonder why the surrender charge declined over the eight-year term. Why doesn't it say at 8 percent forever? The policy has other expense loads built in. Over time, the insurance company recoups the initial cost through these means. This is why between the mortality cost and the expense loads, life insurance is not the best option for building the greatest return.

Policy Owner: More than once in this chapter, I've used the phrase "policy or contract owner." This person or entity owns the policy and may differ from the insured or the annuitant. I am listed as the owner on my life insurance policy, but I have thought about switching that to my kids. In doing so, I remove it from my estate and limit the risks of Medicaid spend-down or other liability issues.

Or consider this: Have you ever heard that lottery winners can get monthly payments instead of lump sums? An annuity traditionally funds these installments through the annuitization feature. The lottery would be the owner of the contract and the winner the annuitant. The owner can be an entity—a trust, a company, the lottery, a city, etc.—but the annuitant or the insured must be a living, breathing person with a life expectancy.

Beneficiary: We briefly discussed this when I explained my daughter's choices in setting up her 401(k). We name beneficiaries for life insurance, annuities, and other qualified accounts, such as IRAs, 401(k)s, and Section 529 plans. When we name a beneficiary, the money will pass directly to that person or entity upon our death, which avoids probate. Probate requires a judge to determine the allocation of assets even if there is a will.

Since a typical beneficiary is one's children, there are two options for naming multiple people as beneficiaries. These considerations would apply anytime we want to name more than one person or their heirs as the people who would benefit by the policy or account.

Per stirpes—means "by roots or branch" in Latin. Relating this to a beneficiary designation, I want you to envision a family tree. When one selects a per stirpes designation, the share of an inheriting person who is no longer surviving would go to the next in line on their branch. This image illustrates how this would work.

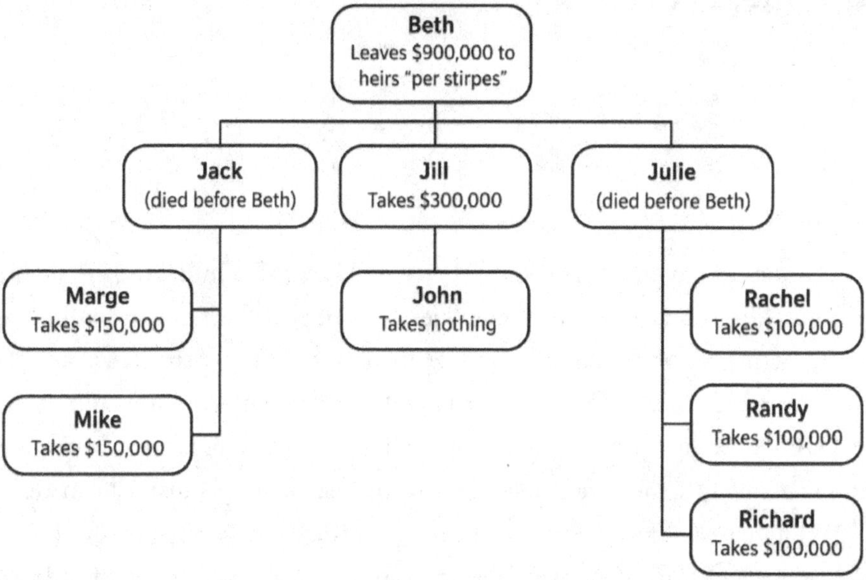

Beth leaves her $900,000 annuity (or IRA, life insurance, etc.) to her three children per stirpes. Jack, her eldest son, has already passed on, so his $300,000 share would go to his two children with equal shares of $150,000 each. Jill, Beth's second child, is still surviving. She'll get the entire $300,000. Her son gets nothing. Some will say, "That's not fair." And maybe it's not, but if Jill manages it well, her son will likely inherit more than $300,000 at his mother's death.

The third child, Julie, passed on before her mother, so her $300,000 was split into $100,000 shares for her three children. All of Beth's grandkids received varying amounts, and if one of the grandchildren died before Beth, their proceeds would go to their children.

Share and share alike—or what is sometimes called "equal shares"—is different. Had Beth selected this option, the full $900,000 would have gone to Jill. Since her siblings have already passed on, they are not here to share with her, and Jill gets it all. As you can see from this example, it is very important to understand the differences in these designations to ensure the people you want to inherit the money receive the proceeds.

THE FIRST IRA

"People always live for ever when there is an annuity to be paid them."
—Jane Austen, Sense and Sensibility

Annuities are the first IRA. They are essentially Individual Retirement Accounts (the original design of annuities is to provide retirement income), and they've been part of the tax code longer than IRAs. They were IRAs before we had IRAs, which is why several of the tax rules for annuities are the same as those for IRAs. Earnings accumulate in an annuity tax-deferred, but if withdrawn before age 59-1/2, they are subject to a 10 percent penalty—just like an IRA.

While all of that is true, the more we've discussed annuities in class, the more it began to resonate with me that annuities are also the first individual pension plans. While one can accumulate money in an annuity tax-deferred, one of the inherent benefits of an annuity is all the annuitization options. To my knowledge, it is the only vehicle where one can collect a guaranteed life income just as they might with a pension.

This is also why annuities are in the insurance section versus the prior chapter about investments. For one thing, they are exclusively offered by insurance companies. Insurers already have actuaries on staff working with mortality statistics for life insurance. Flipping those tables around to calculate life income is an easy maneuver. Moreover, guaranteed life income ensures that our money lasts the remainder of our lives, and that is what insurance does: offer protection for the risks in life.

To better understand the value of annuitization, I've provided an overview of common settlement options:

Life Only—Pays a monthly income for the life of the annuitant. Upon the annuitant's death, payments cease. The risk is that one could die early in the annuitization when the entire balance is not yet paid out. Should that happen, the heirs would not collect anything.

Life with Period Certain—Pays during the annuitant's life with a guaranteed payment for a set number of years. If the annuitant dies, payment continues to the beneficiaries for the number of years that remain in the certain period. Typical periods are five-year increments: 5, 10, 15, 20, but I've also seen seven year-year increments: 7, 14, 21.

Before moving on to the other options, let's consider this question: Between these two options, Life Only or Life with Period Certain, which do you think generates the larger monthly income?

If you are thinking it's likely "Life Only," you would be right. That option has more risk, but as a result, greater reward is possible.

Life with Cash Refund—This option provides life income like the two above; however, here, we do not need to select a specific period to ensure the value to our heirs. If the annuitant dies anytime the entire balance has not yet been paid, it will be given to the heirs in a lump sum. The monthly income for this alternative is also less than the other two.

Joint Survivor—Life-only option based on the life expectancy of two people. Joint Survivor is most customarily used for married people or those in a committed relationship. Using this option, when one partner dies, the same monthly income continues for the surviving person.

Period Certain—Unlike the other options above, this alternative does not offer income for life. It follows a standard amortization schedule and would provide a monthly income for a specific number of years. The entire cash value is paid during this time frame. Upon the annuitant's death, beneficiaries receive any remaining payments. This is the option the lottery would use when it says, "You'll receive a monthly income for 25 years."

IT'S YOUR MONEY

"Don't let money run your life. Let money help you run your life better."
—John Rampton

There is no requirement to "annuitize" an annuity by choosing an option for scheduled monthly income. We can create a distribution instead, and many annuities offer a 10 percent free withdrawal option. Even during the surrender charge period, one could take up to 10 percent of the account value and not pay the penalty. When one creates this sort of distribution, earnings come out first. This is called LIFO—Last In, First Out. The "last" thing in any savings account is the earnings. Due to the deferral, the gains have not yet been taxed with an annuity and will be taxable upon withdrawal.

When we annuitize, however, we spread our taxation out over the term. Each distribution will be a share of the original principal and earnings. As a simple example, imagine you put $40,000 into an annuity. This deposit is made with after-tax dollars, which would be considered non-qualified. Over the years, the account earns another $40,000, so you have a total value of $80,000.

Depending on current interest rates, under a 10-year certain annuitization, $10,000 per year could be collected, but how can that be? Our contract has a value of $80,000. This amount, divided by the ten payments, would be $8,000 annually. Where does the extra $2,000 per year come from, so the total is $10,000 annually?

While annuitized, you will still gain interest on the remaining value in the contract, increasing the payments' value. By annuitizing, only $6,000 of each annual distribution is taxable because $4,000 is one-tenth of the original $40,000 contribution. Since this contribution was taxed before you put it into the annuity, it is not taxed again when it's withdrawn.

COMPOUND TAX DEFERRAL

"Compound interest is the eighth wonder of the world. Those who understand it, earn it. Those who don't, pay it." —Albert Einstein

In the previous chapter, I promised a comparison of the value of tax deferral. This benefit is not exclusive to annuities. We receive it in almost all qualified accounts: IRA, 401(k), Section 529, CVL insurance, SEP, SIMPLE, etc. The more the tax-deferred account earns, the greater the value of this tax benefit.

Please see the image below. You'll see a tax-deferred fixed annuity in the center column and a bank CD on the right. In this example, both are earning 3 percent. In a typical interest rate environment, the fixed annuities would have higher rates than a bank CD, but I want to illustrate the power of tax-deferred growth, so I've left both interest rates the same. Giving the fixed annuity an interest rate advantage skews the illustration of the value of tax-deferred growth.

Years Invested	3% Interest Rate Fixed Annuity	3% CD Less 30% Income Tax Bracket
1	$103,000	$102,100
5	$115,927	$110,950
10	$134,392	$123,100
15	$155,797	$136,580
20	$180,611	$151,536

$156,428
after tax value

Please note that after 20 years of comparison, the fixed annuity now has a value of $180,000 or about $30,000 more than the bank CD, but our work isn't done yet. The $80,000 of earnings in the annuity will eventually be taxed, and if we apply the same 30 percent tax rate to it, we find an after-tax value in the annuity of $156,000, now only $5,000 more than the bank CD, but still clearly an advantage.

Consider this, however: "How likely is it that someone who allowed their contribution to grow over 20 years is simply going to take it all out in a lump sum to pay the tax?" Not very likely. As a result, most people would begin some method of systematic withdrawal, which would allow them the continued benefit of tax-deferred growth on the remaining balance.

FIXED, INDEXED, VARIABLE

"People who buy annuities, it turns out, live longer than people who don't, and not because the people who buy annuities are healthier to start with. The evidence suggests that an annuity's steady payout provides a little extra incentive to keep chugging along."—Steven D. Levitt, "SuperFreakonomics"

Please keep in mind, as we go through this discussion of annuities, each of these structures—fixed, indexed, and variable—can also be used with CVL.

If we look at possible annuity policies based on risk versus reward, the safest position is the fixed annuity. Here, the insurance company guarantees our principal. A fixed annuity also offers a guaranteed rate of return each year and a guaranteed minimum rate.

It is safe and secure with a fixed annuity, but what do we sacrifice for all these guarantees? Correct, an investor in equities might obtain greater gains. If we want higher returns, we could invest in a variable annuity. A variable annuity is like your 401(k), where one can select from various investments under the qualified umbrella. But what's the risk here? The possible loss of principal.

There are riders we can add to a variable annuity that will offer us some guarantees, but that means the policy's expenses will go up. Whenever we want to protect our pennies, it will also cost us pennies. That doesn't mean we shouldn't do it. It does mean we should be aware of it to make an informed decision.

Indexed Annuities (IA) fit right in the middle of the spectrum. Here is the opportunity to capitalize on potential market gains without risking loss of principal. You might be wondering, "Renée, how does an indexed annuity offer stock market returns without risk of investment?" They use options to create the gain. If the index increases, the options pay, and those earnings are added to the client's annuity. If the market goes down, the only amount lost is the cost of options. Part of the proceeds are put into investment-grade bonds to support the guaranteed returns.

You might think, then, "It's a no-brainer. Everyone should put all their money in an indexed annuity (or CVL)." While an IA can be fantastic, buying options can add expenses to the contract, and in lower interest rate environments, it can drag down the overall return. Like everything, it is a good idea to check around and ensure you get the best option for your pennies at any given time.

EASY, PEASY

"Faith makes all things possible... love makes all things easy." —Dwight L. Moody

Before moving on to our discussion about Health Insurance, I want to share some thoughts on two other insurance forms: Property and Casualty (P&C) and Disability Income.

P&C: Typical coverage in this area is auto and homeowners' insurance. Even if you do not have a home, you can still insure your possessions with a renter's policy. If you have unique valuables that are expensive to replace, like a wedding ring or collectibles, riders can be added for special coverage.

I've outlined what P&C generally covers, but I will not spend much time reviewing this area of insurance. I am not licensed in this area, so I don't have a breadth of knowledge to share. Any good agent can review coverage terms and make an adequate recommendation.

To secure your future financial path, I think there are two important considerations regarding P&C insurance:

1. While this form of insurance is not as glitzy as some others, it is vital to have good coverage and keep it in place. Some of the liability challenges one might encounter in life are difficult to overcome. This is why even the wealthy tend to have good coverage and not leave too much of this to self-insuring.
2. That doesn't mean you should pay too much for P&C insurance. Shop around every year or two. I email my DEC (defined below) page with a quote request to several agents in my area. I do an internet search, and if I can't find an email address in their contact information, I generally don't go with them. Emails are far more efficient, and the information is documented.

DEC is short for "Declaration," an overview of the policy terms, including the deductible. It also includes handy information such as vehicle identification number(s) (VIN), which the agent will need to provide a quote. I also do not automatically go with the lowest rate. The agent I have now was so responsive and on the ball that I stopped looking as soon as I found her.

Regardless of how responsive and sharp my agent is, two years from now, I will still shop for coverage again. Every penny counts.

Property—Protects your property from damage, loss, or theft. This can include your home, car, motorcycle, golf cart, rental property, or personal possessions. For example, homeowners' insurance can help pay to repair damage to your home or personal property caused by fire, lightning, windstorms, hail, smoke, theft, and vandalism.

Casualty—Provides liability protection if you're found legally responsible for an accident that causes injuries to others or damages their property. Casualty insurance can include vehicle insurance, liability insurance, theft insurance, workers' compensation insurance, and more.

Disability Income—This insurance coverage is designed to replace your income should you become disabled. While I will not tell you what you should do in this area, I will tell you what I chose to do and why.

When I worked for an employer, I purchased both the group short-term and long-term disability coverage. It was inexpensive enough, and in those years, I was younger without much savings. I was also planning to have children, and these policies replaced some of my income while I was on family leave. You might find that same value if an employer offers you this coverage.

For the last 25 years, while I managed my education business, I never purchased disability insurance. During this stage of life, I had some savings. Mind you, I wouldn't want it to be spent now because I'd rather get some more FREE pennies. I quite possibly was underinsured, but here is why I didn't buy it:

1. Social Security offers disability income. It is hard to qualify for these benefits, and it takes some time. One would have to find a source of income before Social Security Disability begins paying, but it does provide an option.
2. Since much of my work is computer-based, fewer disabilities would keep me from working. Could I still encounter challenges? Yes, certainly. It still remains, however, that I could overcome many obstacles and continue to work.
3. Because my health is good, the most likely reason for disability is accidental. This means there is a high likelihood that other casualty coverage could provide reimbursement for the liability. This could be a car accident or a fall at the mall.

Again, none of these options are automatic, and many would say I was underinsured, but in my mind, the individual plan premium cost was too much compared to my risk. You'll want to make those determinations for yourself. We will now move our discussion to health insurance, which does pose a risk of stealing all your pennies. I was initially going to try to squeeze it into this chapter, and as I began to write it, I realized how much valuable information there is to share. So, it became a chapter of its own—it's time for "The Penny Thief."

CHAPTER THIRTEEN

THE PENNY THIEF

HEALTHCARE IN AMERICA

"America's health care system is neither healthy, caring, nor a system."
—Walter Cronkite

HEALTH INSURANCE

My gosh, does Walter Cronkite have it right? I often wonder how long this can go on before America finally invests in healthcare with genuine compassion. Before offering insight into what you might do with your health insurance component, let me also give you a little perspective on healthcare in the U.S. and the legislation we have in place that is designed to provide better access.

I started my career working at a health insurance company. We offered life and annuities, but our staple was individual medical insurance. When I started in the 1980s, a 20-year-old nonsmoking male in good health could get a $250 annual deductible plan for about $20 per month. Once upon a time, there were different premium rates if you used tobacco. His female counterpart's premium was double that or more because of her maternity risk. Please also note that I rented my first apartment in those years for about $385 monthly. Overall, expenses were much lower than today, but medical care had yet to start the insane increases we've seen in the last few decades.

If either of these people had health conditions, they could be denied coverage, or the insurance company could place a rider excluding coverage on their pre-existing condition. This sort of rider means that if you have a bad knee or shoulder, the policy won't cover anything related to that ailment. Nice, huh?

Some progressive states, like Minnesota, began to make legislative changes. They moved to unisex rates to share the maternity cost with the men. Plans were available for the uninsurable. Coverage for things like chiropractors and mental health care that were typically excluded were now required. If you were on an employer group plan, individuals could not be declined or limited by exclusionary riders, but that did not apply to those on individual contracts.

Fast-forward to the Affordable Care Act, enacted in 2010. The rollout was in stages, but most facets were close to full implementation by January 1, 2014. That was more than ten years ago, and there have been no other significant reforms to healthcare since then. There have been some changes, like increases to the tax credits for those who qualify, and reduced costs for some pharmaceuticals, but nothing major to help all of us.

Meanwhile, the U.S. healthcare cost (HC) is mind-boggling. We have the largest GDP in the world—$29 trillion in 2024—and the most significant percentage of GDP spent on HC compared to any other industrialized nation—approximately 17 percent. Most other countries spend 10 percent or less of GDP on healthcare. That means Americans paid about $5 trillion this year to one of the wealthiest industries.

To put the enormous financial burden of the U.S. healthcare system into perspective, U.S. federal outlays (expenses) for 2023 were $6.1 trillion. This includes Social Security, Medicare, Medicaid, defense, education, DOJ (Department of Justice), IRS (Internal Revenue Service), interest on the debt—EVERYTHING. The federal budget of the United States, which people complain is too excessive, is just one trillion more than our total cost of healthcare. More about that before this chapter ends.

This enormous HC expense might be worth it if we had better-than-average outcomes. Instead, the U.S. has the lowest life expectancy at birth, the highest death rates for avoidable or treatable conditions, the highest maternal and infant mortality, and we have among the highest suicide rates compared to other industrialized, developed nations. The U.S. has the highest rate of people with multiple chronic conditions, and an obesity rate nearly twice the average of the 38 member countries of the Organization for Economic Cooperation and Development (OECD).

The reason our healthcare outcomes are so poor is complex, but ultimately, it stems from two words: **inequities** in the system that we've done little to correct because we have a culture of **individualism** that says you can do it on your own. These two things play off each other—or compete against each other. Even though we know things like racism, sexism, classism, and ageism exist and cause inequities in the system, we can deny this possibility by claiming that people could overcome these challenges if they tried.

The concept of individualism significantly benefits those who experience little impact from the "isms." Adding to the irony and hypocrisy of this idea that we all have the same opportunities are the rules, laws, and favoritism generally granted by the folks who encounter the effects of the "isms" the least—predominantly white men in affluent positions. Their opinion of how we experience success or even what is of value is not universal to all people.

In Joe Biden's July 25, 2024, speech about dropping out of the campaign, he said, "Nowhere else on earth could a kid with a stutter from modest beginnings in Scranton, Pennsylvania, and Claymont, Delaware, one day sit behind the Resolute Desk in the Oval Office as President of the United States, but here I am. That's what's so special about America." Even though Joe comes from modest means, he is still a white man, however. This granted him a leg up every time he walked into a room.

You might point to Kamala Harris, who took over the campaign—her father is Jamaican, and her mother is Indian. She broke two barriers—gender and race—in getting to the top, but Kamala also had something that many young girls of color do not have: highly educated parents. One was an economist, the other a medical researcher. That, too, impacts someone's destiny.

My point is not to say that Joe Biden and Kamala Harris are undeserving. I believe they have offered tremendous value to America. My comments are not intended to diminish the effort and hard work they—or people like you—have put into creating success. I, too, came from modest means and worked hard to build a good life for myself and my children. You likely have as well. Diligence is part of the success matrix.

What I am saying is that all things are not equal. That is the first step. If we are going to do this right, it is essential to recognize the barriers and do what we can so that all people can thrive. If we continue to deny the difference in opportunities caused by "isms," we will never solve critical social problems, and we will continue to miss the richness of elevating all people to an equal voice in the fabric of society.

A GLOBAL PERSPECTIVE

"The right to health is a fundamental part of our human rights and of our understanding of a life in dignity."
—World Health Organization, The Right to Health

Nearly every developed nation, except the U.S., has a universal healthcare system. These countries decided that ensuring access to quality healthcare was a fundamental human right. I know we are told their plans are horrible or the taxes are high, but those are the stories we are told so the rich can keep that $5 trillion in pennies. The whole world would switch to our plan if it were better. The truth is, it's not.

When developing countries like Taiwan decided to enrich their healthcare delivery systems, they did a lot of research. Taiwan initially believed the U.S. offered the best plan and would likely model their healthcare after ours. Their research told a vastly different story. They found that we have a free market, not a healthcare system, and decided that it would not serve their people well.

Instead, they chose to model their system after countries with a more equitable approach.

To see if they overcame barriers to access, in the PBS Frontline documentary *"Sick Around The World,"* the commentator asks, "How quickly could I see, say, an orthopedic specialist?" The Taiwanese official responds, "Would you like to go right now?"

Those countries struggle with the same things we do—providing quick access and quality care at a fair price to the patient, the provider, and everyone in between. It's not easy—it is a balancing act, but it can be done. They all did it by reducing the profit-driven aspects of HC. They negotiate pricing on everything from pharmaceuticals to medical devices. Some, like Japan, even have a price book that tells doctors and hospitals what they can charge for stitches, MRIs, a hospital stay—even a facial tissue. This is how they keep costs down. It is also why you can purchase your prescriptions through an international vendor at dramatically lower prices than you're offered in the U.S.

THE U.S. & OUR PROFIT PROBLEM

"Greed is not a financial issue. It's a heart issue." —Andy Stanley

Healthcare is supposed to "care" just as financial services should "serve," and sadly, due to greed, neither seems able to meet these objectives. When inventor Frederick Banting and the research team discovered insulin in 1923, they refused to put their name on the patent. They felt it was unethical for a doctor to profit from a discovery that would save lives. What a remarkable choice and insight of conscience. The three inventors—Banting, Collip, and Best—sold the insulin patent to the University of Toronto for a mere $1. They wanted everyone who needed the medication to be able to afford it.

Their drug, which many of the 30 million Americans with diabetes rely on, is the quintessential example of pharmaceutical greed. By 2016, about 100 years later, the average price per month rose to $450—and costs continued to rise, so much so that as many as one in four people with diabetes began skimping on or skipping lifesaving doses.

This greed fest continued until the passage of the Bipartisan Infrastructure Law and Inflation Reduction Act in 2022, which required pharmaceutical companies to charge no more than $35—the most prominent beneficiary being Medicare recipients. Congress, the White House, and new players in the market have increased pressure on insulin manufacturers to lower their prices. Many more people benefit from this price reduction, which is good. Typically, if there is a benefit exclusive to Medicare, it has negative consequences for the rest of us. More about this in a few pages.

I want to believe that people can self-regulate—that somewhere in the mix of what each individual needs, we would continue to think of what is suitable for all. Individualism is the killer of this sort of community thinking. The more individualism thrives, the more likely one feels the need to get theirs. When the people around us also believe we have a right to more than others, it becomes easy to focus on the profits and forget about the millions who need this life-saving medicine. The thought becomes, "They'll easily pay anything we charge." Instead of, "How do we make it easier to buy it?"

This brings us full circle, right back to the Flow. When I am connected to the Spirit of the Universe—when I let GOD be my guide—the question is NEVER, "How much can I get?" and inherently becomes, "How can I help?" The Flow connects us. The Flow elevates all—the Great Equalizer, the Great Hope. The more we tap the Flow, the better the world becomes. It had to be the first step in this financial process because, without it, it is easy to lose sight of our Perfect Place—being one among many. The Flow is the Great Connector and the Perfect Vision.

The reduction of the cost of insulin started with a law, yes. Is it possible that the proposer of that law reacted to the Flow? A nudge that said, "People are hurting. You can do this to help." Oh, yes, it's entirely possible. I might say,

"Probable." Did everyone who signed on to this cost-reduction concept have that same motivation? No—some were considering their own selfish aims, but I believe there is a Force ever drawing us toward the Greater Good. We must decide whether to be part of that momentum or ignore the pull.

After the law passed, a few companies decided to drop the price of insulin for everyone. This put their competitors in a tough spot. If they didn't follow suit, they would lose business. This is insulin. One manufacturer does not differ from another. This move forced the entire industry to reevaluate their prices.

What do you believe motivated those first universal price-dropping companies, the ones that expanded the $35 price beyond the law's requirements? I don't know for sure, but I don't think it was advertising or positive public relations because I had no idea of the names of these companies until I did a deep dive for the research in this section. I cannot say what occurred, but something happened that created a universal betterment for many people. That is the Heart of the Flow.

There is a lot more to this story. Before we proceed, however, I believe it is essential to note that if you are unfamiliar with Medicare and Medicaid, you will likely find the information in the coming section surprising. Your thought could be, "That can't be true." Sadly, too many Americans are unaware of the intricacies built into these programs. These details are rarely considered newsworthy, so people are unlikely to learn about them until they are personally affected.

Your other reaction will likely be sadness, anger, or fear. Our system's failures mean that far too many Americans will lose their dignity while they lose all their precious pennies to healthcare. I encourage you to use those emotions to help make a difference.

I joke with my students that they pop into class every two years or so to review this emotionally shocking material, but I am in every class, month after month, year after year. All this information has changed me. I hope you allow it to change you. Let me explain more.

MEDICARE & MEDICAID

"No longer will older Americans be denied the healing miracle of modern medicine. No longer will illness crush and destroy the savings that they have so carefully put away over a lifetime so that they might enjoy dignity in their later years."
—President Lyndon Johnson, Signing Medicare on July 30, 1965

This section will focus on two federally-supported healthcare programs: Medicaid and Medicare. I'll give you a brief overview of each, and then we'll explore how these plans impact you and your pennies.

Medicaid is designed to cover the indigent—those who are impoverished and unable to provide healthcare for themselves. The government pays for a comprehensive insurance plan for those who qualify and are under the age of 65. Paying for private insurance rather than actual healthcare costs reduces taxpayers' expenses and keeps the private market in the mix.

Medicare provides insurance coverage to seniors. Eligibility begins three months before one's 65th birthday. People who qualify for SS disability benefits can also get Medicare. The coverage is comprehensive, covering most medical needs, but has some gaps, so Medicare recipients typically supplement their coverage with a private plan. I'll provide additional information on these coverage terms shortly.

"Both (Medicaid and Medicare) were enacted in 1965 under the Johnson administration, and when combined, they outweigh every other expense in the federal budget. They are more significant than defense, and the only thing larger is Social Security."

That is a standard line from one of my classes. After saying it, we'd look at the federal outlay (expense) figures because, on occasion, people didn't believe me. They would say, "I find that hard to believe." This is a polite way of saying,

"I think you are lying." Or "I don't think you know what you are talking about." It's a little like saying, "Bless your heart." This may sound nice, but it means, "You need blessings because that thing you said or did is crazy."

We'd go through the numbers—proving every word of it. Slowly, healthcare expenses have been inching ever closer until 2023, when they eclipsed the cost of Social Security. Please see the image below. Medicare outlays over the 12-month term are $839 billion, and Medicaid outlays are $616 billion. When we combine them, we arrive at $1.455 trillion. Social Security over the same period, $1.3 trillion. Healthcare spending in 2023 was $155 billion, more than we spent on SS and more than any other segment on this chart.

With Trump back in office, these values have changed. He prioritized defense spending over investments in healthcare. Other expenses, such as those for the Department of Homeland Security (DHS), which were added to the "Nondiscretionary" column, have increased dramatically. Looking at updated values to see new trends might be valuable.

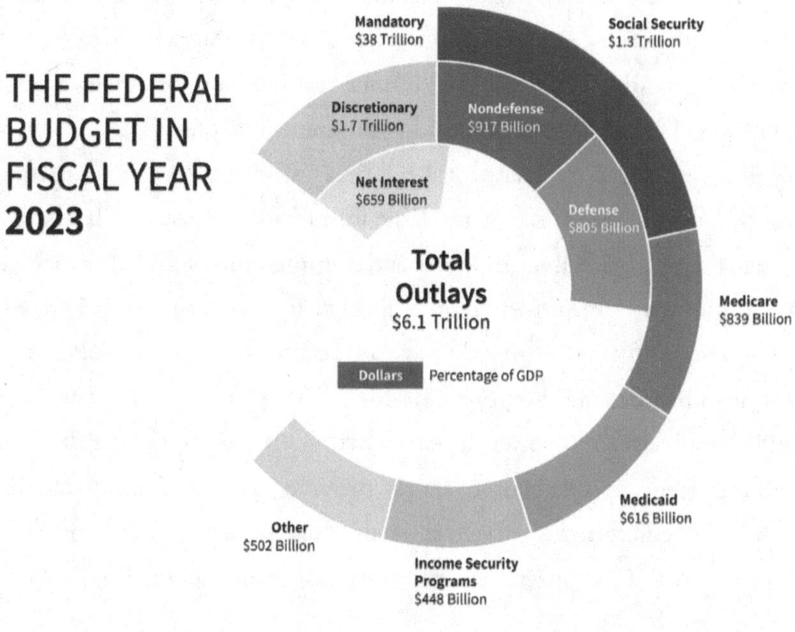

(Source: https://www.cbo.gov/publication/59727)

MEDICAID FINANCING

"I think every program needs to stand the sunshine of righteous scrutiny. Whether it's Social Security, whether it's Medicaid, whether it's Medicare." —*Rick Perry*

It is also important to note that when we see a Medicaid spending value of $616, this is only half the story. When this pivotal legislation was passed, imagine the federal government turning to the states and saying, "We want you to administer a health care program in your state designed to cover the impoverished within your borders. Don't worry; we plan to help you. For every dollar you spend under this important program, we will match it."

Medicaid is a 50/50 sharing arrangement between the federal government and the states—that is, most states and most programs. Some states qualify for more than a 50 percent match from the feds. These states tend to have more impoverished people, but their tax revenue cannot support their 50 percent share. In class, I'll ask, "Which states do you think these are?"

Typical responses are California and Texas. I believe these two states come to mind because people think of the large immigrant population. It stems from the lie that floats around that undocumented immigrants qualify for Medicaid.

I had the word "misinformation" typed in that sentence and changed it to LIE. I understand that some people have innocently shared this misinformation, believing it to be true, but the origins of this disinformation—politicians—know very well this is false. Worse yet, it harms people. It creates further division and can enhance hate. While some states provide coverage and have limited exceptions for emergencies, the fact is that the qualifying rule for Medicaid coverage is to be a U.S. citizen or have proper documentation, PERIOD.

I have encouraged class after class to share any Medicaid enrollment information that dispels this documentation requirement, because I want to give people the truth. Guess how many people have given me information. Yup, ZERO. Not one class member has even said, "I read something in..." From there, we would typically go to the internet and research.

This is just like the Social Security myths we dispelled in an earlier chapter—we hear misinformation without supporting evidence, accept it as accurate, base our choices on flawed information, and then share it with others because it supports a narrative people find useful or comforting in the moment. We are all guilty of this at times, but it is also possible to do better. There are countless quality resources at our fingertips, giving us every opportunity to seek out and rely on the truth.

Here's another fact: California and Texas are both wealthy states. They have larger budgets and higher GDPs than the states that need more federal Medicaid money. States that qualify for more than 50 percent federal funding of their Medicaid programs are typically our southern states. Alabama, Mississippi, Arkansas, and other states can qualify for up to an 80 percent Medicaid match, and the Children's Health Insurance Program (CHIP) also qualifies for a match of more than 50 percent.

This is all to say that the $616 billion the federal government spends on healthcare grows to more than a trillion when we add the states' contributions. But our financial calculations of healthcare in America are not yet complete.

NATIONAL COST OF HEALTHCARE

"Social Security's not the hard one to solve. Medicare, that is the gorilla in the room, and you've got to put all of it on the table."—Joe Biden

Let's do as Joe suggests and discuss all of U.S. healthcare spending—all five trillion.

> Tax-funded health expenditures totaled $1.877 trillion in 2013 and are projected to increase to $3.642 trillion in 2024. The government's share of overall health spending was 64.3 percent of national health expenditures in 2013 and will rise to 67.1 percent in 2024.
>
> (Source: https://www.ncbi.nlm.nih.gov/pmc/articles/PMC4880216/)

There are a few essential pieces of information we can glean from this impactful quote from the National Library of Medicine:

- The number in the quote above is more than Medicare and Medicaid. This is all publicly funded healthcare, so yes, Medicare and Medicaid are included at the federal and state levels. It also includes medical expenses through the Veterans Administration (VA), coverage for public employees, including police and teachers, elected officials, and military personnel, and tax subsidies, such as tax deductions and tax credits under the ACA.
- Over this approximately 10-year period (2013 to 2024), healthcare spending in the U.S. just about doubled. From our earlier penny-doubling math (the rule of 72) a few chapters back, it increased at an average of about 7 percent annually—well above standard inflation. As Joe said, this is the gorilla in the room, and no one is even talking about it, let alone doing anything about it.
- In 2013, the government's share of healthcare spending was slightly less than two-thirds, well over half, of all national spending on healthcare. This percentage rose a decade later, accounting for $3.642 trillion in expenses.
- This also means that individuals (you, me, and everyone else paying all or part of our insurance premiums and medical expenses) and businesses (employers that provide health insurance or other coverage to employees) only account for 32.9 percent. Everything we all pitch in to this ever-growing expense is less than one-third of the $5 trillion annual cost of healthcare.

There are many excellent reasons why we should move to Medicare for All, and right here is one of them—we are so close. Many millions of taxpayers are currently contributing to a healthcare system that few reap the benefits of. I understand that people are frustrated by these numbers, but none of us wants to take Medicare benefits from grandma or take VA benefits from the vets who sacrificed so much for us. Many of us would instead like to see these benefits enhanced for these groups that we believe deserve it.

We seem to direct our ire toward the Medicaid folks. As mentioned earlier, it starts with the (incorrect) notion that some people who don't belong here are racking up all these medical bills (which we've dispelled); then there are lazy people who just don't want to work, so they can get this free healthcare.

Maybe that is true of some people—I certainly don't know everyone on Medicaid. We'll look at some of the income tests for qualification, and they're not the kind of numbers we associate with the American dream. I cannot see the logic of someone intentionally staying in a low-paying job or remaining on government assistance in order to qualify for Medicaid. There's no room to save pennies there. There is also limited dignity and freedom. It is not a grand life that qualifies for Medicaid.

While people like to get worked up about the welfare mom pumping out kids to stay on the system, or some 35-year-old brat living in the basement refusing to work, the data doesn't support this theory. While the most significant number of Medicaid enrollees are in the under-65 market, these individuals are not the lion's share of the program's financial burden. Again, we buy them a health insurance plan instead of paying their healthcare costs, which makes this group annoying to some people, but Medicaid enrollees are not the cost problem.

The cost problem lies with seniors and the disabled. Although they may represent fewer enrollees, they account for the largest share of our healthcare expenses. This brings us full circle again, as we are now faced with the issue of kicking grandma or grandpa off the plan, which is hard for any reasonable person to do. Or kicking off the disabled person who, again, most people would agree is deserving of this coverage, given the intent was to provide coverage for those who could not provide it for themselves.

Yes, a major contributor to these inflated costs is the long-term care (LTC) issue, which is a real mess. Let me explain the downfall I've witnessed over the years.

PENNIES TO THE POOR HOUSE

"Be nice to your children. After all, they are going to choose your nursing home."
—Steven Wright

LTC insurance is a form of daily indemnity insurance, which makes it more like a disability income policy than a standard health insurance policy. With daily indemnity, the policy pays a specific dollar amount for every day a person has a qualifying event. In the case of LTC insurance, a qualifying event is an inability to complete two Activities of Daily Living (ADL): bathing, dressing, toileting, transferring (getting in and out of bed or chair), eating, and continence.

The policy typically covers in-facility and home health care, with different benefit amounts for each. It also typically has inflation protection, so the benefits increase over time as care costs rise. The client chooses the initial benefit amount, and the plan's cost is based on this dollar amount and the client's age. Some contracts offer a rider that returns the premium if the client doesn't use the benefits.

The story of LTC insurance is much the same as that of health insurance, except there was no measure of rescue like the ACA. An LTC insurance policy is fully underwritten, meaning it's difficult to qualify. Agents say, "You should buy it when you're 50." Okay, that possibly gets someone through underwriting, but I am paying 20 years of premiums or more during years I likely won't need it. There is also no guarantee that I can keep affording the premium as I get older. Many of these contracts have experienced dramatic rate increases as the cost of care has risen and more people are using them.

Some older contracts written in the 90s have proven to work okay as seniors age. Another option is to put LTC insurance into a CVL (Cash Value Life) insurance policy. In this case, the death benefit is prepaid if the insured requires LTC, but will only cover care equal to the death benefit. Once that is gone, the client is on their own again. This means using their pretty little pennies to pay for care. For in-facility care, this can be $10,000 per month or more (2025 rates).

DOESN'T MEDICARE PAY?

"I will never turn Medicare into a voucher. No American should ever have to spend their golden years at the mercy of insurance companies. They should retire with the care and dignity they have earned" —Barack Obama

Medicare only covers assisted living if it is medically necessary. The transfer to LTC must follow a three-day hospital stay, and the client must be in a rehabilitative state, effectively improving every day. I'll use my mother's situation as an example.

My mother was diagnosed with cancer in the spring of 2020, the height of COVID-19. They found the cancer because of a tumor in her spine that affected her mobility. They used radiation to shrink it, but after a few days of stabilizing her in the hospital, she was still not mobile enough to go home. They moved her to a transitional care unit so she could receive physical therapy (PT). This qualified for Medicare coverage.

All was well, except my mother didn't improve. They had also provided her with immunotherapy while at the hospital, and my mother had no energy for her PT. Remember, one must be in a rehabilitative (or improving) state to continue getting Medicare coverage for a stay in a care facility. The insurance company allowed her to continue with Medicare coverage for a few days, hoping her decline would be temporary and she would start her PT soon. Since she did not improve, she no longer had insurance coverage for the transitional care unit.

This meant that my mother would now be personally responsible for care costing more than $300 per day. My mother was not a wealthy woman. At the time this happened, she had about $12,000 in savings. We went to the county for assistance through Medicaid, but remember, this program is for those who are impoverished. You might think, "Isn't only $12,000 in savings considered poverty?" Not according to Medicaid.

- Most states have a limit of $3,000 in a cash account. This limit includes retirement funds. Some states have lower limits.
- To qualify, she can only keep specific personal effects, a car, home equity under certain limits, and a burial policy.

We aren't done yet. There are also income limits. To qualify for home health care in Minnesota, the income limit for a single person is slightly more than $1,200 monthly (2023/2024). This is poverty. This monthly income limit doesn't even cover rent in our area, which means that the person qualifies for Section 8 housing, food stamps or an EBT card, heating assistance, and other government programs because one simply cannot live on $1,200 monthly.

People living in a facility in Minnesota are granted a personal needs allowance of $128 (2025), which is supposed to cover all their individual needs: clothing, shampoo, razors, haircuts—everything—for about $100 per month. Any income that exceeds these limits goes to the cost of care first, and no income is exempt. Your state may differ, so you might need to do some research to get the correct numbers. These values are indexed for inflation. As time goes on, they will increase.

Here's my mother, who worked hard to pull together the $12,000. She wanted to get her teeth fixed, but instead she would have to pay $300 per day for about 30 days, when she was down to the $3,000 allowable limit, unless she was released earlier. Upon hearing this, my brother said, "Renée, wait to put in the application until I get that money out of Mom's account."

Wouldn't that be a neat solution? But yeah, they thought of that. The county will review five years of financial records on all accounts as part of the application process. There is no way to escape this process.

Some seniors decide to start giving away their assets. Suppose they transfer their home and savings through sizeable gifts to their kids, grandkids, charities, or trusts, and the transfer was at least 60 months (5 years) before the application to the county for assistance. In that case, it is past the "look-back period" and, therefore, no longer part of their estate for Medicaid eligibility. If the county finds any gifts or transfers within the last five years, it can recapture them to pay for the person's care. The county is clear: they will take any means necessary to recoup this money, including liens on tangible assets or wage garnishment. When people receive these gifts, they need to know that the county could come calling if something happens in those five years.

Not only are there risks to the recipient of the gifts, but I also lose control when I give away my home and money. That is the intent of a gift; however, many seniors do so to preserve some wealth in case they need a nursing home. Also ironic is that many of these same people, moving their assets around, will rage over student loan repayment while forcing young taxpayers to cover their LTC, or screaming about those on food assistance or Medicaid not working hard enough to support themselves. There's that darn INDIVIDUALISM again.

We are the wealthiest nation in the world, and we force people into a degrading process of impoverishment before we offer a solution. To make matters worse, there isn't much you can do about it. Even if you wanted to get insurance to cover long-term care, it's very costly, you might not qualify, and it might not be available for you when you need it because our legislators have done nothing to help with this problem. No one is even talking about it.

In my opinion, this situation is despicable. As I write these words, we are in the longest government shutdown in U.S. history. (That was November 2025, but this record was recently dwarfed by the Department of Homeland Security shutdown in March and April of 2026.) What was at stake? Enriched tax credits under the ACA so that millions of Americans can afford their health insurance. Republicans, who have the majority, are saying (and rightly so), "It's a bigger problem than that." Yes, so where is your idea to solve it?

Democrats are responding (and are just as correct), "Americans need this relief now." Yes, yes, they do. My health insurance premium is about to increase by 400 percent because of this change in credit, and I'm 58 with 7 years until Medicare. Not talking about it, not trying to work through it with the betterment of Americans at the forefront, is not a solution.

What do other countries do, you might ask? They consider LTC part of their universal healthcare. They also do cool things like using the unemployment insurance system to offer paid family leave. The U.S. is one of eight nations worldwide without paid family leave according to the New York Times, October, 25, 2021. Wait until you hear about that!

THE POLAR OPPOSITE

> *"Beginning in the 1800s with the Industrial Revolution, when women started to go into the formal workforce, leaving working at home to working in factories, countries realized they needed to do something. And they started to pass paid maternity leave."*
>
> *—Jody Heymann*

Since he's been a resident of Canada, my son has had some interesting stories to tell about his experience with healthcare. His views have changed now that he sees universal healthcare in action. I believe these personal stories illustrate a rich consideration for Americans. The first is a tender contrast to my mother's cancer story.

A Sick Spouse—The wife of my son's friend was diagnosed with a significant health condition. One afternoon, while they were hanging out, my son asked, "How is your wife doing?" His friend said her treatments were going well. They hoped for a good prognosis soon, but his income replacement had not kicked in yet.

My son asked, "Income replacement?" He replied, "Yes, I can take time off to help my wife, and they'll replace some of my lost wages. We've been waiting a while to receive it." Then my son said, "You're at least lucky you get that. We don't have anything like that in the U.S." (Some states, like Minnesota, have started benefits like this.)

Think about how impactful it is for someone you love who is going through a trying health condition to have a spouse, adult child, or parent there to help care for them and their household. Consider for a moment how impactful this is for better health outcomes and the emotional support of all family members, simply because one can step away from work to be a caregiver with some income replacement and no fear of bankruptcy.

If you are like I used to be, you are likely thinking, "Nice idea, but that is too costly to employers." I'm unsure how Canada finances this benefit, but countries like Japan use the unemployment insurance system, in which employees pay a share of the premium. In the U.S., the employer pays 100 percent of the cost of unemployment insurance, but in Japan, the employer pays 0.7 percent, and the employee pays 0.4 percent of wages.

If we were to implement something similar in the U.S., those earning $100,000 annually would pay $400 per year for this benefit, which would then be provided to every other worker in the country. That's not many pennies for something so impactful. People in class will say, "But I'm done having kids. I don't want to pay for that."

Back to INDIVIDUALISM—did you see how quickly that jumps right in? I understand. Things are tight, and we don't need extra expenses, but I have two thoughts:

1. This benefit is Family Leave. This Canadian man took it because his wife had cancer. I could have used it when my mom was sick. This is more than just a maternity or paternity benefit.
2. As a parent, I want my children, your children, and all future generations to be allowed to pour love, time, and energy into their babies and be present without concern for finances. Growing little people into happy, healthy, and productive big people is the essence of meaningful work.

My son also tells me he can't tell much difference between the taxes he paid in the U.S. and those in Canada. According to the Fraser Institute, the average Canadian will pay about 10 percent of their income in tax for their healthcare plan. So, a family of two adults and two children earning around $169,296 may pay around $16,950.

If you were to calculate all the costs associated with your healthcare in the U.S. (premiums, employer share, deductibles, co-pays, out-of-pocket, etc.), your costs might be about the same or higher than 10 percent of your income. I have a $7,500 deductible plan that costs $500 per month ($6,000 per year). That is just for me and doesn't include other out-of-pocket expenses, such as dental or vision. Here are some other things my son has told me about Canada's plan.

COVID Compassion—My son noticed a stark contrast between his American and Canadian friends at the outbreak of COVID-19. Both groups were nervous about the illness and frustrated with the restrictions, but in Canada, there was less anxiety. They had their healthcare coverage, and it would be there no matter what. In America, we do not have that assurance. For many of us, our insurance, if we have it, is tied to our employment. Amid the pandemic, Americans were uncertain, and rightfully so.

A Business Alternative—My son started his own business two years ago. As he started this venture, he said, "It is so nice to know that I can leave my place of employment and do anything else I want to earn an income, but I don't have to worry about my healthcare coverage. I have enough things to worry about. I don't need that, too." While he said these words, I wondered how many Americans have chosen not to pursue their career dreams because they might lose employer-provided health insurance. The next thought was, "What has society missed out on when a great idea didn't make it to the public because someone couldn't risk the loss of health insurance?"

Damn Immigrants—When my son first got to Canada, he was working on a research project at the University. Plenty of time spent together with Canadians, and the conversation would shift to things outside of the work at hand. When politics would roll around, occasionally someone would say, "Then those immigrants come here, use our healthcare, and pay nothing for it."

My son's first thought was, "Wow—Canadians complain about that too!" The next one was, "Wait, I'm an immigrant!"

This was a real eye-opener on many levels. During one such conversation, my son decided to say, "Ya know what? I am one of those immigrants. Being on this project, I don't earn much money, so I hardly pay any taxes. So, I am one of the people using the system but not paying for it." He followed it with, "Maybe you didn't consider it because I look like you."

My son wasn't mad. He was not offended. He understood their frustration. He had experienced it, too, but he also recognized that we often vent this frustration on people who don't look like us. The University has a diverse population. There were students in attendance representing many shades and countries. While there, he witnessed that most immigrants worked very hard. They realized the opportunity they'd been given and wanted to honor it. Now that he's had this experience, he sees value in helping immigrants succeed. After all, he is one.

COST SHIFTING

"When the government refuses to pay its full share, everyone else must pay more." — Philip Briggs of the Health Insurance Association

Earlier, I mentioned that if seniors on Medicare get a special price break, that isn't helpful to the rest of us. Let me explain what that means. Just as Social Security had financial issues in the 1970s and '80s, so did Medicare and Medicaid. The 1970s were high-inflation years. Healthcare was not immune to these price increases. Something had to be done to keep these programs afloat.

With Reagan's direction, Congress decided the best solution was to pass a law to fix costs. This law told hospitals, doctors, and clinics everywhere (paraphrased, of course), "We can't afford what you're charging. So, listen, this is what we are going to do. We will tell you what we will pay—what we can afford and what we believe is reasonable. If you think you'll get out of this new lower payment structure by denying Medicare and Medicaid recipients, sorry. That won't work either. This law says you must take them."

Some brilliant minds on Capitol Hill thought this would force all healthcare providers to economize and budget more effectively, maybe even reducing costs for everyone. What do you think of that? Do you think that would be your reaction to a mandate to accept a pay cut? Would you budget better? Economize?

Yeah, it's hard to convince anyone by mandate that they'll have to work harder for less money. The universal reaction was not to figure out how to make this more affordable for everyone, but to find a way to keep their income the same.

This is the thing—I've never run a hospital. Probably, you haven't either. We don't know all that is involved, and as much as I can sit here in front of my keyboard blaming a for-profit system, we have no idea where the margins might be that could be cut. Maybe the price is very close to the actual cost.

I don't think the federal government knows the answer to that question without doing a deep dive, yet it has established a price book for what it would spend. In doing so, it had to understand that the reaction to a pay cut would not be a revamping of all healthcare systems. Granted, I don't know how to get such an enormous industry to buy into a price cut, right?

The healthcare industry replied, "Okay, fine. We'll comply as required. We'll shift the losses to everyone else." Thus, a system of cost-shifting was born. They took the Medicare and Medicaid payments, and any losses were shifted to you, me, and everyone else in the private market. We paid higher prices and subsidized these programs with more than just our tax dollars. It's part of the reason private insurance is so expensive.

Unless we make these price breaks universal and applicable to everyone, they will not be helpful. It also means the government must take the time to determine where the abuses are in the system and what can be made more efficient. They must work with the providers to develop the plan. A lot of work needs to be done in the world of healthcare. It can be done; we need our elected officials to get started.

I LOVED IT WHEN I SWITCHED

"That's what the Affordable Care Act is all about. It's about filling the gaps in employer-based care so that when we lose a job, or go back to school, or start that new business, we'll still have coverage."—Barack Obama

Obama was right. The ACA filled that gap, but as we've illustrated, there are plenty more gaps that need filling. ACA was a good start, but more reform is necessary. You might be one of those who are thinking, "Renée, the government messes stuff up. I don't want to be on a government plan." You could bring up VA examples, and some examples are horrible. You might believe the concerns about "death panels," that valuable care will be withheld to save money on the plan. You might have other distressing concerns.

I don't know how a universal healthcare plan would work, but I think there are important considerations to share. Most seniors are relieved when they start Medicare. It costs them less, and seniors are not complaining about Medicare. In our classes, I will ask participants about their experience with Medicare and what they think about the coverage. One woman replied, "I LOVE IT! I couldn't wait until I could get Medicare. I was paying $1,000 per month for a high-deductible plan. Now I qualify for 100 percent coverage for a fifth of the cost."

The typical person isn't that enthusiastic, but overall, all seniors in class who are on the plan and the agents who assist them with coverage believe the plan works well for seniors. Some concerns have been raised about specific coverage areas, such as the prescription coverage list or increased premiums for higher-income individuals, but I think that is to be expected. There are always areas we can improve. No system is ever perfect.

My mother had some out-of-pocket expenses due to her cancer treatments. Still, considering she was an inpatient nearly every day for more than a month after her diagnosis, it's incredible she only had to pay a couple of hundred dollars. That's it—everything else was covered. She was terminal with an expectation of maybe six months. Never once did any medical professional, insurance company, or Medicare communication suggest that it wasn't worthwhile to keep helping her. Tough choices need to be made when someone is dying, and they let my mother and her family make personal decisions with dignity.

Still not convinced? I understand. I wasn't at first, either. When the ACA first came out, I knew what Minnesota and other states like us had done to manage some of the deficiencies in the healthcare system. The ACA, in my opinion, focused too much on insurers and not enough on healthcare providers. Without legislation focused on healthcare providers at every level—pharmaceuticals, devices, hospitals, clinics, etc.—the ACA would not make healthcare more affordable.

The tax credits might make it more accessible, but those tax dollars would go to feed the for-profit healthcare system. It was also costly to roll out, so I was unsure whether it would really help.

It filled more gaps than I thought, and in non-progressive states, it forced them to participate, but too few people realized the benefits. People are still getting caught without coverage when they need it. This is why it is paramount to elect people who understand the complexity of these issues and are willing to take the necessary steps to address our healthcare crisis.

MEDICARE FOR ALL

"The current health-care system in the United States is totally broken. It is totally dysfunctional, and it is extremely cruel."
—Sen. Bernie Sanders, U.S. Capitol Building, May 4, 2023

In 2023, I watched an interview with Bernie Sanders. He was doing his typical jazzed-up stuff about student loans, unions, wages, and more—all he does to help level the playing field for the average American. Then he got to healthcare and said, "There isn't an appetite for Medicare for All right now." You could tell he deflated as he said it. My heart sank.

I hope this discussion has opened your eyes to the potential benefits of a universal system in the U.S. and how close we are to having it. We must do a better job of educating America, and lately, I have been frustrated by two necessary parts of this equation.

Them—Our Elected Officials: In 2021, when they were hashing out the details of the Build Back Better Act (later rebranded and passed as the Inflation Reduction Act), I caught a press conference when Senator Joe Manchin said these words,

> *"I have always said, 'If I can't go back home and explain it, I can't vote for it.' Despite my best efforts, I cannot explain the sweeping Build Back Better Act in West Virginia, and I cannot vote to move forward on this mammoth piece of legislation."*
> *December 19, 2021*

I audibly yelled at the screen, which is why I remembered this quote: "Hey Manchin, if you can't explain it, I can. It's your job to educate your constituents. If you cannot handle it, step aside and let someone else have your job." He might have used this as an excuse for not voting for, as he put it, "this mammoth piece of legislation." But if that is the case, have enough integrity to explain that to the American people. Many legislators who didn't vote for this are now bragging about the bridges and new jobs in their areas.

As you can tell, I get pretty worked up about politics and am immersed in much of it. My job is to teach government policy, and I firmly believe we deserve politicians who will take the time to educate themselves about all these variables and then use that information to empower the voting public. Our representatives should offer us the time and respect to ensure we understand how this works. We also deserve the truth about why they've made the choices they've made regarding specific legislation.

Several people on the Hill do this well. Elizabeth Warren, Bernie Sanders, Katie Porter, and Pete Buttigieg quickly come to mind as excellent political educators. Although I may disagree with his choices, Rand Paul also does a great job at explaining things and maintaining his integrity. We need more like them. This will not change unless more of us demand it.

Us—The Voting Public: I am so disappointed with people who ignore facts and, when presented with an opportunity to learn from someone who might know more about a particular topic, choose to remain ignorant. I appreciate that we do not all approach this from the same experience, intellect, and rationality. I do not expect someone to gain a PhD in economics or to enjoy politics and finance as much as I do.

While we cannot —and should not —approach this in the same way, I would appreciate it if people held their vote sacred and, before casting it, ensured they were well-informed and voted with the best intentions in mind. It's hard to believe that all the millions who voted in the 2024 presidential election relied on facts, common sense, integrity, and solid research before casting a vote. It baffles me that so much corruption and deceit in our political discourse has been normalized, thereby allowing harmful people to hold office. This lack of true righteousness before casting a vote is now negatively impacting the everyday lives of millions of Americans and various people around the world.

There is a concept that helps me navigate a world that often feels divided. I like to think of any group in thirds. One-third of people will immediately see the light in a promising idea. Another third will be resistant at first, but once their questions are answered, they'll join the fold.

But we must accept the reality of the final third. These are the folks who, regardless of the truth, will never move. I've learned not to spend my energy trying to convert them—they keep life interesting, but they shouldn't be the ones setting the pace. Instead, the burden of leadership falls on the rest of us to speak out with a balance of facts and heart.

THE WRAP-UP

"Many kids come out of college, they have a credit card and a diploma. They don't know how to buy a house or a car or health insurance or life insurance. They do not know basic microeconomics." —Jesse Jackson

We are nearing the end of this chapter and this book. There's a good chance you might like some honest advice about health insurance. What sort of plan should you get to cover your family, because gosh darn it, even Bernie doesn't believe there is a current appetite for Medicare for All.

My simple answer is to enroll in the best plan you can. I am a fan of Health Savings Accounts. With this method of insurance, you purchase a qualifying high-deductible insurance plan and then put money into a health savings account—an HSA. As mentioned earlier, the contributions are tax-deductible—technically, lowering your adjusted gross income (AGI). Earnings grow tax-deferred and, when withdrawn to be used for healthcare, are tax-free.

The IRS is quite generous in what it considers medical expenses. These are listed in IRS Publication 502 and include dental and vision. If part of my vision expenses includes contact lenses, the solution for cleaning and storing them is also a medical expense. Mileage to and from the doctor. If I have someone in my family with special needs, even a ramp to assist with access to our home is a qualified medical expense.

IRS Publications with the Qualifying Rules

HSA & Other Tax-Favored Health Plans:
https://www.irs.gov/pub/irs-pdf/p969.pdf
Medical and Dental Expenses:
https://www.irs.gov/pub/irs-pdf/p502.pdf

Yes, HSAs are wonderful, but they don't offer the same value they once did. Typically, when one increases the deductible, their out-of-pocket risk goes up, so the plan price goes down. Over time, the lower premiums for these high-deductible plans have risen so much that they are now close in price to the co-pay plans.

To figure out which health plan offers you the best value, you would add the premium to your expected out-of-pocket costs to determine which policy has the lowest cost. There are mandates on preventative care and various other benefits that make it easy to compare prices today. I've listed a few different things to consider below:

Premium Cost—This is your share of the premium. If your employer pays some of it, or you get a tax credit through the ACA, you should only include the portion you will pay when calculating the overall cost of your healthcare.

Out-of-pocket—The out-of-pocket gets tricky. The safest way to calculate this is to take the full deductible plus any co-insurance. Most plans will define this number for you in the brochure or coverage overview, but if you are reasonably healthy, it is unlikely you'll pay that full deductible or the out-of-pocket maximum. As a result, when comparing plans, I usually take my premium cost plus what I am *likely* to spend that year to compare.

Special Perks—Your employer might offer an HSA contribution, making that plan immediately more attractive with free money. Or you are enrolling on the ACA exchange and qualify for a Cost-Sharing Arrangement, which means your out-of-pocket expenses are reduced. If you get an HSA, you will not qualify for this Cost-Sharing Arrangement.

Network—Another thing to consider is whether your doctor, preferred hospital, or prescriptions are covered in the network.

As a self-employed individual, I enrolled in health insurance through the ACA exchange. Each year during open enrollment, I can review my coverage options.

For years, I automatically picked an HSA. I am blessed that I have been healthy. Besides dental and vision, I don't have much for routine medical costs. I had been having problems with my knee, so last year, I selected a benefit-rich plan so that diagnostics like X-rays, MRIs, and more would not be subject to the large deductible. The same would be true if I needed surgery or to see a specialist.

This benefit-rich plan cost me $100 more per month than the HSA—$1,200 per year. Heck, if I needed an MRI, it could have cost more than that. In the end, all was well. I had an X-ray, which came back normal. My doctor, whom I think is terrific, said, "Renée, you are regularly active. You rode your bike here. It doesn't seem like this knee issue holds you back. Tell me when it causes you problems."

After explaining it to her, it turned out my problem was common. My biking and my choice of weightlifting exercises worked the muscles above my knee more than others. I had to balance this by doing more work with the inner and outer thighs as well as my backside. I hardly have pain now, especially since I incorporated yoga into my workout regimen.

I do not regret getting that plan, though, for that year. I am back on an HSA, making the maximum contribution. For years, I have had more than enough money in the account to cover the out-of-pocket expenses and, I guess, pay for an MRI, too. I just don't want to spend those pennies.

CHAPTER FOURTEEN

YOU ARE RICH

THERE'S NOTHING TO FEAR

"Resilience is all about being able to overcome the unexpected. Sustainability is about survival. The goal of resilience is to thrive." —Jamais Cascio

A GUT PUNCH

My vision for this chapter changed when Donald J. Trump was elected our 47th president. I woke up to the news I feared when I went to bed. I thought, "What is the point of writing a book about financial planning or doing this YouTube channel? The world as we know it is going to blow up." You might have voted for him and do not understand that feeling, but on this side of reality, Trump is a scary man. He caused much damage and chaos in his first term, and now, he can resume with minimal checks due to the Supreme Court's immunity decision.

I could go on, but it's unnecessary. Those who voted for him will likely reject my concerns. If you voted for Harris, you could likely write a book yourself about the dread you experienced after Election Day 2024. I also shouldn't forget the nearly 90 million non-voters, by far the largest voting bloc. I figure many opted out of voting in this election because they are tired of all the drama. Heck, I think most of us are sick of Trump's drama, even many of the people who helped to elect him.

Amid my despondency and uncertainty about the future, my daughter said, "Mom, people will need good financial advice and direction now more than ever." Both of my intelligent kids bless me, because my son later said, "Trump probably won't do half of what he said he'd do. Do we have a wall?" At that, I laughed, and it helped bring reality into perspective. The sky was not falling—at least not today—and before it got that bad, I would likely have time and many options to formulate a new plan.

None of us knows what the future will bring. Life is a gamble, and whether it's another election, a tragic life event, or a devastating financial blow, we have two choices—roll with it or get out of the game. Folding up our cards and walking away brings nothing, but if I step in and submerge myself into the Flow, I find refreshing new energy and direction. The world looks a little brighter, and the work to be done comes into focus.

The following day, after many chats with like-minded souls, I found a new purpose. I was even more committed to publishing helpful, truthful information. The Spirit of Resilience now replaced my dejected fog. Not only would I keep going, but I would do all that I could to help others thrive as well. Much work was needed to ensure a better world for as many people as possible. Who I might influence and how it would look was entirely up to the Flow. Whether poor or prosperous, I find motivation and heightened perspective with the **"7G's of Great Riches"**.

G1: GUIDED BY THE FLOW

"There is no one-way prophecy, no speaking without listening or listening without speaking. The flow must go both ways, or it is not divine flow."

—*Richard Rohr, The Tears of Things*

I opened this book by telling you how vital my connection to the Flow is to my direction in life, and it's only right that we return to it in conclusion. There is little value in any financial achievement until we find peace and purpose. For me, that happens through a connection with God and a focus on a Higher Order—the things that are ultimately, eternally important.

I don't remember the power of the Flow in every waking moment, but I've learned that reconnection only takes an instant. It takes so little effort to breathe deeply and utter a small, grounding statement. "Thank you" is a favorite. It reminds me that, in this exact moment, everything is okay. "Here" does the same—God is here, I am here, and in the now, things are fine. I can resume the work later with greater clarity, but for this moment, a single word like hope, joy, or strength acts as my connection point.

Fear lives in the future. It thrives in the unknown. I frequently have to remind myself that while I don't know what will happen tomorrow, I am okay right now. Over the years, I've realized that the catastrophes I play on a loop in my head have a 0 percent success rate. Not one of those horrific conversations or catastrophic projections has ever actually become part of my "now." They are just twisted stories that give the hamsters in my head running energy—and that energy will never change the outcome of my life.

I only have control over what I choose to do in the present. The miracle is that God exists in the now, too. When I step into that space and acknowledge that God is right here, it becomes much easier to step away from the hamsters and turn my attention to what I am actually called to do.

I want to offer a clarification that might feel counterintuitive: the energy we give those hamsters isn't entirely wasted. Fear may not yield a quantitative value on a spreadsheet, but our feelings are integral to our healing and authenticity. They should be honored, not suppressed.

God loves every single part of us. We live in a society that often prizes cold logic over the worth of our feelings, shaming us for the very emotions that make us human. Those hamsters didn't start running in a vacuum; they're often reciting harmful stories told to us by a world that fears vulnerability. Those stories are written on us, which is why the hamsters are so vocal.

But our emotions are God-given conduits to the Flow. When we appreciate them rather than fight them, they lead us to a place of betterment and wisdom. God wrote a story on us, too. If we quiet the background noise, we can hear that Calm Voice. That Quiet Direction is all we truly ever need.

We have spent significant time discussing the ins and outs of financial products and concepts. During those chapters, I didn't mention the Flow often. To be honest, remembering to invite God in when I'm wrapped up in perfunctory money matters is difficult. It is a constant battle for me to hold onto a Higher Order while balancing financial books.

Yet, I know that developing this connection has increased my security and reduced my fear, regardless of life's circumstances. It has shifted my priorities and redefined what success means to me. This is exactly why the "7G's of Great Riches" are so valuable—they remind us that true wealth isn't just about what's in our accounts, but what's in our souls.

1

Guided by the Flow—In any moment, we can breathe into a new space to find the Flow. GOD is in the now and willing to help us when we choose to connect.

G2: GRATITUDE: A VISION FOR IMPROVEMENT

"For us, material well-being always followed spiritual progress; it never preceded."
—Alcoholics Anonymous, page 127

Gratitude is like rose-colored glasses. If I start to look at things through a new lens that says, "It's good" instead of "It's bad," suddenly what seemed like a bowl full of porridge is now a yummy hot meal. Even as I write that, I realize that is a stretch. Elevating "porridge" to "yummy" with any new lens is challenging. Maybe the rosy hue makes me happy to have a hot meal—that might be all I get out of the deal.

Granted, I have no idea what porridge is—I am blessed enough to have never had to eat it. There's some gratitude right there, and it sounds a tad better than gruel—another unknown food I am grateful to have never been forced to eat. BAM, like that—with a quick snap, I just found a way back to gratitude, which I was quickly able to reinforce by an internet search of these two food products. Yes, "YUMMY" as a descriptor would require super-improved rosy gratitude glasses for porridge or gruel. I still can't believe the search turned up "How to make perfect porridge." My gratitude barometer overflowed when I didn't have to read further.

You, too, are probably grateful that porridge and gruel are not regular staples in your diet. For those fortunate enough to read this book, you had the resources to buy it, the education to read it, the mental capacity to focus, and the desire to learn more about financial matters. This is likely to put you in the top percentile of the global economy. Given that you have enough income and possible future wealth to care about what to do with your resources, it also puts you in the top 50 percent in the U.S.A. Yes, indeed, we have much to be grateful for, even when we don't see it in a particular moment.

To test this, let's run a few numbers past your household. In November 2024, the median income in the United States was $39,700, or about $40,000 (usdebtclock.org). That means half of Americans have a reported income below that number. If your individual income is more than $40,000, you are in the top 50 percent. If we take off our rose-colored glasses and look at the global landscape, the average salary is $1,480 per month, or just under $18,000 per year. Even the poorest people in the U.S. are doing better than many others on this planet.

Even armed with these facts—no porridge today, educated and able, and financially, in the top 50 percent of U.S. earners and top 10 percent of the world—it's hard to find gratitude some days. How is that for a first-world problem, huh? Like all feelings, I think it is vital to consider them, but it is equally paramount to put this in the perspective of our first-world privilege. There are so many people around the world living without fundamental freedoms or the essentials necessary to find prosperity. Today, most Americans still have both of those. Can we do better for all people, those here and abroad? Most certainly, yes. That is why I believe connection to the Flow and moral clarity about money, power, privilege, and our vote are vital to the betterment of everyone and everything GOD loves.

Gratitude reminds me to stay in the now—it also empowers me. Instead of thinking about what I don't have, my rose-colored glasses remind me of the many talents and resources I possess to help me accomplish things to improve the world, even if it is something small like praying for a friend, baking muffins for a neighbor, or texting someone an encouraging word. Our betterments need not be grand. Any loving measure helps to bring the Universe to a healthier place.

Today is okay. GOD is now and will join me in this moment. So, I grab those rose glasses and see the blessing, even in something I might label as "bad." Almost every day, I find myself complaining about something—traffic, a customer, a delivery, a product, or anything—and after a few moments (or maybe more ☺) of this negativity, I stop those hamsters and say, "If that is the worst thing that happens today, it's a good day." The glasses are on, and the world is now a bit rosier.

2

Gratitude: A Vision for Improvement—the brighter world of rose-colored glasses can offer a vision and empowerment needed to take on the challenges of any day.

G3: GOOD IDEAS TURN THE TAP

"Love is the outbound movement that trains people to heal injustice and kindly embrace the world."—Norman Wirzba, Way of Love

The third one is simple—when I think of something kind, helpful, or loving—I DO IT! I don't believe these random thoughts of goodwill are as random as they seem. For example, I am just watering my plants, and out of seemingly nowhere, I think, "You should text (name)." Or I see someone sitting in the park, and I sense I should say something more than just a standard "Hi." Or while grocery shopping, I think, "You should get the stuff for a special dinner and invite (name) over."

I believe these arbitrary prompts are a direct line from GOD. They come from nowhere amid other endeavors, and in my experience, the more I honor them, the more I open the tap to the Flow. By responding with action, GOD knows I am aware and willing, heightening my senses so I can feel which direction GOD would have me pursue.

I am as guilty as anyone of offering excuses in response to these prompts. "You should text (name)," gets a "Why? They never think of me." Encountering the person in the park, my thought is, "Too busy for that." The dinner plans: "It's always me doing nice things for them." Oh yes, I have hamsters with runaway excuses, too. Once those thoughts pop into my head, I can start to ruminate on every grievance on the list.

I have learned that things work better when I avoid that option and tell the hamsters we'll stew on that another day. Then, I do whatever gracious thought comes to mind. Sometimes I feel a little weird, which, in my mind, proves it isn't my idea. Why would I randomly think of something to do that might land me in an awkward situation? That makes no sense. The idea must come from Great Energy, which is trying to move the world to a better place. By honoring it, I am then a willing participant in the Flow.

Have I neglected these prompts? For sure. One that comes to mind is when I was in Phoenix recently. I walked from my hotel to a local fast-food restaurant in 105-degree heat. The 20-minute walk was intense, and when I got there, I noticed a group of four men counting change outside. Judging from their clothing and the dehydrated look of their skin, it was evident they'd been in the heat all day and probably the night.

I saw this and thought, "Renée, you have $20 U.S. dollars you won't need after your flight to Mexico tomorrow. Give it to them." Then a hamster chimed in, "How will they split it? Go in and get change." GOD piped in for one more shot, "Just offer to buy each a lunch."

Another hamster started on a wheel and yelled, "That feels weird. Go get some change." I have no idea why, at that moment, handing each man a five-dollar bill was less weird than saying, "Hey, guys, would you like to come in and cool off? I'd be happy to get you a burger or something." But it seemed too awkward, so I followed the hamster plan, and when I returned, the men were gone. I wonder what happened, because they never made it into the restaurant. My heart sank when I couldn't find them. I had an opportunity to help some people in need, and I worried more about "how" than the "who" or the "why."

I don't know—I'll never know—where those men went that day, but the fact is apparent that I missed an opportunity to do something kind for four men who clearly could have used it. Instead, I live with regret. That regret reminds me that no matter the circumstances or how weird I might feel, it's better to act on kindness immediately. Imagine if everyone followed through on every random thought of a gracious act. How much richer could we make the world?

I have yet to regret following a prompt. Each prompt I've followed brought healing to me and, hopefully, to others. My regrets are only for the missed opportunities. I tell myself, and I'm telling you, "Don't miss an opportunity for random kindness." Just do it—seriously, it's worth it.

3

Good Ideas Turn the Tap—random acts of kindness are opportunities to share our GOD-given blessings and help to energize the Flow.

G4: GENEROSITY OPENS THE FLOODGATES

"Each of you should give what you have decided in your heart to give, not reluctantly or under compulsion, for GOD loves a cheerful giver."
—2 Corinthians 9:7; NIV

Since I am no stranger to a scarcity mentality, I frequently second-guess how generous I should be. Given what I have been through financially (the lack of financial support from key people in my life, and the fact that my income still isn't stable), I suppose a bit of second-guessing is to be expected. To counter this, I use the other principles outlined in this chapter—gratitude, considering what GOD would have me do, and reliance on the Flow. With these tools, I remain generous. I rarely give reluctantly (as the Bible verse above that kicked off this "G" encourages).

I often think about 2 Corinthians 9:7, which tells us not to give under compulsion. Too many pundits and pastors preach the need for routine monetary giving to the church, making it compulsory. Others use guilt or fear to motivate us to contribute to causes. Granted, we should consider if this is what the Universe is asking from us, yet giving under duress or "compulsion" is not part of the Flow. The Flow is cheerful and generous, and plentiful in gifting measures.

Some Bible verses spell out my Faith mission for me, such as Micah 6:8, "And what does the Lord require of you? To act justly, love mercy, and walk humbly with your GOD." Not a word about pennies. Two chapters also resonate deeply. One is John 15—in a word, it's "abide"—be in tune with GOD, the Flow. The other is Romans 12, which is about renewing, changing, or aligning ourselves to see GOD's will. I encourage you to read each and see if anything in the words also speaks to you.

It's in verses 6 to 8 of Romans 12 that I believe we find what GOD asks of us, specifically, about generosity:

> "We all have different gifts. Each gift came because of the grace GOD gave us. Whoever has the gift of prophecy should use that gift in a way that fits the kind of faith they have. Whoever has the gift of serving should serve. Whoever has the gift of teaching should teach. Whoever has the gift of comforting others should do that. Whoever has the gift of giving to help others should give generously. Whoever has the gift of leading should work hard at it. Whoever has the gift of showing kindness to others should do it gladly." —Romans 12:6-8 ERV

We have each been given different resources and gifts. All the work gets done when we give freely from our gifting, as GOD asks. Generosity, like everything else, is not one-size-fits-all. To me, glorious generosity in our Gifts marks our reliance on GOD and is a natural outpouring of the Flow.

4

Generosity Opens the Floodgates—there are no hard and fast rules about giving in GOD's economy. When prompted, we give freely of time, money, and other gifts.

G5: GIFTS OF A NEW NATURE

"How much of this glory can one carry into business?"
—Frank Laubach, Letters by a Modern Mystic, page 67

When I moved to Mexico, a pastor at my church sent me the book, "Letters by a Modern Mystic." It's a collection of letters from Frank Laubach, written while he was a Christian missionary in the Philippines in the early 1930s. It's been a miraculous companion while writing this book and a Spiritual guide for tapping the Flow. Frank's ultimate desire is to stay in constant contact and remain in the Flow. As he explains this process, his thoughts are poignant about how many distractions (and hamsters) hinder our ability to meet this mission.

One of these ideas was expressed in his immediate acknowledgment that the Muslims of the island were far more devout than he was. His willingness to humbly admit this, I found deeply endearing. As Frank witnessed the people around him who were willing to commit more time, effort, and sacrifice to their Spiritual connection, he reconsidered his own practices and purpose.

> "What right then have I or any other person to come here and change the name of these people from Muslim to Christian, unless I lead them to a life fuller of God than they have now. Clearly, clearly, my job here is not to go to the town plaza and make proselytes, it is to live wrapped in GOD, trembling in {His} thoughts, burning with {His} passion. And my loved one, that is the best gift you can give to your own town."
> —Frank Laubach, Letters by a Modern Mystic, page 13

Amazing —"*...that is the BEST gift you can give to your own town.*" And, in my opinion, to yourself, to those you love, and to the world. Could you imagine if everyone could hold to this principle at all times? What a very different place this would be, and maybe what Jesus means by, "Thy Kingdom come on earth as it is in Heaven." This, to me, is a sign of being in the Flow. Too many people profess faith while elevating themselves by looking down on others. Frank instead saw the beauty and lessons in the people around him, and what he wanted to do was to be part of Love. From this observation, he resolved to do two things:

One was to enhance his connection to GOD. He found that throughout the day, he would frequently forget to tap the Flow—to recognize GOD and to create union with the Source. He also found, however, that the more he committed himself to this practice, the easier it became to hold the connection. Ironically, as Frank continued to develop his Higher connection, the Islamic leaders noticed and told their followers that if they had questions about seeking a Spiritual connection, they should ask Mr. Laubach. There are amazing gifts when we remain open to the Source. We see new things, and if we stay humble, others around us witness new things in us, too.

Two, while on this Spiritual quest, he realized that poverty and injustice were tied to literacy. If he were to truly help the Philippine people (and others around the world), he could best enrich their lives by teaching them to read. In that, his Spiritual life's work then became improving literacy on a global scale. When we give from our gifts, and we follow GOD's will, the many needs of the world will draw us in. We'll find ourselves connected to a masterful energy and a bold vision of change.

When considering the Power of the Flow, I often think of an impactful podcast featuring Reverend Dr. Michael Battle, who was ordained a priest by Archbishop Desmond Tutu. Dr. Battle was at the Center for Action and Contemplation (CAC) to discuss his new book, "Desmond Tutu: A Spiritual Biography of South Africa's Confessor."

About midway through the podcast, (if you pull up the transcript, the section is on page 11):

> "...international organizations tried to pressure Tutu to do things morning, noon, and night. And he would say to them, 'What kind of Tutu do you want, and why do you invite him here? If you want him for his communications skills, ebullient personality, and that kind of thing in which he thrives in big groups, if you want that Tutu, you need to respect his need for chunks of silence."

Dr. Battle goes on to say,

> "...it was a pretty easy choice for someone like Tutu to spend seven hours with GOD. Because without GOD, Tutu said he would not be able to be who he was, to do what he did, and to have lasted as long as he did."

For those who have felt the connection of the Flow, you know the Energy of Change it contains. While seven hours of silence is beyond the grasp of my schedule, and likely yours too, constant reminders and attempts to connect get us closer to the Gifts only GOD can bring.

When I consider Tutu's need for time to commune, I paraphrase his perspective as, "What kind of Tutu do you want? A poignant, eloquent, impactful Tutu or a bobble-head bouncing around?" Then, I apply that to myself and my life. What kind of person do I want to be? Poignant, eloquent, and impactful? Or a bobble-head bouncing around? The answer is clear, and in my experience, the more I maintain a connection to the Source, the more impactful are my words and the energy Flow.

5

Gifts of a New Nature—great Spiritual leaders show us that we see the world and our impact on it in a whole new way when we develop strong bonds with the Flow.

G6: GET RID OF FEAR

"Let nothing disturb you. / Let nothing upset you. / Everything changes. / GOD alone is unchanging. / With patience, all things are possible. / Whoever has GOD lacks nothing. / GOD alone is enough."

—Teresa of Ávila

To illustrate the grip fear can have on our future life and why we must get rid of it, let's rely on the main character who runs throughout the book (besides me): Dave Ramsey. He filed for bankruptcy because he couldn't pay his debts.

In my opinion, Dave's main problem was (and is) greed, but that is a topic for another day.

His initial financial failures caused him to believe that debt is bad. But as we discussed and illustrated in numerous ways, debt isn't bad. Debt is a financial tool. When we understand the tool and how it works, we can then use it properly and there's nothing to fear.

So, where did Dave go wrong with his logic? You likely already know. He likely didn't look at the circumstances objectively and tried to determine whether any choices he made caused this—was he somehow responsible? I doubt he thoroughly analyzed the business deals, the market trends, his talents, and various other considerations that I believe help us arrive at healthier conclusions, including "What would GOD have us do?" It's easier to "blame" an outside influence.

We see this all the time—and frankly, I'm guilty of it, too. Many Americans and politicians look at the problems in the Affordable Care Act (ACA—Obamacare) and say, "It's horrible. We should get rid of it." Or, "Immigrants—they're the problem. Get rid of them, too." This thinking is black and white, and does little to solve the problem, just like saying, "Debt is bad."

Working toward truly helpful solutions requires the effort of in-depth analysis into the problem. This also means, at least in my experience, taking an honest assessment of my responsibility, which should include how I might have contributed to the downfall. To fully complete this process, it also means I should work through any emotions I have around the situation (shame, anger, fear, guilt, etc.), recognize what I am responsible for, and work to forgive the actions of others.

I firmly believe the megachurch I mentioned and financial advisors like Dave Ramsey gave me bad (possibly even harmful) advice when they told me to give 10 percent to the church. Does that mean that Dave Ramsey, that church and others like it, have nothing good to offer? Of course not. Would it be rational for me to say all churches are "bad" and should be avoided? Again, no. Nothing is all good, or all bad. Depending on how we perceive something in the present, or by using 20/20 hindsight, sometimes we can see good in the bad, so maybe it's more helpful than we think.

This is why my reliance on GOD and the Flow is so paramount. I do not believe I can do this sort of work adequately without a Higher Power, whom I have come to trust, to rely upon, to challenge what I believe, and to help me break through the walls I've built to protect myself. Having listened to Dave Ramsey's show, I have never heard him refer to any such contemplation or self-examination. None of it is mentioned in his book. From him and others like him, I see the opposite: an arrogance or a false belief that his view of the world is accurate, and those who don't see it that way are wrong. He rarely listens to the opinions of others, and is quite condescending. The irony is that some callers to his show, just like the content in this book, prove he's wrong. Still, he will not consider the possibility of being wrong.

Many claim this idea is overused, but in my opinion, this lack of inner work is at the core of toxic behavior. If I do not take the time to consider my failings, and work to heal the hurts of life, I am destined to let it spill over onto others. In all these years, with mounting evidence everywhere, Dave Ramsey has yet to reconsider his stance on debt and admit he might have been wrong. An inability to admit our faults and then to change seems to be at the heart of toxicity.

I saw a recent article in "Off the Front Page" in which Dave Ramsey claimed that his ownership of more than 15 homes was not excessive, greedy, or contrary to his Christian faith. He went on to claim that "He's managing them for GOD." Since you've made it to the final pages of a book about morality and money, I won't bore you with the many problems with Dave's perspective. Here's one we have not discussed yet: Inner work to determine our failings helps us to see ourselves on equal footing with others. In doing so, it's hard to justify so many houses when others have none.

While I cannot say for certain, it appears that Dave Ramsey and others like him are not operating in the Flow, because GOD will change our perspective about material wealth and the needs of others. It's a natural outcome, and in my opinion, why so many resist truly letting GOD in. The Flow will help us see we are just one of many, and all are loved equally. It's evident there are people outside of the Christian faith that have the Flow working through them, and it's equally evident that there are those who claim the Christian faith who do not let GOD Flow through them. This is why we need not choose or practice a certain faith to allow GOD's Power into our lives.

Multiple times in this book we talked about why we should not be afraid about our finances, the economy, or the future. I'll admit, this is easier said than done. I get scared too. Not all of my financial plans have worked the way I wanted, but here is a little secret for you, and you may already know it to be true. In my life, I only got about 20 percent of what I thought I wanted, but in the remaining 80 percent is where the magic happens. I got stuff that I didn't even know I wanted, and some of it is better than I could have imagined.

The Creator is Love, and Love honors, respects, and protects. Love enriches all things. Love does not tear down and harm others. Love finds a way to nurture and help others feel safe. There is Truth in Love, and the Truth is, no one is perfect, we are all loved, and we are all equal. Love need not fear, because we are all in this together. Love helps bring people to their authentic selves (which is discussed in G7, our next section).

6

Get Rid of Fear—it's work, but we owe it to ourselves, the people we love, and to all those who inhabit this planet to recognize our mistakes and heal our pain. Letting it go makes more room for Love.

G7: GENUINE AUTHENTICITY

"Have faith in you and the things you do. You won't go wrong."
—Sister Sledge, We Are Family

The phrase "You do you" comes to mind. GOD uniquely created you to fulfill specific needs in this world that only you can do. You are important. You are a Superhero. If you don't "do you," that unique, impactful work will never be done. The world needs you!

Let's face it—the world writes on us. Those hamsters picked up their stories from outside influences that are taking us away from our authenticity. When those voices are too loud, we can't hear GOD, and when we cannot hear GOD, we cannot find our genuine selves.

> "There is something in every one of you that waits, listens for the sound of the genuine in yourself, and if you cannot hear it, you will never find whatever it is for which you are searching... You are the only you that has ever lived; your idiom is the only idiom of its kind in all the existences and if you cannot hear the sound of the genuine in you, you will all of your life, spend your days on the ends of strings that somebody else pulls...
>
> Who are you? How does the sound of the genuine come through to you?... Don't be deceived and thrown off by all the noises that are a part even of your dreams, your ambitions ... that you don't hear the sound of the genuine in you, because that is the only true guide that you will ever have, and if you don't have that, you don't have a thing. You may be famous, you may be whatever the other ideals are which are a part of this generation but you know you don't have the foggiest notion of who you are, where you are going, what you want. Cultivate the discipline of listening to the sound of the genuine in yourself." —Howard Thurman, "The Sound of the Genuine," Spelman College, May 4, 1980.

We cannot fully love until we first tame our hamsters and seek out GOD's unique plan for our authenticity. This process is essential so that our hamsters don't seep out and write stories on other people's authenticity. In my opinion, our most important endeavor in life is to heal and be helpful to others. As I look at every ill in the world, it can be traced back to harm that has been done to another, and a lack of restoration to the loving authenticity GOD bestowed in us. We also cannot put our worldly goods into a proper context without doing this very vital work.

You might now think, "Renée, you have gone too far. Suppose my 10-year-old starts telling me they want to be 'furry' or change their gender, or my spouse thinks they should quit their job to do yoga on the beach, or my parents want to give my inheritance to (name a disliked non-profit). In that case, I am not going to help them do it just because of some rule to support authenticity."

I didn't say that you should. I don't know if that would be the right choice, and honestly, you don't either. We do not discover what we should do without listening to the other person and asking GOD for guidance. Then, we must be strong enough to push back the hamsters, have peace in our spirit for clarity about what GOD asks, and tap the courage to do whatever we sense we've been asked to do in order to better the world. That's the conviction we gain when we tap the Flow from our genuine self.

7

Genuine Authenticity—the Flow heals and helps us find our authenticity so that we can help others do the same. Tapping our authentic self brings out our Super Power.

The 7G's of Great Riches

G1: Guided by the Flow—GOD is in the now, and at any moment, I can choose to connect and find the Flow.

G2: Gratitude is a Vision for Improvement—Rose-colored glasses can offer perspective and empowerment to take on the challenges of any day.

G3: Good Ideas Turn the Tap—Random acts of kindness share our GOD-given blessings, and help to energize the Flow.

G4: Generosity Opens the Floodgates—There are no rules about giving in GOD's economy. When prompted, give freely of time, money, and other gifts.

G5: Gifts of a New Nature—We see the world, and our impact on it, in a whole new way when we develop strong bonds with the Flow.

G6: Get Rid of Fear—We owe it to ourselves, the people we love, and to all those who inhabit this planet to recognize our mistakes and heal our pain.

G7: Genuine Authenticity—Tapping into our authentic selves brings out our Super Power and allows us to help others do the same.

TRUDGE THE ROAD OF HAPPY DESTINY

"Abandon yourself to God as you understand God. Admit your faults to Him [Them] and to your fellows. Clear away the wreckage of your past. Give freely of what you find and join us. We shall be with you in the Fellowship of the Spirit, and you will surely meet some of us as you trudge the Road of Happy Destiny. May God bless you and keep you - until then."
—Alcoholics Anonymous, Chapter 11, 'A Vision for You.'

Well, friends, that's it for now. If you enjoyed this final section, an upcoming book, *Tapping the Wellspring,* will include the two chapters removed from this book and will dive deeper into Spiritual concepts that can guide us to the real rewards in life. I hope to release it in 2027.

I am grateful for our paths crossing, and I am encouraged to know that a community of us is seeking morality in money. May GOD guide you, and may the Flow remain vibrant in your life.

If this book helped take the fear out of your finances, I would be honored if you left a quick review. It helps others find their way to the Flow, too. Thank you.

APPENDIX I

WHY THEY?

Those who find their way to this page are here for various reasons. You might be outraged by the decision not to use the masculine pronoun for the Divine (He). You might be inquisitive, just wanting to know my thoughts. Still, others may think, "Heck, yes, it's about time." Regardless of your reasons, I hope you will allow me to explain my thoughts.

TRIUNE GOD

If you happen to be Christian, I do not understand why we don't commonly use "They" to describe GOD. Christianity believes in a triune GOD—the Father, Son, and Holy Spirit—always working together in Perfect Harmony. If this is the fundamental principle of the faith, using "They" to describe this Spiritual Power would be grammatically correct and natural for understanding the Christian GOD. Since we don't, in my opinion, that says more to me about patriarchy and its desire to create more and more self-importance than anything about our Creator. Using 'They' allows me to hear the sound of the genuine in the Divine, unclouded by the binding strings of patriarchy.

IN THEIR IMAGE

In Genesis 1, during the sixth day, GOD created all creatures of the land. In verse 1:26, as GOD begins to make people, the text begins to use plural pronouns: "Let us…in our image, in our likeness…" Interesting. The next verse

(1:27) states that GOD created both males and females at that time, and verse 1:28 says GOD blessed "them"—the two made in GOD's image. Then GOD told "them", male and female, to be fruitful and multiply. Before wrapping up the sixth day, GOD gave "both" instructions, equal and the same. All of this happened in one day—no priority or preference is given to either gender, except that the word male precedes female.

A section quoted more often in sermons is the creation story of the first woman being created from a rib of Adam. This is Genesis 2:20-23. The version that positions women as equal to men comes before this one. In my mind, it holds priority.

I believe the version in the second chapter is more well-known because it has been relied upon by male church leaders to illustrate that men came first and, therefore, should be preordained leaders. The underlying and disheartening side of too much reliance on this story is that women were a GODly afterthought. It is so heartbreaking to be that utterly dismissive of the equally rich benefit of all that is feminine.

Regardless of my personal beliefs regarding reliance on Genesis 2 as the creation's story, if we ignore the richness of Genesis 1, the first story of joint creation, we do not gain the opportunity to benefit from the full context of inherent equality and the plurality of GOD.

In Genesis 1 and 2 and throughout the Gospels, GOD intended women as equal companions. In neither of these two sections during creation does GOD delineate that women are somehow set aside or lesser than their male counterparts.

In the past, using the male pronoun didn't bother me. I understood, and still do, why the references existed. Much of this text was written by men because men deemed themselves superior. They unilaterally made decisions that impacted all of us, including not allowing women to read and write. Men determined women were lesser. Consequently, their opinions were not valued.

Now, with my new lens on, these references feel demeaning. I want to change that sentence to read, "...these references **are** demeaning." But I am concerned about further offending others who do not see it like I do. Using the word HE to describe our Creator discounts the value of anyone who does not consider themselves male. It is also inaccurate. We, men and women and, yes, non-binary folks too, all of us, regardless of race, creed, or gender, are ALL created in Their image. We all have equal value and merit. GOD is not a white dude in the sky, but a pure and holy reflection of ALL of us.

The continued use of the male pronoun as a standard when describing a group of people, including women and others who do not claim a binary gender, obfuscates the transparent, immutable, and intrinsic value of feminine traits to all humanity.

INCLUSION: GOD = UNITY

A third reason I prefer the word They to define GOD: **inclusion**. My faith is Christianity, but I want all people of all faiths to feel that their Higher Power is included in this discussion. While I use some biblical references in this book, I want all those of any faith to feel like this book fits their GOD, too. If you believe in one true GOD (Isaiah 42:5, Ephesians 1:11), we are all connected and referring to the same Divine Entity regardless of faith.

I debated about proceeding with "They" versus "He" as the pronoun for GOD. I know it will make some so uncomfortable that they will not read this book. I hope that doesn't happen to you. This book contains valuable information and several items that will challenge your thinking. I hope you keep reading and go on this Spiritual journey to manage and understand your finances.

SPECIAL FOOTNOTE: As much as my soul feels settled with "They" for "GOD," I know that is not the same for many people, so I was not yet fully committed to the idea. Then the United States Supreme Court rolled back Roe when I wrote this section. After removing national protection for women to control their bodies and their reproductive health, I became even more convinced that our world is much better served when the voice, heart, and soul of women... are equally represented.

GOD loves all—both mom and fetus. GOD also gave us free will. Each of our lives is complex, and a recurring theme in Jesus's teachings was that we not judge others but love and offer mercy. He was not concerned about what the Romans did, but he was very concerned about the religious leaders of the day and how they were failing miserably at crucial tasks. Jesus did not try to change any laws. He was there to change their hearts.

For those concerned that I profess to be a Christian but sound like a pro-choice liberal, I want to clarify this: I am a pro-choice, pro-life, realistic Christ-follower.

When considering abortion laws, I think of Jesus talking to the woman at the well in John 4. He never admonished her. He did not shame her. He spoke to her as a peer, with understanding and sympathy. He knew her life was hard, and she had made difficult choices, and he offered her hope through living water. If we care about babies and little people everywhere, we should follow Jesus's lead, sitting at the well, showing compassion and hope.

APPENDIX II

"For the most part, men are running the world, and it is not going that well."
—Liz Cheney, June 29, 2022, Ronald Reagan Library

WHY BIG GUYS?

Whereas I usually try to keep my tone gender neutral, I used the word GUYS when referring to the rich and powerful. This is because the vast wealth and power are in the hands of a select few—typically white men. They created the system within which we all try to succeed. They control it, and it offers them the most benefits.

Don't believe me? Please take a moment and search for the "Forbes Real-Time Billionaires List." At which number on the list do you find the first woman? Keep scrolling. The first one you see is likely someone who inherited the wealth. Alice Walton, of Walmart fame, is usually in the top 20 at least, but her father founded the company. Although she used to surpass her brothers, Rob and Jim Walton, they are now ahead of her.

Taylor Swift did quite well, right? She's considered a powerful woman. Put her name in the search bar to see where she appears on this list. When I am writing this, October 2024, her $1.5 billion gets her to number 2093 on the list. In perspective, she's only 34, but Mark Zuckerberg, Facebook fame, is number 4 with $204 billion, and he's only six years older at age 40.

To drive this point home just a bit further, put Oprah in the search. Given all her notoriety, people in our class are often surprised that she is still only number 1173 on the list (again, in October 2024) with a net worth of $3 billion. Oprah is now 70 years old and involved in many business ventures but has not yet made it to the top 500 billionaires.

I am not blaming men. I realize that each man independently has little control over the system that gives them the privilege. I fully understand that many people do not see what I am describing. Regardless, we will remain here until those with power realize the value of sharing it and help to level the playing field. Let me share some other considerations.

EMPATHY IS KEY

There was a time when I believed that sexism was the reason more women didn't top this list. It's evident to anyone paying attention and looking at things objectively that women are quite capable of taking over for any one of these captains of industry. The logical reason seems to be that men are keeping them out. While I don't deny that there are plenty of misogynist men who refuse to acknowledge the capabilities of women and may even actively work to suppress them, I've now come to believe that women are participating in this problem.

Years ago, in a psychology course, my professor said, "Research tells us that to the degree one increases their power, their ability to empathize decreases." He went on to say that brain studies show that the neural pathways to our empathy centers atrophy or weaken as we gain more and more control over our environment and the people around us. He never cited his source in this class, but I clung to this idea because we see this function in our world. Those in power do not seem to consider the needs of those under their authority.

Today, science tells us this power dynamic does not affect everyone equally. The book *The Power Code* by Katty Kay and Claire Shipman is an excellent look at the dynamics of power and the differences between men and women. Specifically, in Chapter 3, "Your Brain Power," they use research that says this reduction of empathy is typical for men but not necessarily for women.

> "Of those not primed*—men and women displayed the same level of empathy after watching the video. Of those primed, the women

> displayed substantially more empathy. The researchers posit that because, societally, women are expected to display and use empathy, they tap into it more quickly. So, empathy may be a function of nurture rather than culture. Wherever it comes from, we'll take it because it's an advantage, an essential tool leaders need these days."
>
> —page 82, "The Power Code"

*Priming is a classic technique for behavioral scientists that helps a study participant "feel" a certain way for a limited amount of time, even if that might not be how they typically feel.

POWER < EMPATHY

Maybe the women don't top the Forbes list because they choose to distribute their wealth equally, or getting to the top isn't as important as how they get there. I've heard that Taylor Swift pays out bonuses to the whole crew after her concerts, which have been cited at $100,000 each. This turns out to be multi-millions of dollars throughout her career. Those who received these checks commented, "It's life-changing."

This is not to say that there are not generous men out there. There are. Bill Gates and Warren Buffett are two self-made male billionaires in the top 10 who express much altruism. I am sure others do as well.

Remember how everything is an exchange? How any exchange should be fair and balanced? Think about a person entering that exchange who is considering the needs of the other person, as opposed to someone who is only thinking of what is best for them. Which of the two is likely to offer the fairest deal to both people? It's not hard to answer, and it's also not difficult to see how more empathy in positions of power could change the world.

If our leaders had more empathy, would we have less conflict and fewer people suffering? Could more empathy reduce sexual assault, violent crime, and murders? Would wages rise for the typical worker? Might CEOs reduce their pay to make it happen? You get the idea.

This is not to say that men are entirely at fault. Or if women take over, all our problems will be solved. That is classic "binary thinking," and things don't work that way, but it is undeniable to me that we have not valued what women bring to the table, and we have all suffered for it. Women do not have all the answers, but men don't either. We have our strengths; we also have our weaknesses. We achieve what GOD fully intended only through cooperation and by valuing our differences.

> "Women are looking for men who will honor our uniqueness and realize our gifting is not lesser, it's not weaker, it's just different. It is, in fact, more comprehensive. And it's essential."
>
> *—2017 Ted Talk, Paula Stone Williams*

That is so important; I want to say that again,

"It is, in fact, more comprehensive.
And it's essential."

RESOURCES

Web resources and links were active at the time of publication and may change over time.

CHAPTER 1 — Start Saving NOW:

- "Average Stock Market Return" — Seeking Alpha
  - https://seekingalpha.com/article/4502739-average-stock-market-return
- "S&P 500 Historical Annual Returns" — MacroTrends
  - https://www.macrotrends.net/2526/sp-500-historical-annual-return
- "Financial Peace" — Dave Ramsey
  - https://en.wikipedia.org/wiki/Dave_Ramsey
- "The Richest Man in Babylon" — George S. Clason
  - https://archive.org/details/richestmaninbaby00geor
- "Rich Dad Poor Dad" — Robert Kiyosaki
  - https://en.wikipedia.org/wiki/Rich_Dad_Poor_Dad

CHAPTER 3 — The Heart of the Matter:

- "A New Way to Pay for College" — NPR
  - https://www.npr.org/2022/08/05/1116008536/a-new-way-to-pay-for-college-update

CHAPTER 5 — Tools and the Trade-Off:

- "The Power of Dividends" — Hartford Funds
  - https://www.hartfordfunds.com/insights/market-perspectives/equity/the-power-of-dividends.html
- "S&P 500 Historical Chart Data" — MacroTrends
  - https://www.macrotrends.net/2324/sp-500-historical-chart-data

CHAPTER 7 — A Money Maker:

- "How Elon Musk Financed His Twitter Takeover" — Al Jazeera
  - https://www.aljazeera.com/economy/2022/10/28/how-elon-musk-financed-his-twitter-takeover
- "X (Twitter) Stock Falls" — The Guardian
  - https://www.theguardian.com/technology/2024/jan/02/x-twitter-stock-falls-elon-musk
- "Acquisition of Twitter by Elon Musk" — Wikipedia
  - https://en.wikipedia.org/wiki/Acquisition_of_Twitter_by_Elon_Musk

CHAPTER 9 — Plans for Your Pennies:

- "John Bogle: How Much Do Investors Lose in Charges and Management Fees?" — YouTube
  - https://www.youtube.com/watch?v=0aegXd0Q1CI

- "John Bogle: All You Need to Know About Investing in Three Words" — YouTube
  - https://www.youtube.com/watch?v=A0gQiz0pCyI
- "Jack Bogle: My Essential Advice for Any Investor" — YouTube
  - https://www.youtube.com/watch?v=ETrZX5Ojx_E

CHAPTER 10 — The Government & Your Pennies:

- "Every Falsehood, Exaggeration and Untruth in Trump's and Harris's Stump Speeches" — New York Times
  - https://www.nytimes.com/interactive/2024/09/21/us/politics/trump-harris-2024-election-speech.html
- "Historical Highest Marginal Income Tax Rates" — Tax Policy Center
  - https://www.taxpolicycenter.org/statistics/historical-highest-marginal-income-tax-rates
- "U.S. Historical Marginal Tax Rate Chart" — Wikimedia Commons
  - https://commons.wikimedia.org/wiki/File:USA_Historical_Marginal_Tax_Rate_for_Highest_and_Lowest_Income_Earners.svg
- "U.S. Economy-The Envy of the World" (October 2024) — The Economist
  - https://www.economist.com/special-report/2024-10-19
- "U.S. Bank Prime Loan Rate" — YCharts
  - https://ycharts.com/indicators/us_bank_prime_loan_rate
- Social Security Administration — SSA.gov
  - https://www.ssa.gov/
- Internal Revenue Service — IRS.gov
  - https://www.irs.gov/

CHAPTER 11 — More FREE Pennies:

- "Correlation Coefficient Explained" — Investopedia
  - https://www.investopedia.com/terms/c/correlationcoefficient.asp

CHAPTER 13 — The Penny Thief:

- "Medicaid Eligibility (Seniors & Medicare Enrollees)" — Medicaid.gov
  - https://www.medicaid.gov/medicaid/eligibility/seniors-medicare-and-medicaid-enrollees
- "Personal Needs Allowance" — Medicaid Planning Assistance
  - https://www.medicaidplanningassistance.org/personal-needs-allowance/
- "Why Is Insulin So Expensive?" — Vox
  - https://www.vox.com/2019/4/3/18293950/why-is-insulin-so-expensive
- "Insulin Price Cap Explained" — CNN
  - https://edition.cnn.com/2024/01/01/politics/insulin-price-cap/index.html
- "Family Medical Leave" — Ontario.ca
  - https://www.ontario.ca/document/your-guide-employment-standards-act-0/family-medical-leave
- "Sick Around the World" — PBS Frontline (YouTube)
  - https://youtu.be/h4rg-DJBd34?si=SpUj0PgD7gZVKwbU

- The New York Times Historical Archives (TimesMachine)
  - https://timesmachine.nytimes.com/timesmachine/1982/03/03/issue.html
- "Reagan Deregulation and Rising Healthcare Costs" — The New York Times
  - https://www.nytimes.com/2018/06/04/upshot/reagan-deregulation-and-americas-exceptional-rise-in-health-care-costs.html
- "U.S. Health Care from a Global Perspective" — Commonwealth Fund
  - https://www.commonwealthfund.org/publications/issue-briefs/2023/jan/us-health-care-global-perspective-2022

CHAPTER 14 — You Are Rich:

- "Global Wealth Perspective" — BBC
  - https://www.bbc.com/news/magazine-17512040
- "Real Estate Wealth Commentary" — Off the Front Page
  - https://offthefrontpage.com/dave-ramsey-says-owning-15-20-houses-isnt-greedy/
- "Letters by a Modern Mystic" — Frank C. Laubach
  - https://en.wikipedia.org/wiki/Frank_Laubach
- "Amnesia and the Big Picture" — Center for Action and Contemplation
  - https://cac.org/podcasts/amnesia-and-the-big-picture-with-rev-michael-battle/

APPENDIX II — Why the BIG Guys?:

- "Real-Time Billionaires List" — Forbes
  - https://www.forbes.com/real-time-billionaires/
- "Taylor Swift Bonus Payments" — Forbes
  - https://www.forbes.com/sites/kellyphillipserb/2023/08/04/taylor-swift-says-thank-you-to-eras-tour-workers-by-handing-out-checks/
- "The Power Code" — Katty Kay and Claire Shipman
  - https://www.goodreads.com/en/book/show/63076680-the-power-code

www.ingramcontent.com/pod-product-compliance
Lightning Source LLC
LaVergne TN
LVHW040517210926
848480LV00007BA/1491

9798995449706